Sunset Travel Guide to
WASHINGTON

By the Editors of Sunset Books and Sunset Magazine

Lane Books · Menlo Park, California

Hours, admission fees, prices, telephone numbers, and highway designations in the editorial content of this book are accurate as of November 1973.

Maps have been provided in each chapter for the special purpose of highlighting significant regions, routes, or attractions in the state. More detailed maps of Washington are available from auto clubs, oil companies, or the Washington State Highway Commission, Olympia, Washington 98501.

Acknowledgments:

Research for this travel guide was expedited in many helpful ways by the following individuals and organizations: Bobbi Bennett, Tri-Cities Visitor and Convention Bureau; Nancy Davidson, Northwest Editor, *Sunset* Magazine; Randall S. Downing, Industrial Development Division, Spokane; Roy Franklin, San Juan Airlines, Friday Harbor; Al Hunter and Donald M. Richardson, Travel Development Division, Washington State Department of Commerce and Economic Development, Olympia; Chester Higman and Tony Preity, Bureau of Indian Affairs, State of Washington; Frank M. Hiteshaw & Associates, Beverly Hills; Jane Johnson, Expo '74, Spokane; Irwin Kaplan, Graphic Studios, Seattle; Donald W. McKeehen, Cleveland & McKeehan, Inc., Seattle; George Responté, Jr.; Everett Stokes, Port of Seattle; Harald Sund; U.S.A. Corps of Engineers, Walla Walla; Frederick Walsh; Ralph White, Washington State Ferries, Seattle.

Edited by Robert Bander

Design: John Flack

Cartography: Roberta Perez-Dillow, Tim Kifune, and Jack Doonan

Covers—*Front:* Fishermen busy themselves on Clear Lake in Pierce County near Tacoma. Private residences line the far shore of the lake, and Mt. Rainier forms a Fujiyama-like backdrop. Photo by Doug Wilson. *Back:* All-weather clamming absorbs a pair of sportsmen on Long Beach. Photo by Keith Gunnar.

Executive Editor, Sunset Books: David E. Clark

TOTEM POLE at left stands on Admiral Way in West Seattle, was carved by Robert Fleischman and Michael Morgan.

Contents

Washington's Water World

WINTER FISHING for steelhead trout in fog-hung waters of Snoqualmie River near Seattle.

CHURNING RAPIDS of Wenatchee
River near Leavenworth
make kayak bounce vigorously.

RIVER RUNNING on inner tubes offers convenient water diversion for many Washington residents.

MEDITATION seems appropriate for father and son in primeval setting of Green River Gorge.

NOISY POWERBOAT storms ahead in annual Sammamish Slough competition.

WHEN SUN, sail, and water combine, Puget Sound takes on tropical glow.

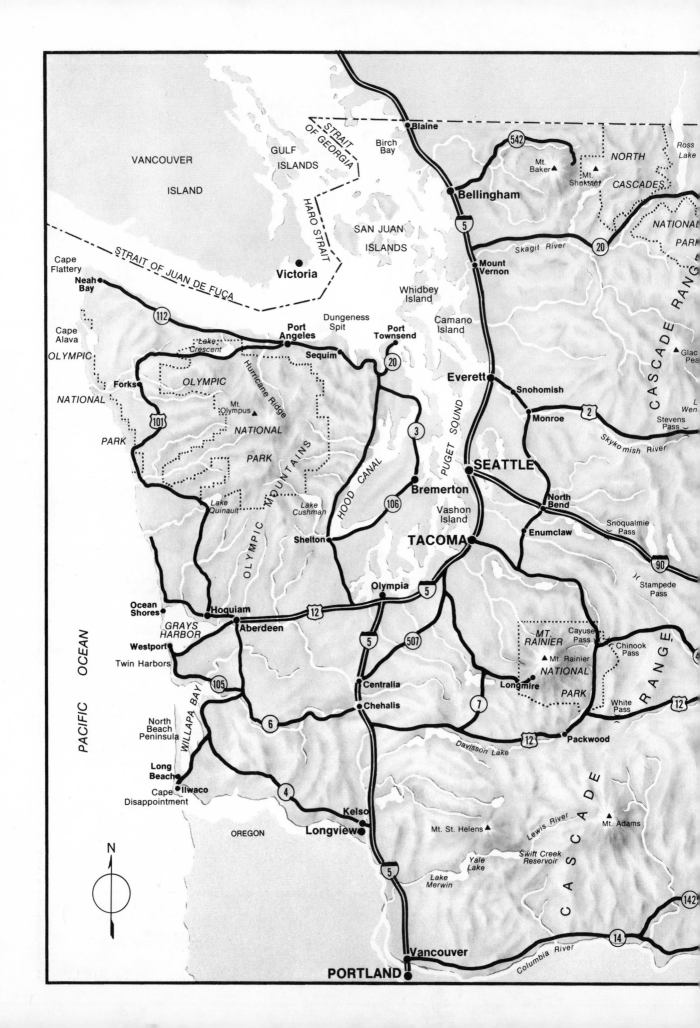

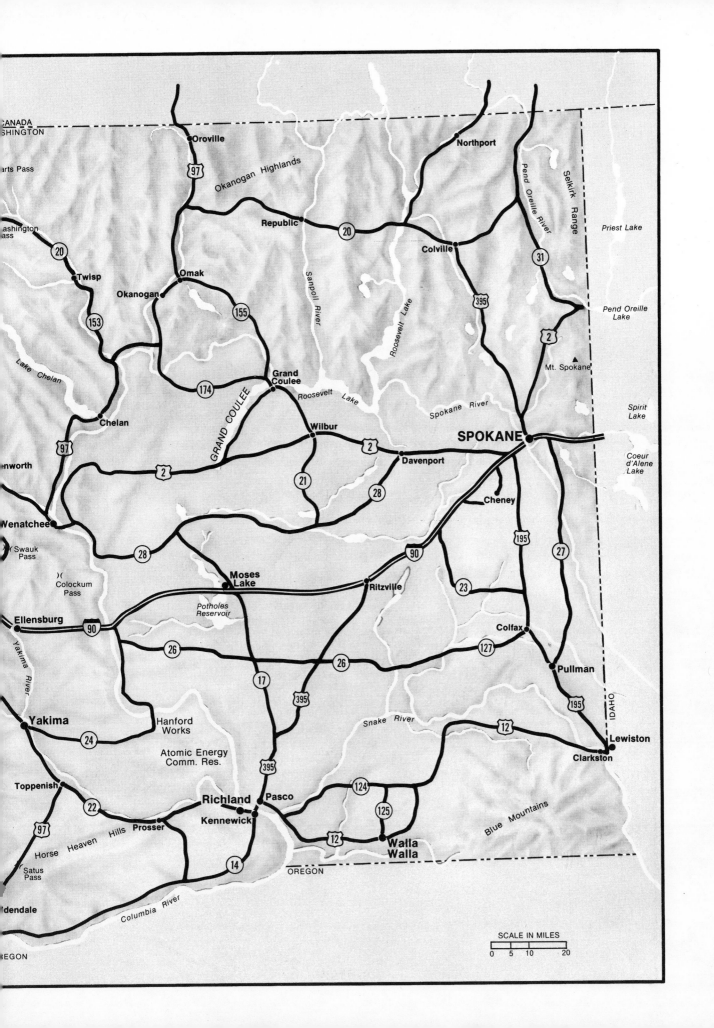

Introducing Washington

Humptulips, Queets, Lilliwaup, and Hamma Hamma seem like Indian names that might come from the great American Southwest. Yet these are names from a far different region, one rich in surprises for the curious traveler. The region is the Pacific Northwest; the state, Washington.

Why is the exciting quality of life in Washington so little heard about outside its borders? One reason may be that the state is geographically somewhat off the beaten track, tucked away in the upper left hand corner of the conterminous United States. Then, too, Washingtonians recognize a good thing when they live it, and understandably most of them want it to last. Some of the citizens of Seattle lend more than whimsical support to an unofficial organization called Lesser Seattle. It is dedicated to making the city a better place to live for the people who have already moved there and—not incidentally—to keeping Seattle a secret from the rest of the world.

And they have a point. For every state needs extensive recreational resources and wilderness areas that soften the stresses of urban life. Washington has them—in abundance.

THE FACE OF A STATE

What gives Washington its personality—its character? What are its topographical features and climate like? What is the economic base of this important Pacific Northwest state? What special scenic treats lie in store for you here? The next few pages explore these questions.

(continued on page 10)

SCUDDING SEA FOAM washes up the sand at Second Beach near La Push on the Olympic Peninsula. Some of many offshore sea stacks are topped with trees.

(continued from page 8)

It's wet . . . and it's active

A visitor to coastal Washington can't help but be impressed by the overwhelming presence of water. Water in many forms, many settings, is a major element. The Pacific Ocean froths along Washington's shores; Puget Sound is a heavily trafficked network of arteries; lakes are plentifully scattered; the Columbia is the West's largest river. Seattle is bordered by salt water on the west, fresh water on the east, and a series of canals and waterways in between. In this city—America's answer to Venice—status derives not from having two cars but from being a two-boat family.

Along with water, Washington brings to mind the word "activity." The state's abundant recreational resources kindle a spirit of adventure equally in residents and visitors. They water ski on Puget Sound, tube down the Yakima River, trudge through Mt. Rainier's ice caves, pick blueberries in North Bend, ski at Snoqualmie Pass, kayak near Leavenworth, scull on Lake Washington, hike, fish, clam, crab, run rivers, rockhound.

Climate and terrain

The majestic Cascade Range, extending the length of the state and on into Oregon, divides Washington into two distinctly different regions. Down the crest of the range marches a line of imposing,

WATCHING automobiles debark from docked ferry at Seattle's Ferry Terminal is bonus for onlookers.

white-topped volcanoes. From north to south, the major ones in Washington are Mt. Baker, Glacier Peak, Mt. Rainier, Mt. St. Helens, and Mt. Adams. Combined with other mountain giants, these magnificent outcroppings form an extensive recreation area easily accessible from both east and west.

West of the Cascades, the climate is moist and the vistas evergreen. Here the weather is also influenced by the Olympic Mountains on the Olympic Peninsula. These mountains shelter the cities around Puget Sound from the heavy rainfall that blankets the ocean side of the peninsula. Average yearly rainfall in the Puget Sound area totals about 35 inches; on the western slopes of the Olympic Mountains it averages 60 to 138 inches. Heaviest rainfall is in the winter. Because western Washington's skies are frequently gray throughout the year, bright sunshiny days are welcomed with more than usual attention.

Winters in western Washington are mild, and summers are cool. Snowfall and below freezing temperatures are rare in the cities, although the nearby Cascades fill up with snow well before Christmas.

East of the Cascade range, though, the terrain presents a startling contrast. The valleys of central Washington are very dry—almost desertlike—though laced with rivers, lakes, reservoirs, and man-made waterways. Rainfall increases toward the eastern edge of the state, encouraged by the Rocky Mountain chain that is visible east and north of Spokane. And the temperature range in the state's heartland is greater than that west of the Cascades.

Washington's economy

Washington is a treasure chest of natural wealth. You can see it in her forests — 24 million acres, occupying roughly one-third of the state. Forestry and wood products, particularly the manufacture of paper and paper goods, figure importantly in the economy of the western and northern areas.

In the Palouse country of eastern Washington, grain is the byword; more bushels per acre of wheat are grown here than in any other area of the world. Fruit is also vital to the state's economy; fruit orchards are centered in the northcentral and southcentral regions. Dairying in western valleys is another important activity. Washington's fishing industry earns over $100 million a year, falling just short of the record marks set by California and Massachusetts.

One of the state's great wonders—the salmon-rich Columbia River—roughly bisects the state and runs for 300 miles along the Washington-Oregon border. Harnessed by the Grand Coulee Reclamation Project and a series of dams, the Columbia provides a virtually inexhaustible water supply for irrigation and a vast source of electric power. But progress also has its drawbacks. Once a free-flowing recreational river, the Columbia is now a placid chain of lakes with no real "white water." (The Cascade

LOOMING COOLLY, lordly Mt. Rainier stands sentinel over Mercer Island Floating Bridge across Lake Washington in Seattle.

Mountains were named for the Columbia's boiling rapids that Lewis and Clark saw on their way to Astoria.)

In the Puget Sound area, the aerospace industry is concentrated. Boeing's factories in Seattle and Everett employ one of the Pacific Northwest's largest work forces. Added to the aerospace activities are canning plants, lumber mills, and pulp and paper plants. Petroleum refineries of four major companies also operate here, and aluminum and atomic energy are young, growing industries.

Its scenic delights

Added to Washington's cornucopia of natural resources are its impressive scenic wonders, many of which seem naturally to call up superlatives in their description. Here is towering Mt. Rainier—thought by the Indians to be a god. Here is the place where one of the wettest sections of the country is found: the Olympic Peninsula's dense rain forests. And here is Puget Sound, a sprawling inland sea, set with islands, whose shoreline serpentines into a succession of picture postcard bays.

Because of its fortunate location and historical associations, Washington has an abundance of parks, forests, and historical sites—many of which have been preserved only through the efforts of

hard-working conservationists. You'll find three national parks in the state: Olympic, Mt. Rainier, and North Cascades (the most recently designated United States National Park). There are also three national recreation areas—Ross Lake, Lake Chelan, and Coulee Dam; five wilderness areas; 16 wildlife refuges; and three national historic sites — Fort Vancouver, Whitman Mission, and San Juan Island National Historical Park.

In addition, Washington offers seven national forests, as well as sections of two more totaling more than 9½ million acres. Once you've exhausted all of these national domains, you'll still have your choice of more than 110 state parks to visit.

A TOURIST'S SAMPLER

Washington's third largest industry—tourism, both by state residents and out-of-state visitors, amounting to approximately $2 billion in spending—is the real subject of this book. We're concerned with providing answers to the question, "What *people* interests does Washington particularly appeal to?"

One answer might be, "Just about anything—from backpacking to backgammon." But a more discriminating reply would have to focus on four activities that the state is especially strong in: boating, fishing, hunting, and skiing.

MONORAIL CAR (below) traveling between downtown Seattle and Seattle Center pulls into stylish station. Ice pellets fly (right) as climber chops out steps on glacier in Mt. Rainier National Park.

Boating in Washington

Whether you own a boat, charter one, or simply ride the ferries, boating waters in Washington are seldom far away. Moorages, ramps, rentals, and other facilities are plentiful enough to be where you need them without being so numerous that they encroach on the beauty of the surroundings. And they are well used: Seattle has more boats per capita than any other area in the country.

Washington is unique in its vast areas of protected salt water. The San Juan Islands cluster in the northern waters on the Canadian border, while the Strait of Juan de Fuca extends west to the Pacific and below stretches the 100-mile-long Puget Sound with its own popular islands. All this salt water is in addition to the ocean that forms Washington's western boundary.

Don't count on tanning and swimming weather, though. In these waters the attractions are forested shores reflected in blue coves, the glimpse of a whale or porpoise, a catch of crab, clams, or salmon, or a stiff breeze for sailing. At sunset, you can choose rustic cottages or a few luxury resorts, but a campfire on a secluded beach or an anchorage with a view of snow-capped mountains are more common, for these waters have miraculously escaped a tourist invasion. Boating practices in

these salt-water areas are governed by U. S. Coast Guard regulations.

Although a boatman could spend a lifetime fishing and exploring these coastal waters, a multitude of fresh-water lakes and rivers dot the state. Some of the most popular areas for boating are the Columbia River, the lakes of the Cascade Mountains, Lake Chelan in Central Washington, and the Columbia Basin in southeastern Washington.

Fishing

From the snow-fed lakes and streams of the Cascade Mountains to the salt water of the Pacific Ocean and Puget Sound, Washington waters once ran thick with fish. And fishing is still good for those who know the places and understand the techniques.

Licenses are required for fresh-water fishing except for children under 16 and in national parks. A 7-day non-resident fishing license is available. No license is necessary for salt-water fishing, but fishermen must record catches on punch cards that are issued at marinas, sporting goods stores, and other places where licenses are sold.

Fresh-water fish found in lakes, rivers, and streams all over the state include 11 kinds of trout, many stocked by the Game Department in the

An Interest Index to Activities in Washington

Wherever your interests lie—from birdwatching to beer making—you'll find something to liven your stay in Washington. Here's a miscellany of suggestions; but remember, this is only a start:

Archery: Aim your arrows straight at the Blue Mountain Archers' practice targets in Fort Walla Walla Park.

Beer making: Sample the product at the Tumwater Olympia Brewery or tour Sick's Rainier Brewery in Seattle.

Birdwatching: Sight the lovely trumpeter swan in your binoculars at Turnbull Wildlife Refuge south of Spokane. On the western coast, Leadbetter Point at Willapa Bay is a prime spot for viewing migratory birds.

Blueberry picking: Ripe berries are especially plump on the north slopes of Mt. Adams, accessible from the Randle-Troutlake road.

Canoeing: Rent a boat at the University of Washington crewhouse for exploring waterways at the edge of the arboretum.

Clamming: Go after these fast-disappearing morsels on Pacific sands at Grays Harbor beaches or Kalaloch Beach on the Olympic Peninsula.

Crabbing: Although there is no closed season or closed area for crab raking in Washington, the best times are spring and summer in most areas. Some dependable spots are Anacortes, Birch Bay, Dungeness, Dosewallips, Quilcene Bay, and the San Juan Islands.

Farm living: For an unusual and inexpensive family vacation, you might enjoy boarding for a week or more on a working farm on one of Puget Sound's islands, outside Seattle, or inland. Local chambers of commerce (see Appendix) can put you in touch with farm families who are willing to serve as your hosts.

Feeding ducks: The most sociable (and gluttonous) waddlers inhabit Green Lake in Seattle and Manito Park in Spokane.

Fossil hunting: Digging in the Horse Heaven Hills southwest of the Tri-Cities might reward you with 50,000-year-old bison remains.

Herb gardening: Examine unusual species at the Grace Campbell House in Spokane or at the University of Washington specialized pharmaceutical garden.

History: Best glimpses into the past are at Vancouver or Walla Walla.

Ice skating: Wintertime temperatures freeze many of the lakes around Spokane.

Mini-yachting. Take your pint-sized sloop to races on Green Lake in Seattle, Medical Lake near Spokane, or Tacoma's Waughop Lake. Check with the North American Model Boating Association, 228 Culp Avenue, Hayward, Cal. 94544.

Pack trips: Two of the many areas that lend themselves well to pack trips are the Cougar Lakes alpine country area on the east slope of Mt. Rainier and the Cathedral Rocks area, east of North Cascades National Park and quite close to the Canadian border. To arrange for trips, first select an area you'd like to explore, then write to national park or national forest headquarters (see Appendix). They will send you names of guides who have been given permission to lead pack trips.

River running: Kayaking is "in" at Tumwater Canyon near Leavenworth; a refreshing pastime on a warm summer day in Ellensburg is to float down the Yakima River on an innertube. Or start at Clarkston with a jet boat or rubber raft to run the rapids of the Snake River through Hells Canyon (America's deepest gorge).

Salmon fishing: Small fleets of charter boats—highly organized for the visiting fishermen—fill the harbors at Ilwaco, at the mouth of the Columbia River, and at Westport, on Grays Harbor near Hoquiam and Aberdeen. Cost for an 8-hour charter, including bait, averages about $20 per person. If you need fishing equipment, it can be rented inexpensively.

Tidepool exploring: Look but don't touch the Olympic National Park seashore area's bright red sea cucumbers, scuttling hermit crabs, and elusive octopi.

Totem poles: If you're looking for the real thing in an authentic setting, search the forests around Lake Quinault on the Olympic Peninsula.

Water skiing: Try the spot where the champions compete—the Columbia River's Lake Wallula in the Tri-Cities.

Wilderness camping: If you want to get *really* close to nature, head for Pasayten or Glacier Peak in the North Cascades, Goat Rocks and Mt. Adams in the Cascades closer to Oregon, or the Wenaha Backcountry in the Blue Mountains near Walla Walla.

Wine tasting: Taste-test at the winery on Hartstene Point off State 3 near Shelton.

most heavily fished waters. Warm water fish, such as bass, crappies, and perch, inhabit the Columbia Basin lakes and reservoirs, as well as the lowland lakes and sloughs west of the Cascades. Small-mouth bass are found mainly in the Snake River area of southeastern Washington.

Salmon, steelhead, and cutthroat are among the most prized Washington game fish because they run so large and put up a remarkable fight. These are migratory, anadromous fish that travel from salt water to fresh water. Steelhead and salmon runs are found in the Columbia and Snake River systems, as well as in the waters of the Pacific coast and Puget Sound.

Although you don't need a license to harvest shellfish, you must be aware of daily per-person possession limits. There is a season for razor clams and a limit of 15. Daily limit on geoducks is three; 20 pounds in the shell is the limit for other clams and mussels. Crabs can be taken year round, but they must be male and at least 6½ inches across. The oyster season is also year round, with a limit set at 18.

For information on shellfish, salmon, and other fish, contact the State Department of Fisheries, 115 General Administration Building, Olympia, Washington 98504. For current regulations on fresh-water fishing (as well as hunting), write the Washington State Department of Game, 600 North Capitol Way, Olympia, Washington 98504.

Hunting

Hunters in Washington will find opportunities to sight both small and big game. Some of the most popular include deer, elk, and bear, as well as waterfowl and other game birds. Check with the State Department of Game or license dealers for seasons and limits which are established annually.

Most blacktail deer are hunted in western Washington, white-tailed deer in the northeast counties, and mule deer on the eastern slopes of the Cascades and in the northeastern and southeastern mountain areas. The Yakima-Kittitas area and the Blue Mountains of southeastern Washington are the hunting grounds for Rocky Mountain elk, while Roosevelt elk roam the more remote regions of southwestern Washington and the coastal counties.

Black bear inhabit most of the state's timbered regions and have been declared a predator in the Olympic Peninsula area because of damage to growing timber. Here they can be hunted during a special bear damage season in spring, as well as during the regular fall season. Check with the game department (see address in previous section)

for detailed information on the bear season. More rare big game animals are moose, big-horned sheep, antelope, woodland caribou, and an occasional grizzly.

Migratory bird populations proliferate on the coast and in Puget Sound, as well as in the eastern farming areas of the Columbia Basin. Ducks and geese are most abundant, but mourning doves, snipe, and the band-tailed pigeon are also hunted. Resident game birds include grouse, quail, chukar, Hungarian partridge, and the popular Chinese pheasant.

Although some Indian reservations permit hunting, permission must be obtained, and a fee is usually charged. No hunting is allowed in national parks or wilderness areas.

Skiing

Snowplowers and schussboomers alike will find that heavy Washington snowfalls make the skiing season one of the longest in the country—sometimes at higher elevations extending from October to July.

Here are some of the most active skiing areas in the state:
• East of Bellingham, an average snow pack of 250 inches at the Mt. Baker ski area often extends the

ETHEREAL LIGHT of setting sun gives Biblical tone to this scene of a sheepherder near Mt. Adams moving his flock across country road. Horse seems pleased with orderly sheep.

ski season to July. Early-season skiers can usually find snow at Baker before the other areas are open. Another northern slope is Mt. Pilchuck, east of Everett.

• At the crest of the Cascades, the challenge of Sno-Country/Stevens Pass attracts the experts. An area for ski touring stretches immediately north of the pass. Yodelin, farther east on Highway 2, also has good facilities.

• At Snoqualmie pass, the ski slopes are just east of the summit. Ski Acres is a learning area, with lots of slopes for lessons. Hyak has lifts on both sides of the mountain; the longest and most rigorous ski runs are at Alpental, north of the summit and reached by a 1-mile gravel road. All of the areas at Snoqualmie offer night skiing, but Ski Acres claims the most extensive lighting.

• Crystal Mountain, just outside the northeast entrance to Mt. Rainier National Park, provides varied terrain with miles of touring slopes. Paradise is a smaller facility inside the park that also encourages sledding and tobogganing.

• East of the Cascades, in the northern part of the state, Loup Loup Summit and Sitzmark are small but active slopes.

• Near Wenatchee, Mission Ridge offers the most extensive skiing facilities, as well as a spectacular view of a string of Cascade peaks. Leavenworth, 20 miles west of Wenatchee, is known for its jumping competition. Other small areas in the vicinity are Squilchuck and Badger Mountain.

• To the south, White Pass Village and Satus Pass attract skiers from around Yakima.

• Near Spokane are Snowblaze on Mt. Spokane, complete with condominiums, and 49° North on Chewelah Mountain. Both are slated for major development.

• Hurricane Ridge on the Olympic Peninsula is a small area with a fine view of the Bailey Range and Mt. Olympus when it's clear. Trails for ski touring are nearby.

Probably the liveliest *après ski* resorts are found at Alpental, Crystal Mountain, Snoqualmie, Ski Acres, and White Pass Village. Tourists can rent cars with ski racks, snow tires, chains, and antifreeze at airports in Seattle, Spokane, Wenatchee, and Yakima.

Write to the Department of Commerce and Economic Development, General Administration Building, Olympia, Washington 98504, for a complete list of ski areas and facilities.

Driving through Washington

You can cross Washington state from north to south and from east to west on interstate highways that are multilane, divided expressways. Interstate Highway 5 runs north from Vancouver, Washington, through the state's most densely settled area —Olympia, Tacoma, Seattle, Everett, and Bellingham—ending at the Canadian border. Washington's second major expressway, Interstate 90, cuts east through the center of the state, from Seattle

CONTESTANT in Leavenworth ski-jumping tournament eyes slope as crowd below waits for his leap.

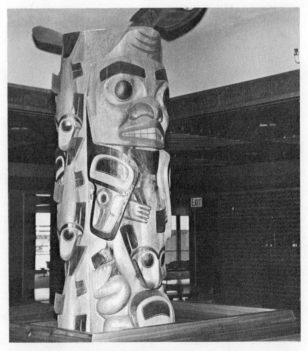

ARTISTIC RENDERING of familiar Pacific Northwest totem pole motif stands in new Sea-Tac Airport.

SALMON FISHING can be highly rewarding, as this sturdy catch in waters off Westport testifies.

RHODODENDRON, Washington's state flower, grows lushly along Hood Canal, framing Olympic peaks.

across the Cascades and past Ellensburg and Moses Lake on its way to Spokane and the Idaho border.

Other stretches of divided highway in the state are State Highway 8, connecting Olympia with Aberdeen on the Pacific coast, Interstate 82, linking Ellensburg and Yakima, and other limited sections of road near Olympia, Tacoma, Seattle, Kennewick, and Spokane. The rest of Washington's highway system is principally two-lane.

Five east-west roads now traverse the scenic Cascades. From north to south, State 20 cuts through the North Cascades, U.S. 2 through Stevens Pass, Interstate 90 through Snoqualmie Pass, State 410 through Chinook Pass, and U.S. 12 through White Pass.

The speed limit in Washington is 70 miles an hour during daylight hours unless otherwise posted, 60 miles per hour at night. In Washington a right turn after a full stop at a red light is permitted.

Though you'll encounter many slower-moving camper vehicles and logging trucks on the roads, they don't slow down traffic too often.

Accommodations and resort areas

The most popular resort areas in Washington—with accommodations that are typically comfortable but rustic, rather than elegant—are located chiefly along coastal areas and in the Cascades.

Along the coast, the 18-mile-long strip of beach-land just north of Grays Harbor, running between Ocean Shores and Copalis, is popular in summer. So is the 28-mile-long Long Beach peninsula, which extends north from just above the mouth of the Columbia River to Willapa Bay.

If island exploring is something you enjoy, you'll be pleased with the prospects in the Puget Sound area. The Puget Sound islands—particularly Whidbey, Camano, and Orcas—are fine vacation fare.

For many travelers, the San Juan Islands are the best that Puget Sound has to offer. With an equitable climate and very little rainfall, the San Juans move at an extremely leisurely pace—geared perhaps to the deliberate speed of the ferries that navigate between them. The hundreds of explorable San Juan islands mean that here you might find for a weekend the ultimate in privacy: an island of your own.

In the Cascades, Washington's first-ranking ski resort area is Crystal Mountain, near Mt. Rainier National Park. On the eastern slopes of the Cascades, dude ranches have been burgeoning recently from Ellensburg up to Okanogan. Along the Columbia River and in the Columbia Basin area near the Tri-Cities, boating is popular and sightseeing increasingly interesting.

Hotel and motel accommodations are usually easy to find in the main cities and towns and along principal highways. In the resort areas, though, reservations are advisable, particularly during the height of the season.

LOGGING TRAINS along roadside tell tale of Washington's lumbering prowess. This locomotive near Humptulips is only for viewing; one in Forks is unfenced for climbers.

Reservations can be made through a travel agent, through local resort associations, or by writing to a specific resort. Many local chambers of commerce will provide information about resorts in their areas; look for a list of Washington chambers of commerce in the appendix.

Camping

Campers will find excellent facilities in most vacation areas. There are free public campgrounds in Olympic and Mount Rainier national parks. Nine national forests offer camping facilities. Most are free, although there is a nominal fee for camping in improved campgrounds.

The state of Washington provides overnight camping facilities in many of its parks. Fees are charged per night per car for camping and for house trailers where special hookups are provided.

Since campgrounds in Washington tend to become filled to capacity during summer months, tourists might better plan their camping trip for early spring or following Labor Day in September, the month when Washington's climate is best.

For a list of campgrounds in Washington, consult the Sunset *Western Campsite Directory*.

How to use this book

Sunset's *Travel Guide to Washington* has been edited with two kinds of people in mind: those who are primarily interested in learning more about the state and those who are actually traveling over its highways, along its air lanes, or on its waterways.

When you are reading ahead about Washington, possibly thinking of making a trip to the Northwest, such sections of the book as the Introduction, photo essays, and sidelights will give you important—often colorful—background information.

Once you've moved from your armchair to the driver's seat, though, other sections of the travel guide will come into play. Each chapter outlines the state's most appealing tourist attractions. Especially helpful are the automobile Loop Trips found in several chapters and listed on the Contents page. These tours, in addition to routing you through some of Washington's most remarkable regions, give illuminating facts about points of interest along the way. Provide yourself with an up-to-date road map to supplement the small loop tour maps.

This book first focuses on those sections of the state west of the dividing Cascade range, then those located east of it. Spotlighted are two of Washington's most impressive travel developments of the 1970s: the completion in September, 1972, of the North Cascades Highway (State Highway 20) through magnificent North Cascades National Park, making a long-planned fifth pass through the Cascades a reality (see pages 93 to 95); and Spokane's Expo '74 (see page 157), America's first ecologically conceived world exposition.

What Makes Seattle Special?

Seattle *is* a special kind of city in the Pacific Northwest—or, for that matter, along the entire West coast. Here are some of the reasons why this is so:

• **First, its history.** Because it was a jumping-off place for adventurous types during the 19th century Alaska gold rush, Seattle has kept alive some of that excitement. Its unmistakable aura of local color can best be felt in Pioneer Square, along the dock area, and in the environs of 1st Street and the Pike Place Market. Because Seattle has jumped from the frontier to the space age in a sudden leap, the old and new here present a vivid contrast.

• **Second, its people.** In its own way, Seattle is as cosmopolitan a city as San Francisco. The importance of the Indian tribes of the northwest to Seattle's makeup is underlined by the fact that those vital transportation links in Puget Sound— the ferries—all bear Indian names. Seattle itself was titled after an Indian chief who sold to settlers for about $16,000 the right to use his name (he fared better than the less sophisticated eastern Indians who turned Manhattan Island over to the Dutch for $24). Recently, Indians took over a section of Seattle's Fort Lawton in which to build and operate an Indian Cultural Center.

Europe and the Orient, too, have made their mark here. A proud community of Norwegian and Swedish families lives in Ballard, where good Scandinavian restaurants are worth looking into. And the Scandinavian influence is just a beginning. You can buy pastry in a Swiss bakery or have a deliciously ethnic meal in an Italian, German, Chinese, Japanese, or Czech restaurant.

• **Third, its setting makes Seattle special.** Like Rome, it was originally a city of seven hills: Capitol, Magnolia, Beacon, First, Queen Anne, West Seattle, and Denny. But in a project begun in 1906, the steep precipices of Denny Hill were washed away to make room for further city expansion.

Sharing the same latitude as Newfoundland, Seattle benefits from its proximity to the Japan Current. The city is protected by the Olympic

SPACE NEEDLE topped by revolving restaurant in Seattle Center distinctively punctuates skyline.

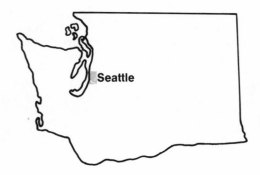

Mountains to the west from heavy winter rains and blocked by the Cascades to the east from the frigid continental winters. Rarely has the temperature been noted to reach 100 degrees, and city records reveal virtually no zeros at all.

Though high mountains make up the distant view from Seattle, this is a water-oriented city. Seattle is nestled between two long arms of water —Elliott Bay on the west and Lake Washington, a 32-mile-long natural lake, on the east. Green Lake and Lake Union lie within the city, and a man-made ship canal crosses the city from Lake Washington to Puget Sound, with locks that operate as readily for small pleasure craft as for freighters.

Leaving Seattle's piers, ships navigate 125 nautical miles through Puget Sound and the Strait of Juan de Fuca, the majority of them Orient-bound, the rest pointed toward European, Alaskan, and eastern ports.

Seattle's interests and industries have always been centered around the water. Yesler Way was the original "Skid Road," a log chute ending at Yesler's sawmill. Today, the most important Seattle industry is jet airplanes, missiles, and space vehicles; but wherever you turn, the city shows its past—fishing, Alaskan shipping, lumbering.

• **Fourth, its efficiency.** Seattle *works* as a city— perhaps because it is a manageably medium-sized metropolis of about 525,000 people. The streets are generally clean; the bus system is brisk and dependable; Seattle Center is a model development for culture and recreation. The fact that the bus running between downtown Seattle and the admirably conceived Seattle-Tacoma Airport is named the "Hustlebus" neatly pinpoints the quality that makes visitors to Seattle forget power failures they may have known.

Exceptions exist, of course. Blessed with a large and potentially lovely lake within city limits (Lake Union), Seattle has allowed it to become industrialized to its detriment as a natural resource. But even here, steps are being taken: the site of an old gas works on a point overlooking Lake Union is being turned into a park.

• **Fifth, Seattle's friendliness gives it a special distinction.** Despite occasional evidence to the contrary, the word "unspoiled" keeps running through a visitor's mind. This is a human city—a folksy city, even. You collect proof on all sides: the typed words taped to a secretary's wall—"This above all, to thine own self be true..."; the phrase in a Seattle tourist guide describing modern aircraft "traveling at a speed that would shock the socks off our grandparents"; the short order cook who really *cares* whether or not you like her hot cakes.

CIRCULATING THROUGH THE CITY

Seattle is both a compact and sprawling city. Its historical and modern business districts are compact; its outlying residential, recreational, and cultural sections are widespread. Because of Seattle's physical layout, its texture can be best experienced by taking both short auto tours and brief walking tours. Bicycling around its lakes brings still another perspective.

TURNING ITS TAIL to silent forest of masts, lone duck glides purposefully across twilight waters of the Shilshole Bay Marina.

Four scenic city drives

More than 400 neat blue-and-green trident signs mark four scenic drives, totaling 117 miles, through Seattle. They take you past most of the favorite views. If you have the time, take all of them, but if your time is short, work out your own combinations of scenic drives 1 and 2 or parts of them.

Drive 1 takes in Woodland Park, discloses wide views of Puget Sound and the Olympics, passes two salt-water parks, Shilshole Bay Marina, the locks, the fishing fleet, and the Seattle Center.

Drive 2 swings through Volunteer Park, along Portage Bay to the University of Washington, goes through several pleasant residential districts, and then curves along Green Lake back to city center.

Drive 3 goes to Beacon Hill and Seward Park, then follows the shore of Lake Washington to the University of Washington Arboretum, and returns to downtown by way of Volunteer Park.

Drive 4 has more residential and industrial driving than the other three drives, but it does offer superb views of the harbor. It loops around West Seattle and takes you to Alki Point, Lincoln Park, the Duwamish Valley, and Beacon Hill.

Or take a walking tour...

At least five colorful areas of Seattle need to be strolled through to be truly appreciated. Take good walking shoes and an appetite for adventure with you, for your time afoot in the city may prove to be more rewarding than your time in a passenger car.

Walking Tour 1: The Pioneer Square area. A morning walk through the 18 square block section at the south end of 1st Avenue in downtown Seattle holds much fascination. Because it is well-stocked with exotic restaurants, the area being restored around Pioneer Square will also be a good place to relax over lunch. (Pioneer Square is described in more detail on pages 24-25 and in the Special Feature "Underground Seattle," page 28.)

Walking Tour 2: The Seattle waterfront. The Alaskan Way is an evocative name for the street that winds along Seattle's waterfront. Start your stroll at the foot of Yesler Way, the downtown street that edges Pioneer Square on its descent to the dock area. A six-block walk from Pier 51 to Pier 57 will give you a smorgasbord of lively impressions. (See pages 25-26 for further information on Seattle's waterfront.)

Walking Tour 3: The Pike Place Market. Like the first two walking tours, Tour 3 lies right in the downtown area, just below 1st Avenue on Pike Street. Located on a bluff overlooking the waterfront, the market is on two levels: its upper level is filled with fish, meat, and produce stands, its lower level with individualistic shops. Stalls can be rented by the day. Secondhand shops and modest restaurants in the immediate neighborhood of the market are also worth exploring. (A fuller description of Pike Place Market appears on page 32.)

Walking Tour 4: Seattle Center. It's easy (and fun) to travel out to Seattle Center from downtown by monorail. Board the ultramodern overhead car at the monorail station at Westlake between 4th and 5th streets. The ride to Seattle Center, a distance of a mile, takes only 96 seconds. Both the monorail and the Center were built for Seattle's 1962 World's Fair. The varied cultural and recreational facilities on this 74-acre site are described on pages 36-38. (For a visual preview of the Center, look at the photo essay on pages 40-41.)

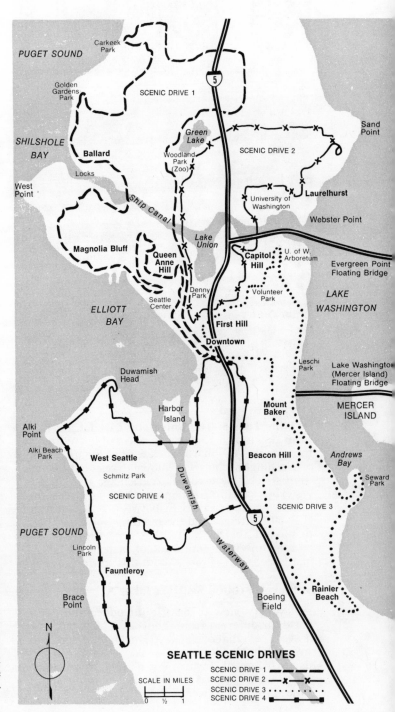

SEATTLE SCENIC DRIVES

SCENIC DRIVE 1 — — —
SCENIC DRIVE 2 —×—×—
SCENIC DRIVE 3 ·········
SCENIC DRIVE 4 ▪▪▪▪▪▪

SCALE IN MILES
0   ½   1

HERE, there, and everywhere, bicycles roll through Seattle. Left, student happily pedals past mod shops in the "U district." Above, cycling family pauses at Green Lake in autumn.

Walking Tour 5: The University District. Farthest from downtown (but easily accessible by bus) is the area that lies just a block west of the University of Washington campus—known to residents as "the 'U' district." Here you'll experience a rich slice of waterbed culture in shops and eating places that line University Way N.E. between N.E. 40th and N.E. 50th streets. And the bustling university campus itself invites a stroll. Its partially Gothic architecture will remind you of eastern Ivy League institutions. (Read more about this area on page 31.)

Or bicycle around Seattle's lakes . . .

A bicyclist's view of Seattle introduces him to a world far different from the world of a motorist—or even from that of a pedestrian. Moving fleetingly through shifting locales, the biker intensely senses his environment. In turn, his gliding presence has a noticeable effect on those he passes. Some smile; some wave; some swerve; some bark.

A prolonged view of water as you bicycle adds pleasure to the activity. Giving facts about bike tours around lakes in or near Seattle, the following paragraphs might be considered a bicyclist's mini-almanac. Trips are listed in order of increasing cycling distances:

Green Lake. *Cycling distance:* about 3 miles. *Time:* 12-20 minutes. *Where to begin:* Large parking lot near east end of lake, near Evans Pool. *Joys:* All paths, no cars, views of ducks, joggers, engrossed lovers. Amenities include drinking fountain, snack bars, rest rooms, mildly steep hills, and the hum of nearby civilization. (Hungry riders often stop at a restaurant at the lake's southeast corner for fish and chips.) *Hazards:* Chiefly the pedestrians on the path, sometimes walking five abreast, oblivious to bicycles. The half mile or so of gravel along the path is gradually being paved. Dogs are seldom a problem. *Interesting side trip:* Woodland Park Zoo —½ mile southwest, uphill.

Lake Union. *Cycling distance:* 7 miles. *Time:* 1½ hours. *Where to begin:* Parking lot of the public boat ramp on North Northlake Way. *Joys:* More scenic than you would imagine for a city-bound lake. You'll enjoy views of downtown Seattle over the lake and the pleasure of crossing two drawbridges. You won't have to pump up many hills or be besieged by dangerous dogs. And if you work up a thirst, a tavern is a comforting stop at the south end of University Bridge. *Hazards:* Traffic can be heavy in places, especially at the drawbridges during rush hours. Steel gratings on the bridge are really not as treacherous as they seem beneath your bike. Try the wooden sidewalk, though, if the grating makes you nervous. *Interesting side trip:* Cycle ¼ mile to the old gasworks at the north end of the lake. This is the site of a planned park that will preserve some of the ominous black structures as observation towers and a link to the past.

Lake Sammamish. *Cycling distance:* about 25 miles. *Time:* 3-5 hours. *Where to begin:* Leave cars at Lake Sammamish State Park at the south end of the lake near State Highway 10 and Issaquah. *Joys:* The Great Outdoors. Here is bucolic sub-suburbia. Wooded hills rise above a fjordlike lake. At its north end is the pleasant town of Redmond. Try the strawberry shortcake in the big restaurant on the main street. *Hazards:* Some heavy traffic near Redmond, as well as a small but significant number of fast and feisty canines. Best defense against these is to stop and jump off your bike, keeping it between you and the witless warrior. Speak soothing words and move slowly. After a sufficient show of courage and display of duty done, the dog will probably grow bored and return to his guard post. *Interesting side trip:* Pine Lake, 4 miles extra, roundtrip. Look for a Pine Lake sign about 2 miles north of the southeast corner of the lake (heading counterclockwise around Lake Sammamish). At Pine Lake you'll come upon King County Park—a tiny, friendly pond where you can swim and picnic.

Lake Washington. *Cycling distance:* 50 miles. *Time:* 6-10 hours. *Where to begin:* Seattle's Seward Park; or, east of the lake, Kirkland's waterfront park.

Europe's Outdoor Cafes—Seattle Style

Until recently, that popular European institution, the sidewalk cafe, was not to be found anywhere in Seattle. Besides the problems of frequently uncooperative weather, an antique city ordinance actually prohibited sidewalk cafes in the city.

But recently, after restaurant owners said they would brave the threat of rain and wind to give the sidewalk cafes a try, the ordinance was amended to allow them to operate under permit. Now, four sidewalk cafes—all extensions of larger indoor restaurants—are in business in downtown Seattle at least during the summer season and some of them also earlier and later.

• *Brasserie Pittsbourg*, 602 First Ave., (206) MAin 3-4167; authentic French cuisine. Operates sidewalk cafe daily on warm, sunny days and will set up tables and umbrellas on other occasions if enough people request them.

• *Brown Bag Store*, 1400 Madison St., (206) EAst 9-7300; soups and sandwiches. Operates sidewalk cafe during warm weather season only.

• *Das Gasthaus*, 303 Occidental Ave. S., (206) MAin 2-5870; fruit plates, stews, soups, salads. Daily sidewalk cafe service available spring, summer, and fall.

• *Jan's Cafe*, 909 Fourth Avenue (downtown YMCA building), (206) MAin 3-1555; mixed menu with emphasis on seafood. Operates daily under awnings, rain or shine, spring, summer and fall.

ELEGANT al fresco *lunch on Occidental Avenue.*

CURIOUS SHOPPERS peer through windows of restored bank with gleaming facade near Pioneer Square.

GINGERBREAD GALORE characterizes the ironwork of Victorian pergola set in Pioneer Square.

Joys: Again, more scenic than you could believe if you had previously seen most of it through a car windshield. This ride offers great variety: city streets, deep woods, small towns, sublime parks, bridges, factories, and views over majestic Lake Washington. *Hazards:* Routing problems: South of Bellevue take 60th S.E., then turn left (north) on 119th Ave. S.E. to avoid a dead end on Lake Washington Boulevard. Study a map carefully for the Kenmore to Lake City stretch. Then wide Sand Point Way is best.

Just beyond the University of Washington, cross the quaint Montlake drawbridge, then point east on Lake Washington Boulevard to reach the shore of the lake again and the delightful University of Washington Arboretum. The Lake Washington floating bridge may be used to divide this trip into two parts, one half each day. *Interesting side trip:* The biker may want to become a hiker for awhile in Bellefields Park, a marshland left in its native state, but made walkable by guided foottrails.

(If your visit to Seattle is too brief for you to explore by auto, bicycle, or on foot, take advantage of the excellent overview of the city you can get on one of the bus tours.)

WHAT TO SEE AND DO

In addition to its urban pleasures, Seattle offers many of the attractions that can be found elsewhere in the state. Here you can try boating, fishing, swimming, ice skating, taking nature walks, and even—on some of the steeper city streets—previewing what a mountain climb is like.

All of the following places will be well worth your while to visit, the activities worth the effort to participate in. Taken together, they make up the quintessential Seattle.

Pioneer Square . . . the oldest and the newest

Seattle's most important historical site, Pioneer Square was once a little island (later filled in) on which Arthur A. Denny established the city on February 15, 1852. The square's worldly atmosphere is enhanced by a restored glass-roofed Victorian pergola that stands side by side with a soaring totem pole.

The heart of old Seattle is compact. You can park your car in a garage or parking lot and stroll past the shops and markets, the historical monuments, and the ornate old buildings around Pioneer Square. It's not hard to find your way — avenues run parallel to the waterfront, whereas streets lead east and west, to and from the bay.

Pioneer Square was the center of Seattle during the city's first few decades when it was a bustling mill town. Nowhere else can you recapture the feeling of early Seattle quite as well. Remarkably consistent in their ornate iron and masonry scrollwork, the massive old buildings in the surrounding blocks were built immediately after the disastrous fire of 1889. Take time to stroll the streets bordering the square. You'll find Seattle's oldest restaurants, some with their original white-tiled floors and embossed ceilings.

But near Pioneer Square you'll also find what is newest in Seattle: elegant buildings, echoing the city's past, restored with tasteful restraint. You'll find a sidewalk cafe or two; art, antique, and craft galleries; a bank remodeled in turn-of-the-century style; wholesale fine furniture galleries. The Grand Central on the Park shopping and dining structure (a former hotel) is a smaller-scale version of San Francisco's Cannery complex. Occidental Square, paved with cobblestones, has a fountain and benches. This is all part of the Pioneer Square Historical District, in which no building can be torn down or have its exterior altered without permission from the city. Occidental Avenue is a good example of the result—a paragon of redevelopment that is one of the brightest elements of the new Seattle.

Near the square, Smith Tower, at 2nd Avenue and Yesler Way, is a good place from which to view the city. Express elevators take you to the Chinese Observatory, 42 stories above the street. From the narrow platform that surrounds the tower on four sides, you can view the city with its backdrop of mountains. Inside the observatory is a replica of a Chinese temple, with elaborately carved teakwood screens and handsome furniture. There is a nominal admission charge.

The Northern Life Tower on 3rd Avenue has a glass-enclosed view room open to the public without charge. Stop at the manager's office on the fifteenth floor to pick up a pass.

A few blocks southeast of Pioneer Square—roughly bounded by 4th and 8th avenues and Main and Lane streets—is a concentration of Oriental business establishments. Try the inexpensive Chinese and Japanese restaurants in this area where knowledgeable Seattle residents flock to dine. It's not far from the railroad station.

Small stores serve the local population and are not keyed to the tourist trade. Plain brick and wooden structures push up to the sidewalks, and the occasional splash of a tong balcony or silver-and-red shop front seems all the more vivid because it overlooks drab streets and weathered buildings.

Don't keep your eyes focused only on what you see at street level. Some of the most interesting sights are three stories up, where gilded lions guard balconies fringed with lanterns and supported by carved balustrades.

Scouting the waterfront

If film directors have not discovered the Seattle waterfront as a prime location site, it must be chalked up to pure oversight. For the piers are stocked with more than enough of the necessary ingredients—a winding waterfront road to hold a police chase or a docking ferry to reunite lovers—to encourage those familiar commands, "Lights! Camera! Action!"

EVERYBODY EATS on Seattle's bountiful waterfront. Top, hungry sea gulls get sustenance from both land and water. Bottom, diners feast at Pier 70 as ferry passes outside on Elliott Bay.

In yet another mood, the dock area may bring to mind the plaintive sounds of Billie Holiday singing "I Cover the Waterfront." It offers both high drama (a fireboat sirening into action) and low (two seagulls contesting a prize catch); even comedy of sorts (a father buying a fish to pacify his son who didn't catch one.) It all depends on the unfolding events, your mood of the moment, and the time of day you choose to visit.

You can reach the waterfront by driving or walking downhill toward Elliott Bay from almost anywhere downtown. At the base of the hill are the waterfront and Alaskan Way. Overhead is the ponderous double-deck Alaskan Way viaduct. Beneath it are railroad switching tracks and convenient nose-in parking with one and two-hour parking meters.

Walk across the busy street between you and the water; immediately you'll sense the excitement in sounds and smells of a busy seaport.

Most ocean-going vessels today berth at more modern piers south of downtown or on Harbor Island. But big freighters still nose alongside these ancient piers on Alaskan Way, close enough almost to touch.

Stretch your legs on the waterside sidewalk. In the space of a few blocks, you'll pass fishing boats, fireboats, sightseeing boats, freighters, ferries. On the way, you can look over the tempting fish displays in the open-air market — everything from Dungeness crabs and halibut to octopus and ink fish. If you prefer your fish in motion, there's also a waterfront aquarium.

Suited for browsing is Ye Olde Curiosity Shop. Don't let the proliferation of cheap souvenirs put you off; you'll find everything from carved walrus tusks to rare Tlingit basketry. At import shops, you'll see an equally wide range of unusual shopping buys from all over the world.

In addition to satisfying your shopping urge along the waterfront, you can also appease your appetite. Seafood restaurants (one with a nautical snack bar), a Polynesian dining place, a spaghetti house, a hotel that serves one of Seattle's best Sunday brunches—all are on or just off Alaskan Way.

At Fire Station No. 5 at the foot of Madison Street, you can tour the fireboats *Duwamish* and *Alki* daily. Saturday or Sunday during summer between noon and 1 p.m. the fireboats go out into the bay for pumping drill—a splashy sight.

From Pier 56 the jaunty little sightseeing boats of Seattle Harbor Tours make several one-hour trips around Elliott Bay daily. A loudspeaker provides a running commentary, and the skipper seems to know the name, home port, and cargo of every ship in port.

Pier 57 is prized by both youngsters and adults: it is Seattle's official public fishing pier, a place from which you can bottom fish to your heart's content. From here there's a good chance of hooking cod, flounder, perch, sole, or other bottom-dwelling fish at any time of the year.

Quite a bit farther along the waterfront is one of its newest and most ambitious projects: Pier 70. Housed on the Ainsworth and Dunn wharf in a 70-year-old structure once used to store canned Puget Sound salmon, Pier 70 now contains some 40 or more colorful shops. These offer foreign-made pottery, furniture, wines, health foods, cut flowers, plants and garden supplies, leather goods, yarns, clothes, books, toys, antiques, and assorted imports. Completed in 1973, Pier 70 bids fair to become one of Seattle's most exciting shopping complexes.

Specialty food bars sell ice cream, peanut butters, tacos, and the like. There's a large, comfortable, end-of-the-pier restaurant whose windows look out to Elliott Bay and the Olympic skyline and back to a corner of the city. And carousers note: a tavern and chowder house adjoining the restaurant offers dancing to live music Monday through Saturday nights.

Modern Seattle

Controlled growth: this is what is apt to come to mind when a visitor sees Seattle for the first time. Certainly the city's skyline is changing—but not at the headlong pace that is characteristic of the Tokyo, San Francisco, or New York skylines.

The downtown business district of Seattle is one that is easily encompassed. Major hotels and office

DOWNTOWN SEATTLE

DOWNTOWN SEATTLE fits between Interstate 5 (foreground) and waterfront. Across Puget Sound rises the Olympic Mountain range.

buildings are mostly within a 9-square-block area. Outlying offices are rarely more than a $1.40 taxi ride from the city's center.

For years, the 42-story Smith Tower (built in 1914) was the single most conspicuous building on the Seattle scene. In 1962, though, the 607-foot Space Needle—"the Eiffel Tower of Puget Sound"—provided some upthrusting competition. With its completion in the late 1960s, the 50-story, dark glass shaft of the Seattle First National Bank Building came to dominate the skyline. (In it you'll find a permanent art exhibition and, on the 46th floor, a French restaurant.) By the mid-1970s, though, it will be joined by a number of other upward bound structures, including the 20-story Peoples National Bank of Washington Building, the 26-story Royal Crest condominium, the 37-story Federal Office Building, and 42-story Bank of California Center.

Another major project scheduled for Seattle is the $40 million King County Stadium, rising south of the business district. Due for completion early in 1976, it is expected to generate up to $50 million in annual business. And by mid-1976, downtown Seattle's skyline will be changed dramatically by the 40-story, $35 million Commerce House tower to be built in the White-Henry-Stuart block.

On the planning boards for several years—and soon to become realities—are two major park projects. A $5 million Waterfront Park has been designed to stretch along the central waterfront. More unusual is the Freeway Park that will be developed: the park, complete with a major water-fall and canyon, will grow atop a bridge covering about two blocks of Interstate 5 as it cuts through downtown Seattle.

Interstate 5, the city's relatively new freeway, is essential to the functioning of modern Seattle. Veining its way north-south close to the business district, the freeway clogs with heavy traffic on work days at 8 a.m. and 5 p.m. But it serves city motorists well by allowing them quickly to head out to the university district to the north, Snoqualmie Pass to the east, and Seattle-Tacoma Airport to the south.

One reason that Seattle does not appear to be an extremely overcrowded city may be that much of its work force lives in such satellite bedroom communities as Bellevue, Kirkland, Lake Sammamish, and Renton.

Along with a number of other American cities, Seattle has participated in a federally subsidized Model Cities program to upgrade depressed areas of the city.

And, of course, Seattle's monorail gives it a firm claim to modernity. Though a monorail winds through Disneyland in Southern California, only Seattle among American cities maintains a monorail as an integral part of its rapid transit system.

Different hills—different scenes

Each of Seattle's six hills has special characteristics that set it apart. You may enjoy knowing a few of the reasons for the hills' individuality:

CENTURY-OLD sidewalks, storefronts, and water system are pointed out on underground tour.

Underground Seattle

Say the words "underground city" and almost instantly an image of Roman catacombs or Parisian sewers races across your mind. But Europe is not unique in having subterranean history to explore. In the United States, Seattle—alone among American cities—has an underground past that is open to visitors.

The story of how Underground Seattle first came to be is a delightful episode in superpractical city planning. In Seattle's early days, the often-soggy climate, lack of drainage, and the unpaved streets of the downtown area combined to form virtual rivers of thick mud, impassable for much of the winter. City government, compelled to find a cheap and quick solution after the drowning of a small child in a mud puddle in a downtown street, struck upon the solution—raising the streets and sidewalks.

Incredible though it may sound, this is precisely what was done. What is now underground Seattle is the result of the sidewalks and first floors of the then-existent buildings being covered up by the new, higher streets and sidewalks. The old sidewalks became underground passageways; the first floors of the buildings became basements. In all, there are approximately 8 miles of underground, though only a small fraction are open to the public.

Tours of the underground start at the Blue Banjo, a vividly-decorated saloon in Pioneer Square. The State Liquor Board has allowed the saloon to maintain "classroom" status during the hours of the tour; no alcoholic beverages are served during the tours, and children are welcome. Tour guides—all well-informed about early day Seattle—begin the tour with a lively introduction to the early history, highlighting the talk with slides and colorful facts about Seattle's flamboyant founding fathers.

Setting off on the tour, you are conducted through the dimly-lit subterranean passages. (Though there is generally enough light, it might be helpful to take a flashlight to probe dark corners.) At points along the way, the city of Seattle has supplied street signs to orientate you in the maze of passages.

Underground Seattle is unique for the insight it gives you into people and places past: glimpses into turn-of-the-century buildings, resplendent in their marble and iron grillwork; the hollow sound of footsteps on the original wooden sidewalks; storefronts and forgotten stairways. Going underground gives you an insight into Seattle's lively past.

To get information on the tour (for which there is a charge), call 682-1511. For reservations, the number is 682-4646. Because hours for the tours vary, be sure to telephone ahead.

Magnolia Bluff. Misnamed by an explorer who mistook the madrona trees for magnolias, this hill with its fine residences offers panoramic views of mountains and water from its encircling boulevard.

Queen Anne Hill. The tallest of the six hills, Queen Anne is a good restaurant area and offers spectacular views from its heights; Seattle Center is at its base. Seattle Center (for details, see p. 36) should not be missed; from art gallery to amusement park, it holds something for everyone.

First Hill. Nicknamed "Pill Hill" because of its many hospitals, this is the Old Seattle area, filled with many historical buildings and location of the major downtown business area.

Capitol Hill. Site of huge, ornate, turn-of-the-century homes, Capitol Hill is also where Volunteer Park is located. The hill was named in sure anticipation that the capitol of the Territory of Oregon would be situated here. With its gardens, art museum, and concerts in the summer, the park has become an oasis for both residents and visitors.

Beacon Hill. Originally part of the central business district, Beacon Hill is today largely residential. In summer (or year-round, if you're brave), you can swim at the beach of Seward Park, a peninsula-shaped park jutting into Lake Washington.

West Seattle. Accessible by only one road or by boat, this hilly peninsula was the landing spot of the first settlers. A marker can be seen on Alki Point. Fishing at the public piers is good.

A cultural exposure

Several outstanding museums and private galleries in Seattle offer both permanent and changing collections:

The Seattle Art Museum in Volunteer Park has on permanent display one of the world's finest collections of Oriental art, as well as American and European art and exhibits that change each month. At Seattle Center, the **Seattle Art Museum Pavilion** has displays of contemporary and Northwest art and sculpture and selections from the museum's permanent collection.

The Thomas Burke Memorial State Museum at the University of Washington focuses on peoples of the Pacific Rim and on man in relation to plants and animals. In a hall of its own is a presentation of the Northwest Coast Indian.

Found also on the university campus is the **Henry Art Gallery,** housing contemporary paintings and sculpture, Northwest and Japanese folk pottery, and a fine print collection.

The Museum of History and Industry, at 2161 East Hamlin, a few blocks south of the University of Washington campus, tells a story of Seattle's first 100 years in a manner that brings history vitally alive.

The Frye Art Museum, 704 Terry Avenue at Cherry (on Capitol Hill), features 19th-century European paintings and other changing art exhibits.

INDOORS OR OUT, art often enlivens Seattle scene. Left, fountain at Seattle Public Library shows Far Eastern influence. Below, Seattle Art Museum in Volunteer Park mounts fine Oriental work.

Picnic, sun, or splash in the great outdoors

About 3,500 acres of recreation land are included in Seattle's extensive park system for the enjoyment of residents and visitors. Hiking and riding trails, tennis courts, swimming pools and beaches, picnic areas, bowling greens, horseshoe courts, ball fields, and archery ranges are all among the offerings. Boating enthusiasts will find public launching ramps, moorages, and rental facilities. Most beaches are backed by a park, picnic grounds, and changing rooms.

SECOND OLDEST park in Seattle, Volunteer Park has formal garden, paths for walks along reservoir.

Perhaps more outstanding than any other feature are the lovely park gardens. There's no better place to spend some time on a sunny afternoon, and gardeners will find them especially fascinating.

Here are some of the larger parks and those that are of special interest:

Carkeek Park, on Puget Sound at Northwest 110th Street, is a beautiful natural park with a beach, picnic area, and outstanding views across the Sound to the Olympic Mountains.

Golden Gardens Park, at Northwest 85th Street, is another good view spot. It has a picnic area, boat launching ramp, and fine salt-water beach with changing rooms.

Woodland Park, Seattle's largest, at Phinney Avenue North and North 55th, has almost 2,000 birds and animals in its zoo. There's also a children's zoo and children's play area with recreational facilities, including a miniature railway. The Woodland Park Rose Garden is in peak bloom in June.

Green Lake Park adjoins Woodland Park in the heart of Seattle's residential north end. Nearly a mile long, the lake is ringed with a park of trees and rolling lawn. A bicycle path circles the lake, and you can rent bicycles nearby. Bathing beaches, an indoor swimming pool, a fishing pier, boathouses, and other recreational facilities make this park popular. Every Fourth of July, Seattleites gather for a display of fireworks over the lake.

Volunteer Park, at 15th Avenue East and Prospect, is on the crest of a hill. On its rolling lawns, dipping to the east and west, stand clusters of handsome trees—dogwoods, elms, maples, oaks, pines, firs, and hemlocks. In this park, the view, the conservatory, the Seattle Art Museum, and the gardens

AWAITING DELIVERY to many world airlines, jet planes manufactured in Boeing's Everett plant stand in regimental lines.

compete for visitors' time and attention.

The Volunteer Park water tower on Capitol Hill is at the highest point on the ridge between Lake Washington and Lake Union. You can climb 151 steps up the large covered platform at the top of the tower, where bronze arrow markers identify the tallest peaks in the Olympics and Cascades.

Denny Park, Dexter Avenue and Denny Way, was the city's first public park, established by David Denny, who gave 5 acres of his land for the purpose.

Leschi Park, on Lake Washington, is one of the city's oldest landscaped parks. Some splendid trees, most of them planted in the 1880s, make this spot especially worth visiting.

Seward Park, on Lake Washington Boulevard South at South Juneau Street, is a forested peninsula. It has a beach, picnic areas, trout-rearing ponds, and small Japanese garden designed around a stone lantern. The lantern was presented to Seattle by the people of Yokohama in gratitude for assistance after the earthquake of 1923. Kwanzan cherry trees line the approach to the park and present a handsome display of rosy pink blooms in May.

Alki Beach Park, at the entrance to Elliott Bay, has a sandy, salt-water beach, picnic tables, changing rooms, and outstanding views.

Schmitz Park, east of Alki Point, is a 54-acre tract of forest.

Lincoln Park, Fauntleroy Avenue Southwest and Southwest Rose Street, is a popular salt-water beach park with wonderful views across the Sound and a good swimming beach. Swimmers who find the Sound waters too chilly can enjoy the warm-water outdoor swimming pool.

Huskyville: the University of Washington

The Pacific Coast's oldest state university occupies almost 600 acres in northeast Seattle. First classes here were held in late 1861. Growing from a nucleus of 20 halls that originally housed part of the 1909 Alaska-Yukon-Pacific Exposition, the 100-plus buildings on the campus today display a variety of architectural styles, from the bright modern of the student union building to the older buildings' Gothic. The campus is set on a bluff against a background of woods, water, and the distant, looming shape of Mount Rainier.

Not only is this the largest academic institution in the Northwest but also it is a leader in sports. Its football team, the Huskies, often draws 55,000 fans to the rakishly designed university stadium. Its crews are almost always leaders in intercollegiate rowing and more than once have brought home Olympic titles.

The Drama School operates three campus theaters: the Playhouse, the Showboat, and the Penthouse. The Penthouse is a theater-in-the-round. The Showboat is just what its name implies: a replica of an old Mississippi showboat.

The Pacific Northwest Collection at the library is one of the main sources of Northwest Americana in existence.

FUTURISTIC sculpture, "Broken Obelisk," emphasizes University of Washington's architectural contrasts.

University of Washington Arboretum

In the Montlake District, south of the Lake Washington ship canal, you'll want to explore the University of Washington Arboretum, one of the most outstanding arboretums in the country.

Enter from Lake Washington Boulevard at Madison Street or at Calhoun. A slow-traffic road takes you through part of the grounds in your car, but to get the most from your visit, you should stroll the paths. Stop at the office for a map or join a guided tour.

You can take a general tour of the entire arboretum or concentrate on specific plantings of rhododendrons and azaleas, dogwoods, hollies, magnolias, crabapples, species roses, brooms, tree peonies, flowering cherries, flowering quince, or oaks.

Japanese tea garden. This 4-acre garden in the arboretum is the largest Japanese tea garden outside of Japan. There is an authentic teahouse, where occasional tea ceremonies are held. The garden is open daily from 10 a.m. to sunset (weekends only in midwinter). Admission fee is modest.

FLOATING PATH at University of Washington's Arboretum is for pedestrians and bicyclists only; no motorized traffic is allowed on this half-mile zigzag walkway south of Union Bay.

Foster's Island. A tiny island in Union Bay has been set aside by the arboretum as a bird sanctuary. During a half-hour walk around its 7 acres, you'll see many species of land and water birds. To reach the island, drive through the arboretum to the Broadmoor gates next to the golf course. Park here and cross the pathway that links the island to the mainland. The island is almost ideal as a natural shelter. Water birds nest in the marsh area along its shores, and land birds inhabit the open grassy fields, dense brush, deciduous and evergreen groves, and the arboretum's center planting of oak, pine, and birch.

Floating path. You can explore the marsh along the south shore of Union Bay on a floating walkway that angles through this city marsh yet leaves it virtually untouched. Winding among tall cattails and scrub willows, this experimental urban nature trail represents the first phase of the arboretum's waterfront footpath network. The ½-mile walk begins at the parking lot of the Museum of History and Industry on East Hamlin Street.

Pike Place Market has personality plus

A haphazard cosmos of arcades and stalls, weathered old Pike Place Market sits irreverently under the nose of Seattle's modern skyline. A jumble of sights, smells, and accents, it suggests at once a 19th century immigrant neighborhood amid the grayness of the Pacific Northwest.

Since opening in 1906 as a place for truck farmers to sell their goods without a middleman, the market has served as the great equalizer, equally available to skid road inhabitants and housewives. It may be the most democratic institution in Seattle.

Vegetables and fruit splashed shiny with water and stacked in yellow, green, and red echelons still visually dominate the main concourse of stalls. Customers at fish counters lean across barrels of fresh clams and crabs to receive a king salmon, which they carry off cradled like a baby. At several of the seafood markets, you can arrange to have a Puget Sound salmon shipped anywhere in the country.

On one side of the brick street that threads through the market, an aging Bolivian cafe owner spoons out bowls of searing hot shrimp soup made from a secret South American recipe. In the main arcade, bearded young men hawk handmade leather purses next to an old woman selling old-time political buttons. A Greek restaurant pumps German beer and serves Filipino dishes, and a tavern with a French name has the best selection of Irish songs in town on its juke box.

This polyglot bazaar, unduplicated anywhere in the West, was the subject of a burning controversy in Seattle for nearly 10 years. Many business people, and some members of the city government, wanted to see it torn down or largely changed to make room for a modernized shopping arcade and hotel-apartment complex, financed in part with urban renewal funds.

Only after a public referendum in 1971 was the market declared safely within a 7-acre historical district, where changes must harmonize with existing structures and be approved by a board of planners and architects.

Today, Pike Place Market is still very much alive. On the crest of a waterfront bluff, it is the dominant feature at the end of Pike Street on the western edge of Seattle's downtown.

Take a look at the level below the produce market, too. Passages lead to musty basement shops where you can buy a 1938 Bing Crosby record or get the equipment to make your own wine and beer.

Yet no matter how tempting the Pike Place merchandise may be, most people come away with the feeling that the market's most colorful display is the people who shop and sell here.

Marketing the Pike Place Way

SATISFIED SHOPPER strides homeward after busy foray at Seattle's unique bazaar, Pike Place Market.

SHOES, SHIPS, and sealing wax—whatever you are looking for, try Pike Place's lower level shops.

DILIGENT CLERK measures out exotic coffee beans in one of market's most pleasantly aromatic stores.

SMALL PURCHASES, social conversation go hand-in-hand at stalls displaying lustrous vegetables.

The locks and the ship canal

Seattle's locks and the Lake Washington ship canal first began operating in 1916. The original idea was to open the fresh waters of Lake Union and Lake Washington to ocean shipping. A short stay in the lakes cleaned an ocean freighter bottom of barnacles, saving the cost of a drydock hull cleaning. Today the locks still open for ocean-going vessels, but the heavy traffic is in fishing boats and pleasure craft.

This interlocking system of fresh and salt water connects Puget Sound through the Lake Washington Ship Canal with a large, freshwater harbor composed of Salmon Bay, Lake Union, Portage Bay, and Lake Washington. The locks separate fresh from salt water at the western end of the ship canal.

The total shoreline of this protected, placid water recreation area measures about 100 miles. Portage Bay has unique houseboat communities; Lake Union moorages shelter huge old ocean-going freighters.

Although the Hiram M. Chittenden Locks are no longer among the largest in the world, they handle more vessels each year than most others. The large lock is 825 feet by 80 feet; the small lock is 150 feet long and 28 feet wide. Vessels leaving fresh water for Puget Sound travel 8 miles from deep water in Lake Washington to the end of the ship canal, dropping between 6 and 26 feet (depending on tides) as they pass through the locks.

The locks were designed with visitors in mind. The grounds have 7 acres of gardens, and spectators on Saturday or Sunday mornings can watch flotillas of small boats crowd into the lock, then drop to salt-water level. Sunday evening, when the boats come home, is the busiest time of all. Sometimes leaping salmon passing through the locks along with the boats add to the traffic.

Children like to cross over the locks on the pathway formed by the closed lock gates.

Once a day, from May 31 until mid-September, the *M.V. Sightseer* makes a round trip from Leschi Park on Lake Washington to Elliott Bay on Puget Sound. The trip takes 2½ hours one way. Highlights are the downtown waterfront, the ship canal passage, and the Lake Washington cruise. The ship has a coffee shop, snack bar, steamer chairs on deck, lounge chairs indoors. Loudspeakers inter-

WATER RISES in Hiram M. Chittenden Locks as boats, traveling between Puget Sound and Lake Washington, tie up at wall to await passage.

mix music with running commentary on passing sights. In midsummer, it's wise to make this trip on a weekday. Weekend trips are often jam-packed.

Test a floating bridge

The only way to prove that the floating bridges across Lake Washington really float is to walk on one of them. (You can walk out on the Mercer Island Bridge, but pedestrians are not permitted on the Evergreen Point Bridge.) The bridge pontoons, anchored firmly in place, move so imperceptibly that you can't feel them in a car, even when the wind is strong enough to send spray over the roadway. But as you walk, even on a calm day, you'll feel enough rise and fall to convince you the bridge is floating.

Along the Mercer Island Floating Bridge, sidewalks run on both sides, with four auto lanes between. Small boats pass under the elevated end spans that connect with the floating span. For large boats and for ships, a section of the bridge close to the Mercer Island shore opens. This bridge is a good place from which to watch the sailboat races that take place on Wednesday afternoons in summer a mile north.

Evergreen Point Bridge is the second floating bridge across Lake Washington. This is the world's longest floating bridge, with 35 pontoon units. It crosses the lake north of the University of Washington Arboretum and connects with Evergreen Point on the opposite side of the lake.

Seattle's Seafair festivities

Seafair is a hectic but exhilarating annual 10-day celebration held in late July and early August. It is best known for its salmon-fishing derby and the hydroplane races on Lake Washington, which climax the week's festivities. But a crowded schedule

RIDING THE CREST of the granola boom, salesgirl in "U district" health food shop shows wares.

JAPANESE GARDEN in University of Washington Arboretum has picturesque Turtle Island (left of ducks), topped with red pine.

SEATTLE'S SKYLINE forms backdrop for typical nautical scene as motorboat, powerboat, and sailboat converge at dock fronting Elliott Bay in West Seattle.

PLEASING SPIRALS of parking garage, elegant curve of terminal at new, $150 million Sea-Tac Airport.

of parades, street dances, water shows, Oriental festivals, band concerts, and fireworks offers many other amusements.

If you visit Seattle during Seafair, make your hotel reservations well in advance. For a detailed schedule of events, write to Greater Seattle, Inc., 1102 Northern Life Tower, Seattle 98101.

Seattle Center: a stunning leftover

With vigor and imagination, Seattle has transformed its old 74-acre World's Fair site into a new kind of city park. It includes a performing arts center (like the Los Angeles Music Center and New York's Lincoln Center), an amusement park, a mix of eight museums and galleries, perhaps the most exuberant array of fountains this side of Rome, acres of lawn for lounging, avenues of trees. There's an overhead bucket sky ride that reminds you of Disneyland, a general air of relaxation and activity that reminds many visitors of Copenhagen's Tivoli.

Seattle's great park is easy to find. From downtown or any approach to downtown, just look for the Space Needle and head in its direction. (Or park downtown and walk to the Westlake and Pine monorail station.)

Many of the buildings erected for the 1962 Century 21 Exposition now house cultural and civic attractions. The Opera House and the Seattle Center Playhouse are busy all year with theatrical

Side Trips from Seattle

East, west, north, south on the compass—in all directions, points of interest crop up close to Seattle. These are some:

Carnation Milk Farms. Any young milk consumer should enjoy a visit to the Carnation Milk Farms, some 25 miles from Seattle in the valley of the Snoqualmie River. Open daily (except Sundays and holidays), the dairy offers a well marked do-it-yourself tour that leads you past calf and cow barns, milking sheds, dog kennels, wild game bird pens, an old wagon exhibit, rose gardens, and a large statue of the world's champion milk cow.

To reach Carnation Farms, drive out the old Redmond-Fall City Highway (State 522) for 5½ miles; turn left on Ames Lake Road. Ames Road is well marked with signs directing you to Carnation Farms.

There is no admission charge. The best time to be on hand is 2 p.m., when milking begins.

Seattle-Tacoma International Airport. If you fly into Seattle, you're almost certain to experience one of the Pacific Northwest's newest manmade wonders—sparkling Seattle-Tacoma International Airport. But if you drive, you might miss seeing what is probably the West Coast's most comfortable, efficient, and esthetically pleasing airport—unless you make a short side trip. Sea-Tac is located between Seattle and Tacoma off Interstate 5.

Passenger capability of the new airport is now from 12 to 15 million travelers a year. Future satellite expansion by one-third will accommodate a total of 20 million passengers by the 1990s. The new Sea-Tac took about 5 years to complete and cost roughly $150 million.

The result? Sea-Tac is to the West what Dulles International Airport is to the East: an integrated, well-designed facility. The new airport is all the more remarkable because it was built around the shell of the former airport without causing an interruption in passenger service.

Blake Island. A westbound excursion boat leaves the Harbor Tours dock at Seattle's Pier 56 from June to Labor Day for Blake Island and a Tillicum Indian village tour. The ticket includes transportation, a barbecued salmon dinner cooked in traditional Makah style, and a program of Northwest Indian songs and dances.

Blake Island is so small that you can walk completely around it in two hours, viewing botanical specimens and the Seattle skyline.

Boeing Company, Everett. Visitors may arrange to tour the impressive Boeing plant located about 30 miles north of Seattle. Touring is possible from Monday through Friday between 9 a.m. and 1 p.m. No children under 12 years old are admitted.

Green River Gorge. Green River Gorge resort, picnic tables, and wooden stairs leading to a trail and the river below have weathered into charming rusticity and exude a nostalgic, museumlike appeal.

The gorge itself presents a look farther into the past. Cutting through more than 200 feet of sedimentary strata, it provides a glimpse at millions of years of geologic history—as well as offering a fine setting for a spring outing.

To get to the gorge (it's about 30 miles southeast of Seattle), take the Maple Valley Highway (State 169) to Black Diamond, where a large sign marks the cut-off at Lawson Street. Continue 4 miles east to a bridge spanning the gorge; across it is the resort.

THUNDERING FALLS, massive rock outcroppings fascinate explorer at Green River Gorge.

EACH GENERATION follows its special interest in Seattle. Top, flute seller in Pike Place Market demonstrates product. Bottom, serious rockhounds inspect specimens at their kind of rock show.

productions, symphony concerts, recitals, ballets, and lectures. Seattle's Repertory Theater performs in the playhouse. The Coliseum offers sports events and special shows. The Arena has a public ice skating rink and is also used for concerts and displays; hockey games played here explode with vigorous local color.

Focal point of the Center is the Space Needle, which offers a panoramic view from a restaurant and observation platform on top. There's a nominal fee for riding up on the elevator. Once atop the Needle, you can buy a light snack on the observation deck or a more complete meal in the revolving restaurant.

The Center's fountains are a grand surprise. It's easy to miss some of the best ones—but you shouldn't. Go to the Playhouse entry plaza to see the great fountain by sculptor James FitzGerald, a tall, abstract sculpture.

The great International Fountain runs through a 90-minute repeating cycle, afternoons and evenings, with music and water action programmed together.

Many visitors especially like the flower fountains you look down upon in the Science Center water court. Each "flower" is 16 feet in diameter with water jets rising 6 feet in the air.

Stop by some of these other attractions:

Pacific Science Center is spread through five large, handsome buildings arranged around a delightful water garden with pools, fountains, walks over water. Here you'll find a science show unlike any other in America. A big attraction is the Moon Walk. You can also experience lunar gravity (one sixth of that on earth) in a special harness, take a ride in an air-cushion vehicle, and work a "master-slave manipulator" used in atomic research.

Northwest Craft Center is an art and handicrafts sales gallery packed with the unusual. It features work by artists and craftsmen from the 11 western states and Western Canada.

Seattle Art Museum Pavilion, a branch of the main museum in Volunteer Park, has rotating regional and international contemporary exhibits.

Mural Amphitheater is a sylvan outdoor stage area where "all-join-in" folk dancing occurs in summer.

Hall of Fire Engines attracts boys of all ages and their fathers to inspect fire-fighting equipment from the mid-19th century to World War II.

Hall of Aviation displays historic planes, including an early Sikorsky helicopter and an F-5 jet fighter. For a small charge you can "fly" in a hooded Link trainer.

Food Circus and International Bazaar, together in one large building, offer you a choice of some two dozen inexpensive restaurants, as well as a shopping arcade downstairs where you can buy loden coats, lederhosen, silks from India, Korean brass, Scandinavian cookware. Also located in the Food Circus building: Jones Fantastic Museum; Pullen Alaska Museum; Pottery Northwest Workshop.

HOUSEBOATS nestle at base of University Bridge on Portage Bay. Tubbed plants provide cheery touch in this water-based enclave.

Fun Forest is an amusement park with rides and games for every age level.

If you write to Seattle Center, Special Activities, 305 Harrison Street, Seattle 98109, you'll get back an up-to-date map of the center.

Things you might not think of

Here are a handful of sights or activities—and one important address—to give added dimension to your trip to Seattle:

Sailboat races. At Shilshole Bay Marina, sailboats race in all kinds of weather. It's an exciting spectator sport, too—though Golden Gardens, the park next to the marina, is crowded during summer. Drive west on 45th Street to reach Shilshole Bay. (Near here are the locks, and Ballard is close.)

"Get-away" ferry trips. A number of short but delightful ferry trips leave the Seattle Ferry Terminal, Pier 52 at the foot of Marion Street, for the Kitsap Peninsula (gateway to the Olympic Peninsula) and Bainbridge Island. From the Fauntleroy Terminal in West Seattle, you can take a ferry to Vashon Island and the Kitsap Peninsula. Take advantage of the excursion rates. Write Washington State Ferries, Ferry Terminal, 98104, or phone 464-6400 for details.

Children's zoo. Turn in by the rose gardens at Woodland Park and you'll find yourself at the Poncho Theater, where plays are often performed and where you'll hear an introductory lecture on the Children's Zoo. If zoos in general charm you, this Children's Zoo will multiply the effect.

Houseboat peeking. Along Portage Bay (off Eastlake Avenue nestled under University Bridge), a colorful community of houseboats has sprouted. Exploring these cheery floating homes, many with tubbed gardens on their porches, will give you an insight into an inviting lifestyle. Houseboats here have been featured in architectural publications. (There are over 500 houseboats in Seattle, housing over 1,500 people.)

Undersea gardens. It's well worth the nominal fee at the Shilshole Bay Marina to see this unusual, submerged aquarium where Puget Sound specimens live in their natural habitat. (This experience is scuba diving for those with neither the equipment nor taste for the real thing.)

International Friendship Grove. Trees representing 71 nations from all over the world were planted during the 1960 World Forestry Congress held at the University of Washington. The grove fills the center strip on the Campus Parkway.

Hydrofoil to Canada. For a special thrill, try a trip aboard the revolutionary new hydrofoil "H.S. Victoria," which leaves Seattle's Pier 64 daily for Victoria, B.C. The 2½-hour Puget Sound ride leaves Seattle at 9 a.m. and departs Victoria at 4:30 p.m. daily except Monday. Telephone 682-1851 for prices and reservations.

Seattle Visitors' Bureau. No book could answer all the questions you might have about Seattle, but the Seattle Visitors' Bureau can. Visit them downtown at 1815 7th Avenue or telephone them at 622-5022. They'll advise you about accommodations, sightseeing, local and regional trips—even about the unique, 24-hour Emergency Language Bank (telephone 622-6900) that Seattle maintains to give instant translation help to visitors who are not fluent in English.

Seattle Center: a People Pleaser

SPRAWLED on lawn beneath arches of Pacific Science Center, audience listens to folk music concert.

TWO of Center's top attractions: orchestrated fountain (music and lighting are added); Space Needle.

RAUCOUS FUN *for all ages on the roller coaster ride, popular in Center's Fun Forest section.*

BONUS *from Seattle's 1964 World's Fair, former exhibition hall is now Seattle Art Museum branch.*

DINING OUT *takes on a new perspective when your table is set in the revolving restaurant atop 607-foot-high Space Needle. While dining, you'll get 360-degree view.*

CAPACITY AUDIENCE *anticipates Opera House performance.*

Puget Sound: Its Cities, Its Islands

When you first come upon Puget Sound, your reaction may be to wonder how an area with so many natural riches has escaped industrial and recreational exploitation.

Yet it has. Despite its many tempting assets—protection from (yet easy access to) the Pacific Ocean, dozens of superb natural harbors, scores of habitable islands, abundant fishing and timber resources, hundreds of miles of valuable coastline—Puget Sound has not been spoiled. Its cities have not spread together to form a faceless urban mass; its waters have not turned brown; its air remains clean and clear; its tourist facilities are surprisingly uncluttered. The Sound (named for Peter Puget, one of Captain Vancouver's lieutenants) is still very much for visiting.

CITIES AROUND THE SOUND

In addition to Seattle, a number of other distinctively Washington cities have sprung up around the Sound. Seven of them (Bellingham, Anacortes, Mount Vernon, Port Angeles, Port Townsend, Everett, and Poulsbo) are above Seattle; two (Bremerton and Tacoma) are below Seattle. Some tourist attractions of interest in these cities are mentioned below. (Olympia, the state capital and southernmost city on Puget Sound, is discussed separately on pages 83-84.)

Bellingham . . . gateway to Canada

The last major city in the northwestern corner of the United States before the Washington coastline meets the Canadian border, Bellingham has diverse economic interests. It boasts a cold storage center, fishing port, boat building industry, lumber processing and pulp and paper manufacturing plant, as well as an oil refinery and an aluminum plant.

Of interest to tourists is the fact that Bellingham is the headquarters for Mt. Baker National Forest. You may also want to visit Western Washington

FOLLOWING one of the world's most scenic routes, a ferry navigates through forested San Juan Islands.

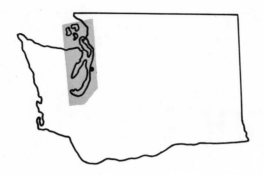

State College campus here. The Whatcom Museum of History and Art is inviting. And don't overlook the Lummi Aquaculture Project (6 miles northwest of Bellingham on State Highway 540). In these Indian-operated fish and shellfish ponds, oysters, trout, and salmon are raised and seaweed is harvested. In June, a Lummi-Stommish Indian water festival takes place at their Sea Farm.

An island city—Anacortes

Situated at the northwest tip of Fidalgo Island, Anacortes is strategically connected to the mainland by State 536. The city's ferry terminal is the popular starting point for excursions through the San Juan Islands.

Fidalgo Island itself offers much of recreational appeal. Visitors particularly enjoy Causland Park, Washington Park, and Mt. Erie. An annual Arts and Crafts Show is held in Anacortes during the first weekend in August. Authentic Indian totem poles are carved and for sale at Totem Pole Lane, 2101 9th Street, Anacortes.

The northwest's Mount Vernon

Named for George Washington's Virginia plantation, Mount Vernon was developed by thwarted gold seekers who turned to logging and farming. The city is located near the Skagit Delta, rapidly becoming a tulip-raising center.

On Little Mountain, southeast of the city, a 35-foot observation tower atop the 927-foot peak overlooks the San Juan Islands and Skagit Valley and is surrounded by a 480-acre forested park.

Port Angeles: an Indian village expands

Once a small Indian village, Port Angeles has grown into a center for shipping and tourism. Ediz Hook, a 3-mile-long sandbar, forms a harbor that makes the city the first American port of entry for many ships entering Puget Sound from the Pacific.

Port Angeles is the headquarters and jumping-off spot for Olympic National Park. And from the city atop the Olympic Peninsula, ferry trips depart for Victoria, B. C., just 17 miles away across the Strait of Juan de Fuca. At Port Angeles' annual Salmon Derby, held on Labor Day weekend, Friday is children's day.

STROLLING ARM IN ARM along the waterline is a common activity on the Whidbey Island side of Deception Pass State Park. Driftwood bonfires require permits. At left: Fidalgo Island.

Port Townsend turns back the clock

At the northeast tip of the Olympic Peninsula, Port Townsend was once an active port visited by stern-wheelers and sailing vessels. Now it is a farm and paper mill town, with ferry service connecting it to Whidbey Island.

But Port Townsend's chief tourist draw is its unusual number of preserved Victorian buildings, refurnished in the style of the 1800s. Other features include Old Fort Townsend Historical State Park and the Crown Zellerbach plant, which offers an industrial tour.

Ships and planes at Everett

Sheltered by Whidbey and Camano Islands, Everett is rapidly developing into a major Pacific Coast port. The city's harbor is located where the Snohomish River empties into Port Gardner Bay. Another distinction of Everett: here you'll see the plant in which Boeing's 747 is manufactured and assembled.

From Everett, tourists have easy access to Whidbey Island to the west by ferry from Mukilteo, to Granite Falls to the east by State 92, or to Mt. Baker National Forest to the north by Interstate 5, connecting with State 530.

Poulsbo . . . Little Norway

Poulsbo, a fishing village north of Bremerton on the Kitsap Peninsula, was settled by Norwegians who found the region resembled the forested hills and waterways of their native land.

Annually in May they celebrate their heritage with a Viking Fest.

The navy town of Bremerton

Bremerton beats to the pulse of its Puget Sound Naval Shipyard. This community, surrounded on three sides by water, is devoted almost entirely to the needs of the base. With its six drydocks, Bremerton is considered a home port for the Pacific fleet.

Of special importance in the Naval Shipyard—itself worth a visit—is the *USS Missouri*, the historic World War II ship on whose deck the formal Japanese surrender took place. Look, too, for the informative Naval History Museum in Bremerton's Ferry Terminal Building.

What makes Tacoma tick?

Set halfway between Seattle and Olympia near the southern end of Puget Sound, Tacoma provides shippers with one of the world's best harbors. In addition to its more than 400 industries, Tacoma houses major railroad and shipbuilding yards. Here are located the University of Puget Sound and Pacific Lutheran University. Nearby are two important military installations: the Army's Fort Lewis (12 miles southwest on Interstate 5) and the Air Force's McChord Air Force Base (9 miles southwest on Interstate 5). The Nisqually entrance to

VISITORS at Whatcom Museum in Bellingham, left, examine loggers' axes. Above, Gig Harbor, at southern end of Puget Sound, offers protected harbor for fishing craft, pleasure boats.

Mt. Rainier National Park is 56 miles southeast of Tacoma on State 7.

The present Narrows Bridge between Tacoma and the Kitsap Peninsula represents an engineering feat; an earlier bridge was ripped away by riptides and winds. Across the bridge on State 16 at Peacock Hill, the Scandia Gaard country restaurant and gift shop is patterned after a typical Scandinavian farm. Folk dances from the Scandinavian countries are presented there in mid-June at the traditional Midsommarfest. Below is picturesque Gig Harbor.

In Tacoma, tourists can see one of the world's tallest totem poles, carved from a single cedar tree by Alaskan Indians. Of added interest: Wright Park, which contains approximately 1,000 trees of 111 varieties; the State Historical Society Museum, with its excellent collections of pioneer relics; and 638-acre Point Defiance Park.

The Puyallup Valley Daffodil Festival, which takes place in April in Tacoma and in nearby Puyallup and Sumner, features a floral parade with floats.

Birdwatching (Snow Goose Division)

SNOW GEESE, above, swoop past marshy fringes of Skagit Wildlife-Recreation Area near Mount Vernon. Left, birdwatcher peers through binoculars at migratory birds that winter over in broad delta of Skagit River.

One of the most important wintering grounds for migratory waterfowl along the Pacific Flyway lies southwest of Mount Vernon in the broad delta of the Skagit River.

The Skagit Wildlife-Recreation Area is year-around home to scores of birds but most famous for the thousands of snow geese that winter here. You can see the great white birds in large numbers in February and March, along with Canada geese, black brant, and hundreds of other species.

For the best views of snow geese, time your visit during a high tide which will enable the feeding birds to come close to the shoreline. Find a high vantage point for an overall panorama.

Binoculars are standard bird-watching equipment, as are warm clothes, gloves, waterproof boots, and rain gear. For novices, a helpful paperback guide to bird identification is *Washington Birds: Their Location and Identification*, by Larrison and Sonnenberg (Seattle Audubon Society, Seattle, 1968; $3.95).

The state game department, which manages the area, has a brochure that explains how to get there, lists important species of birds by season, and includes a map showing road access points and parking. For a copy of the brochure, write to the Washington Department of Game, 1100 E. College Way, Mount Vernon 98273.

To get to the wildlife area, leave Interstate Highway 5 at the Conway Exit and follow Fir Island Road west 1½ miles to Mann Road. Turn left (south) and drive a mile to the delta.

Tacoma's Point Defiance... Stanley Park South

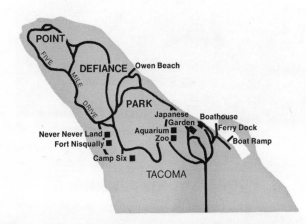

HUMPTY DUMPTY waves hello at entrance to Never Never Land, children's joy in Point Defiance Park.

FRIENDLY OCTOPUS shakes hands with attendant as monkey leans in for closer view in park aquarium.

YOUNGSTERS peek inside colorful Indian canoe at Fort Nisqually, former Hudson's Bay Company post.

PUGET SOUND FERRIES

One long blast—two short blasts: that's the standard Washington State ferries' signal. And if it succeeds in luring you onto one of the system's 21 roving vessels, consider yourself lucky.

The fun of a ferry

You'll feel the thrill of docking when the Seattle skyline seems to rise suddenly around you in the curve of Elliott Bay, pulling your head back irresistibly. The ferry roars on as though heading for some secret subterranean passage, and for a moment you get the feeling that both it and you are going to glide right under the city. Then at the last moment, the engines throb into reverse and the ferry coasts meekly into its slip.

It's an old experience, yet it never grows stale. And it's the sort of thing that makes so many Puget Sounders and visitors enthusiastic about the ferries that crisscross the Sound and the Strait of Juan de Fuca—offering marvelous opportunities to sightsee and to sample the romance of the sea without having to make the commitment of real ocean travel.

On later winter weekends, for example, you can watch a storm roil the Sound into a frothing blue-green turbulence, then retreat to the ferry's warm interior to relax over a cup of coffee and imagine the feelings of Captain George Vancouver and his men as they explored these waters 180 years ago.

On a sunny day you can explore Vashon, Bainbridge, or Whidbey Island or take a cruise to the San Juans.

FERRIES LARGE AND SMALL cross Puget Sound. Top, jumbo ferry MV Spokane *resembles ocean liner. Bottom,* MV Klahanie, *former San Francisco ferry, seems minute by comparison.*

FERRY ROUTES

Washington State Ferries

1. Anacortes, Skagit County, to Sidney, B.C., via the San Juan Islands, with stops at Lopez Island, Shaw Island, Orcas Island and Friday Harbor on San Juan Island. (Note: On some trips, ferries do not make all stops, nor do all ferries terminate at Sidney.) 3½ hours.

2. Mukilteo, Snohomish County, to Columbia Beach, south end Whidbey Island; 15 minutes.

3. Edmonds, Snohomish County, to Kingston, north Kitsap County; 25 minutes.

4. Seattle Ferry Terminal, Piers 52–53, to Winslow, Bainbridge Island; 25 minutes.

5. Seattle Ferry Terminal, Piers 52–53, to Bremerton, Kitsap County; 25 minutes.

6. Fauntleroy, West Seattle, to Vashon Heights, north end Vashon Island, and from Vashon to Southworth, Kitsap County; 30 minutes.

7. Tahlequah, south end Vashon Island, to Pt. Defiance, Tacoma; 15 minutes.

Other ferry routes

All year service:

8. Anacortes to Guemes Island. Operated by Skagit County; 7 minutes.

9. Port Angeles to Victoria, B.C. Operated by Black Ball Transport, Inc.; 1 hour, 25 minutes.

10. Steilacoom to Anderson Island (30 minutes), Ketron Island (15 minutes), and McNeil Island (10 minutes). Operated by Pierce County.

11. Gooseberry Point (Bellingham) to Lummi Island. Operated by Whatcom County; 10 minutes.

Seasonal service:

12. Port Townsend to Keystone, west side Whidbey Island. Service from April through October. Operated by Olympic Ferries, Inc.; 35 minutes.

13. Seattle Ferry Terminal, Pier 64, to Victoria, B.C. Service from May to September. Operated by Canadian Pacific Rail; 4 hours.

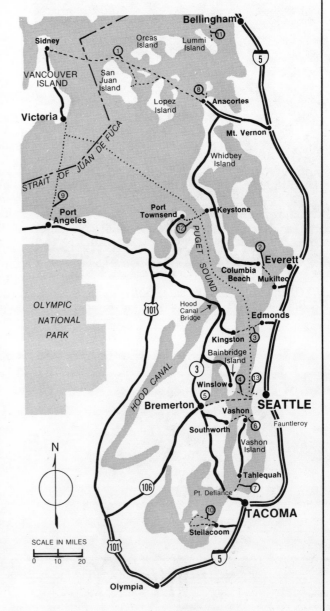

If Washington's weather is varied, so is ferry travel. You can travel as a foot passenger, leaving the car at the dock; or bring your bicycle, motor scooter, or auto to help you investigate your destination. You can cruise for an hour or two or (during the summer months) take a full-day package tour to Victoria, B. C.

Perhaps you'll want to ride one of the two new jumbo ferries that began service in 1973—the *MV Spokane*, traveling between Seattle and Winslow; and the *MV Walla Walla*, cruising through the San Juan Islands between Anacortes and Sidney, B. C. Each is a double-deck, 440-foot-long giant with room for 206 vehicles and 2000 passengers. Or you can enjoy the relaxed simplicity of slower, older craft, such as the seven ferries brought to Puget Sound from California when they were retired from service on San Francisco Bay.

*BEYOND ABUNDANT Puyallup Valley daffodil fields,
Mt. Rainier towers majestically in the distance.*

Vital water highways

Although Puget Sound's ferries are a highly pleasurable novelty to many tourists, to the area's residents they are an indispensable part of the highway system. (Signs on Interstate 5 direct motorists to turnoffs that will lead to the ferries.) Some ferries cross unbridgeable waters; others provide short-cuts; all happily release a driver from his intense focus on the road and let him concentrate instead on his environment as he is moved from point to point.

All-year ferry service connects major western Washington highways with 13 islands, the Kitsap and Olympic peninsulas, and Vancouver Island. Washington State Ferries' bustling green-and-white fleet has the lion's share of the business (seven routes); six independent companies have one route each. The British Columbia Ferries company operates a number of routes, connecting the Gulf Islands with the Tsawwassen terminal on mainland British Columbia and the Vancouver Island docking points of Swartz Bay, Crofton, and Nanaimo. (These routes are not shown on the ferry map.)

On all the routes except those through the San Juan Islands, Port Angeles-Victoria, and Seattle-Victoria, ferry travel takes little planning, but it does call for patience. Still, departures are so frequent that you seldom have to wait more than 45 minutes. No advance reservations are taken, except on the summer-only Canadian Pacific Railroad's *Princess Marguerite* (which carries cars but is not the usual double-ended reversible ferryboat) between Seattle and Victoria and some B. C. ferries.

On busy summer weekends, traffic jams are usual at some of the ferry landings, especially on routes serving the Olympic Peninsula, San Juan Islands, and Whidbey Island. To avoid long waits behind homeward-bound weekenders at Columbia Beach, Kingston, Winslow, or ports in the San Juan Islands, arrive at the ferry landing as soon after noon as you can. Extra vessels are usually put into service when traffic is heavy and will continue to load (despite printed schedules) until all waiting cars are loaded.

Most ferries start running at about 6 a.m. and tie up about midnight. There are a few exceptions, however. The last departures from Sidney, B. C., for Anacortes, Victoria for Port Angeles, and Port Townsend for Keystone are in the late afternoon.

In daylight hours, the coffee shops on regularly-scheduled Washington State Ferries (and Black Ball Line's *Coho* between Port Angeles and Victoria) serve hot meals, except on the Point Defiance-Tahlequah route. You'll find vending machines for in-a-hurry hunger and thirst.

Ferry trips without a car

Any ferry ride is a delightful (and inexpensive) cruise without a car. All vessels carry pedestrian passengers. You don't need a destination; you can go round-trip. For example:

*STEEPLE of venerable church in Port Ludlow returns
to position in a way first builders never imagined.*

Bremerton Navy Yard. The Navy conducts guided tours of its extensive repair facilities and the battleship *USS Missouri* (10:30 a.m., 1, 2:30, 6:30 p.m. from May 1 through September 30; 1 p.m. only in winter). Take the Bremerton ferry from Seattle Terminal (Marion Street and Alaskan Way); Bremerton Navy Yard entrance is a short walk from the ferry slip.

Twilight cruise. Board a Bremerton or Winslow ferry at Seattle Ferry Terminal in the early evening to enjoy the long northern summer twilight and splendid views of Mt. Rainier. Have dinner in Bremerton or Winslow and return by late evening ferry.

Anderson-McNeil islands. Board the tiny Anderson Island ferry at Steilacoom for a leisurely, two-hour round trip, calling at McNeil Island (Federal Penitentiary; passengers are not allowed to debark without permission of penitentiary authorities), and pastoral Anderson Island. Anderson Island is a good place to ride a bicycle. (Bicycles travel free of charge on the ferries.) There are no designated picnic grounds on the island, but many of the cross-island roads terminate in a strip of beach ideal for picnicking. If you don't take your lunch with you, you can pick up ingredients at the Yoman Dock ferry landing.

Automobile-ferry loop trips

Here are some of the ways you can combine ferry trips with automobile sightseeing on Puget Sound. Many other combinations are possible depending on your interests and the time you have to spend.

Remember to ask for bridge (or ferry) credit slips when making a combined bridge-ferry trip in Puget Sound. This will give you a roundtrip reduction in the combined fare.

Vancouver Island-Olympic Peninsula loop (two days minimum). From Seattle, drive to Anacortes; ferry to Sidney; drive to Victoria. Or take a Canadian Pacific *Princess* liner direct from Seattle to Victoria. Return by Black Ball ferry from Victoria to Port Angeles; drive via Hood Canal Bridge and Edmonds-Kingston ferry to Seattle. Approximate highway mileage (via Anacortes): 180. (For Olympic Peninsula points of interest, see pages 63 to 77. For what to see and do in Victoria, consult Sunset's *Travel Guide to Western Canada.*)

Whidbey Island-Port Townsend loop. Drive to Mukilteo; ferry to Columbia Beach on Whidbey Island; ferry from Keystone to Port Townsend. Return by way of Hood Canal Bridge and Winslow-Seattle ferry. Approximate highway mileage: 106.

Kitsap Peninsula loop. Take the Seattle-Bremerton ferry, return on the Winslow-Seattle ferry. Approximate highway mileage: 29. (You can add as many miles as you wish exploring the roads of the peninsula or the shores of the Hood Canal.)

Vashon Island-Tacoma loop. Take the Fauntleroy ferry from West Seattle to Vashon Island, then the Tahlequah-Point Defiance ferry to Tacoma. Return

WILD BLACKBERRIES, sweet enough to eat just with cream, grow on Galiano Island in the San Juans.

to Seattle via Interstate 5. Approximate highway mileage: 63.

FIVE ISLANDS JUST OFFSHORE

What American city wouldn't leap at the chance to have easily accessible islands—perfect for one-day excursions or mini-vacations—located only a few miles from its city limits? Seattle and her sister cities along Puget Sound's eastern coastline do.

A short ferry ride (often a holiday in itself) or a waiting causeway leads coastal Washington's city dwellers to a dramatic change of scenery and makes possible many recreational diversions. Tourists to the Puget Sound area can also plunge into the pleasures of island hopping. It's easily done, and the rewards are many.

For some of them, read the descriptions of the shore-hugging islands of Vashon, Bainbridge, Camano, Whidbey, and Fidalgo given below:

Vashon Island: suburb in paradise

To certain very satisfied Seattleites, Vashon Island is a suburban haven with a difference. Not much farther than a stone's throw from downtown Seattle, Vashon nestles between Kitsap Peninsula and the Puget Sound coast just south of Seattle. You can reach its northern tip by ferry from Fauntleroy, its southern tip by ferry from Tacoma.

FROG ROCK, part of the local color on Bainbridge Island, gets a fresh coat of paint every spring.

EARLY MORNING FOG shrouds this visitor to Coupeville's ancient wooden pier on Whidbey Island.

What makes Vashon Island especially desirable as a place to live is its soothing rural quality—its forested heights, steep banks, and sandy beaches. As a place of habitation, it attracts both professional people and counterculturists. Its fertile soil is just right for growing berries and fruit.

If the natural attractions of Vashon aren't enough, visitors can test their ingenuity on two local mysteries. A village of Chinese fishermen, called Hongkong, flourished near Manzanita (east shore of Quartermaster Harbor) in the early 1880s. Reportedly it had 3,000 inhabitants, but they suddenly vanished during the race riots elsewhere in Puget Sound, leaving most of their possessions behind. About a mile north of Burton, the main road crosses Judd Creek. Somewhere along its banks a cache of $800 in gold was buried in 1877; the treasure was never recovered.

Go treasure hunting, speculate on the fate of Hongkong's citizens, or just enjoy Vashon's peaceful, relaxed atmosphere.

Bainbridge Island . . . strawberries and scotch broom

Tucked into a hollow on the eastern shore of the Kitsap Peninsula, Bainbridge Island is a convenient blend of country living with nearby metropolitan culture. Commuters ride the Winslow-Seattle ferry to the city; the Agate Pass bridge connects the northern end of the island to rural North Kitsap.

State parks are situated strategically on each end of the island. From Fay Bainbridge Park, on the northeastern peninsula, campers can look over the Sound toward Seattle. On the southern tip of the island Fort Ward, founded in 1910 as a military reservation, now has picnic facilities.

Bainbridge is home for many talented people. In Winslow there's a large co-op and crafts gallery with high quality merchandise. The Potlach Theater is also here. (Patrons and many of the performers ride the ferry over from Seattle. A package tour includes dinner, ferry ride, theatre ticket, and a nightcap in Seattle.)

Besides lovely homes, Bainbridge retains a scattering of small farms. Roadside stands sell freshly picked strawberries and raspberries in season. You may see Chinese pheasant, quail, and deer.

Two celebrations liven the island: Fourth of July and the Scotch Broom Festival. The festivities on the Fourth are like those held most places, but the Scotch Broom Festival isn't anything like the lilac, rhododendron, and daffodil ceremonies of other areas.

Tourists sometimes enjoy the bright yellow flowers of shrubby broom thriving everywhere; residents hate it. On Bainbridge Island they accept allergy attacks every spring gracefully. On a Friday afternoon in May, when the super-hardy weed blooms once more, Winslow merchants lock up their stores, twist garlands of yellow broom into floats, collect an assortment of musicians, and dub an unsuspecting bystander queen.

For a sheltered retreat, try Camano Island

The bulk of Whidbey Island across Saratoga Passage acts as windbreak for smaller Camano Island, just off the eastern shore of the Sound. Residents can live a relatively secluded life here; visitors are able to sample its beaches and hills by stopping at Camano Island State Park.

From Interstate 5, go west on State 532 over the bridge spanning the slough that separates the mainland from the island. About 4 miles on is Terry's Corner junction, with a large island directory. To the right of the directory billboard is a pioneer cemetery. From the junction, travel 8 miles southward as far as Elger Bay. The park is 2 miles to the west.

The 200-acre park was developed by island residents. Its coarse grass and madrona trees edge rocky beaches littered with driftwood. At high tide, the beaches almost disappear. On the slope above the beach grow soaring sturdy firs and hemlocks—the piles used to build the San Francisco docks were Camano and Whidbey Island trees. In addition to lush greenery and spectacular views, the park offers a nature trail, picnic facilities, and space to camp.

History comes alive on Whidbey Island

Visitors find Whidbey Island both a favorite summer travel destination and a fine place for a winter drive. Whidbey is sheltered from incoming weather fronts by the Olympic Mountains to the west and averages only 18 inches of rain a year, compared to Seattle's 35. The dry weather makes it more fun to tour the island's historic sites, many preserved in public parks. And Whidbey's mixture of jutting headlands and deep bays and coves ensure that you are never far from a wilderness beach.

Fastest approach from Seattle is by the Mukilteo ferry, 9 miles northwest of Interstate 5 on State 525. The ferry leaves daily every 25 minutes beginning at 6 a.m.

South Whidbey State Park. This 87-acre salt-water park, 5 miles northwest of State 525 on Bush Point Road, offers 76 picnic spots and 52 campsites among thick woods overlooking Puget Sound and 2 miles of sandy beach where you can walk, dig for clams, or cast for steelhead. Few salt-water parks so close to Seattle can match its uncrowded appeal.

Fort Casey Historical Park (4 miles west of State 525 on State 113). With batteries at forts Worden and Flagler, the guns of Fort Casey once stood watch over Admiralty Inlet, helping to guard Bremerton Navy Base and south Puget Sound cities. During World War II, its unusual disappearing carriage guns were scrapped, and the fort was decommissioned in 1951. Now it's a state historical park with interpretive center and four remounted guns. There are also boat launches, 104 camp and picnic sites, and 2 miles of beach to explore.

Ebey's Landing. This inconspicuous spot, easily missed (drive 1½ miles north of Fort Casey on Engle Road to junction with Ebey Road and follow the signs), marks where Colonel Issac Ebey was beheaded near his home by Haida Indians in 1857. The house is gone, but a stone memorial near the Ebey Road about 25 feet above the beach tersely recounts the deed. Just off nearby Sherman Road, to the west, a pioneer graveyard sits quietly beneath the firs. Across the road is a restored blockhouse and an interesting headstone dedicated in Gaelic to Mary Barret Maylor, from Ireland, who died in Whidbey in 1861.

Coupeville. Founded in 1850, this seaport village is one of Washington's oldest towns. Many pioneer structures remain, including the Methodist Church built in 1894 and the Alexander Blockhouse, one

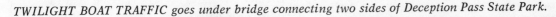

TWILIGHT BOAT TRAFFIC goes under bridge connecting two sides of Deception Pass State Park.

A Seagull's View of Puget Sound

CIRCLING *the eastern coast of San Juan Island before landing at Friday Harbor Airport is this* *Piper Aztec operated by San Juan Airlines. Fly-ins are gaining in popularity in the San Juans.*

Well-seasoned travelers to the Pacific Northwest often declare the best way to see the Puget Sound area is the way the seagulls do—from the air.

It's easily done. Several small air transport companies can give you the twin pleasures of flying in a light plane and witnessing an unparalleled view of islands, lakes, mountains, and cities beneath you.

Here are a few of the ways to get around Puget Sound by air:

San Juan Airline flies twice daily between Seattle-Tacoma International Airport and Friday Harbor in the San Juans. One-way fare is under $20. A passenger may make a reservation to stop at any of these other points: Shaw, Crane, Blakely, Safari, East Sound, Stuart, Waldron, Roche Harbor, Decatur, or Lopez. Planes normally fly directly from Sea-Tac to Friday Harbor; passengers then transfer to lighter planes for hops to other islands. Telephone 624-0215.

Gross Aviation offers scheduled service from Sea-Tac to Tacoma, Olympia, Aberdeen, Hoquiam, Shelton, Centralia, and Chehalis. But they also arrange for charters and scenic tours of the Sound. Beechcraft flights of 15 minutes at $5 per person or of one hour at $34 for three people are available. Telephone 838-1017.

Cross-Sound Commuter Airline schedules flights to Bremerton and Fort Lewis from Sea-Tac. Telephone 243-4886.

Pearson Aircraft flies from Sea-Tac to Port Angeles on the north coast of the Olympic Peninsula. Telephone 622-6077.

Harbor Airline can put you in a light plane for Oak Harbor (Whidbey Island) and Bellingham. Phone them at 622-2557.

Execuair serves the Tri-Cities area—the communities of Pasco, Richland, and Kennewick. Telephone 946-6179.

For information about schedules and fares for any of these six commuter airlines, phone the helpful coordinating Air Commuter Center (242-2995) at Sea-Tac. To make reservations on scheduled flights or to arrange for scenic tours or charter flights, get in touch directly with the airline itself.

of seven original blockhouses that once ringed the town. In the spruced-up, century-old buildings on Front Street, overlooking quiet Penn Cove, you can browse in antique or gift shops, study the old architecture, or stop for lunch. An arts and crafts exhibit on Front Street, Indian canoe races on Penn Cove, and an Indian salmon barbecue in the city park spotlight the annual Coupeville Festival in August.

Deception Pass State Park. Here are miles of beaches to walk, trails to hike, camping and picnic facilities, a children's playground, marshlands and tidepools for nature studies, Cranberry Lake for canoeing or sailing, and a superb view from Deception Pass bridge.

You can cross to Fidalgo Island here and return to the mainland by continuing north on State 525.

Fidalgo: named for a Spanish explorer

Fidalgo is one of the few Puget Sound islands with a sizeable city: Anacortes. (See page 44 for additional information about the town.)

If you drive to the northern end of the island, perhaps on your way to the San Juans, you might take a few minutes to visit Causland City Park, at Seventh Avenue and M Street, one block west of Commercial Avenue.

What makes this little park worth stopping to see is the ornate rock mosaic wall that rims it, rising at one point into a sort of cut-stone and crushed rock gazebo. In the wall, small and medium-sized rocks are arranged in stripes, geometric designs, and even stylized flower patterns.

Though it's a striking and unusual effect here, the wall may look familiar to anyone who has traveled in rural France. Similar designs executed both in stones and flowers are seen in parks and squares in French villages.

Another attraction at the north end of the island is Mt. Erie, a 1,300-foot-high spot near Anacortes, offering comprehensive views of the Cascades from Rainier on the south to the Canadian border and beyond on the north.

On the last weekend in July, the Anacortes Chapter of the Society for the Preservation and Encouragement of Barbershop Quartet Singing in America holds a salmon barbecue, show, and novice competition.

On Fidalgo Island's lovely beaches, try clam digging, crabbing, or gathering oysters. Both salt and freshwater fishing are excellent — set hooks for salmon, cod, bass, halibut, or steelhead.

Next to the Similk Beach golf course are large oyster beds, rock gardens, and a rock collection.

Perhaps the most striking spot on Fidalgo is Deception Pass. Reservation Bay's Rosario Beach, just off the highway leading over the Deception Pass Bridge, is nestled in thickly forested hills. Here you can visit a salmon hatchery, picnic, hike, or swim. The Pass itself is spectacular: steep cliffs drop deep into swirling waters speckled with wooded, rocky islands.

SAILING A SMALL skiff on Washington's waterways can take you to many spots motorists can't reach.

ON ORCAS ISLAND, weekend cyclists pedal along a quiet road near Eastsound toward Moran State Park.

A TRAVELER'S JOY— THE SAN JUAN ISLANDS

Many travelers have had their most memorable experiences on the world's islands. Whether it is Sicily, Mykonos, Rhodes, Cyprus, Crete, Maui, or Ibiza, an island can often smooth a furrowed brow more swiftly and surely than many other travel destinations.

The San Juan Islands have much of the same mystique. Tightly grouped together, their Douglas fir and madrone forests offer the sort of water-directed vacation that Northwesterners take for granted. If they were as close to Southern California as Catalina or as accessible to San Francisco as the Sacramento Delta, the islands would be famous and certainly more crowded.

Where the islands are located

Puget Sound officially includes the area between the entrance to the Hood Canal and the southern-most tip of the sound. However, in popular usage Puget Sound has come to mean most of the inland sea to the north as well. The San Juan Islands, although not actually in Puget Sound, are often considered to be a part of it.

The islands are scattered like stepping stones throughout the arm of the sea that reaches north-ward from Puget Sound. A few of them are settled. Many are uninhabited. Some are for sale.

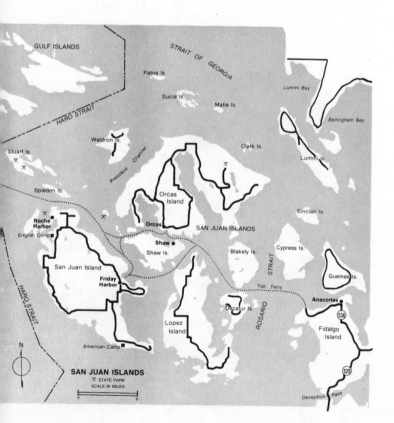

What they are like

The San Juan and Canadian Gulf islands number in the hundreds (the exact count depends on whether the tide is in or out). They're occupied by a rela-tively small number of farmers, retirees, ex-urban-ites, fishermen, and part-time vacationers. To Northwesterners who vacation here yearly, every island still unvisited remains a challenge.

The ragged-edged islands offer a fabulous wealth of harbors, coves, and beaches. Areas exposed to the wind are lined with piles of driftwood that have weathered to a silvery gray. Bottom fish lurk in the rocky kelp beds, and salmon run in the deeper waters farther out. Few beaches on the Pacific coast expose so much life at low tide—great sea urchins with long spines, vivid orange sea cucum-bers, crimson sea plumes, gorgeous sea anemones, giant chitons with turquoise lining, jellyfish, scut-tling crabs, clams, mussels, long ropes of kelp.

On summer evenings, the island shores are dotted with the bonfires of beach picnics, clam bakes, and fish suppers. Inland, there is boating, swimming, or fishing for trout on a handful of lakes.

Life on the islands is slow-paced. Come in your old clothes. There are no sightseeing tours, practi-cally no "night life." You are left pretty much alone to see the islands in your own way. Although you'll find many resorts (a preponderance of housekeep-ing cottages), they are not deluxe by any fast-moving mainland standards. One major exception: Rosario, on Orcas Island's East Sound, is posh.

Though Northwesterners often undersell these islands, they're sometimes guilty of overselling the weather. They'll tell visitors, especially those from Arizona and California, that because the islands lie in the rain shadow of Vancouver Island, the sum-mer weather is balmy and warm. Listen politely but bring a rain poncho. Don't expect to do a great deal of swimming or to take home an impressive tan. The weather can be glorious, but if it isn't, call it a welcome break from summer heat at home.

Meet four of the San Juans

Here is an advance introduction to four of the San Juan Islands you'll be likely to experience:

Orcas Island. Largest of the islands, Orcas is the most resort-conscious (but in a thoroughly easy-go-ing fashion). Eastsound has a few homes, a school, restaurant, and general store. There are stores at other settlements around the island. At 5,035-acre Moran State Park, you'll find improved campsites, good swimming in Cascade Lake, and rowboats for rent. Trout fishing is good here and in Mountain and Twin Lakes. A paved road leads to the summit of Mt. Constitution, highest point in the San Juans (2,409 feet); from the top you can enjoy a spec-tacular, 360-degree panorama of the islands. For resort information, write Orcas Island Resort Asso-ciation, Eastsound 98245.

Lopez Island. Lopez is a fairly flat island. Dairy and poultry farming are the main industries. Most of

the population is settled around the town of Lopez on all-but-landlocked Fisherman's Bay. You'll find camping facilities at Odlin Park, about a mile from the ferry slip on the main road. For information about resorts, write to Lopez Island Resort Association, Lopez 98261.

Shaw Island. This is the smallest of the San Juan Islands reached by ferry. You can camp at Shaw Island County Park, about 2 miles from the ferry landing. No resort accommodations are available.

San Juan Island. Most businesslike of the islands, San Juan is also most populated. Friday Harbor is the county seat of San Juan County (which includes all islands west of Rosario Strait). It has a customs house where mariners check in or out across the international boundary, a salmon cannery and packing house, and the only hospital in the islands. The University of Washington Oceanographic Laboratory, 1½ miles north of Friday Harbor, is open to visitors afternoons on Wednesday and Saturday during the summer; you can inspect live specimens of marine life taken from nearby waters.

The British Union Jack flew on San Juan Island until 1859. That year an American settler, finding a pig rooting around in his garden, seized his gun and took aim. Since the pig belonged to a member of the British Hudson's Bay Company, there was an angry dispute. Both the Americans and British set up garrisons to fight what has been labeled the "pig war," the real issue of which was whether Haro Strait or Rosario Strait was to be the western boundary of the United States. In 1872 Kaiser Wilhelm I of Germany, as arbitrator, designated Haro Strait as the boundary, thus awarding the San Juan

LADEN WITH DUFFEL, young campers debark from ferry at Orcas Island for summer holiday in San Juans.

TUGBOAT PULLS a large log raft across the gleaming waters of Puget Sound in the San Juan Islands. Washington's extensive waterways are vital in transporting lumber.

Islands to the Americans. The English and American camps are now national historic monuments.

Camping is permitted at San Juan Park, across the island from Friday Harbor. Overnight accommodations are available at several places on the island. For information, write: San Juan Island Chamber of Commerce (address in appendix).

Cruising through the islands

Your travel can be as much fun as your destination when you move over water through the San Juans. Take yourself—or be taken:

By ferry. Probably the most celebrated ferry trip in the Northwest is the three-hour cruise between Anacortes, Washington, and Sidney, B. C. During the summer (until September 30), there is one round trip daily. The route meanders through the islands, skirting wooded shorelines and stopping at small island communities on Lopez, Shaw, Orcas, and other San Juan islands. Not all ferries leaving Anacortes go all the way to Sidney. In addition to the international schedule, three trips daily connect Anacortes and Friday Harbor.

By smaller boat. To offer guests a sampling of the excellent small boating conditions, most resorts have available rowboats, outboard motorboats, or perhaps a sailboat for day trips. A few larger resorts offer day charters on inboard motorboats.

Going by private boat simplifies your vacation itinerary. Scattered throughout the island groups are marine parks with facilities for visitors arriving by boat: piers, mooring buoys, campsites, fresh water, and bathroom facilities. Several are accessible only by water.

Some of the most popular in the San Juans are on Stuart, Sucia, Matia, and Jones islands. In the Gulfs (some residents call them the Canadian San Juans), there are marine provincial parks on Tent Island off Kuper Island, at Montague Harbor on Galiano Island, at Beaumont Park on Bedwell Harbor, and at Sidney Spit on Sidney Island.

If the clear, deep water of a sheltered cove holds promise of succulent crab for supper, drop anchor. The calm, soft twilight lingers in these northern latitudes almost until it's time to go to sleep. You can spend the night aboard or at a campsite ashore.

It's not uncommon to see boats as small as 14 feet moored at buoys or at pierside. Smaller boats with their shallow draft are easier to take close to shore. Most large boats tow or carry a small dinghy.

To exchange pleasantries with other sailors, head for one of the resort marinas. Roche Harbor on San Juan Island, site of an old lime kiln, has a vine-covered, turreted hotel built in 1886, with a heated pool and restaurant. Rosario on Orcas Island is an extensive resort. Original owner of the property was Robert Moran, a ship builder and early mayor of Seattle. Both resorts charge mooring fees.

The most spectacular mooring is the free public dock across from Victoria's stately Empress Hotel, within earshot of the summer concerts at dusk in front of the provincial parliament building.

Crossing the international border, you must clear customs. You can enter Canada through Sidney, Bedwell Harbor on South Pender, or Victoria, where customs is one block north of the public dock. Coming into the United States, you can stop at Roche Harbor, Friday Harbor, or Anacortes.

Why Not Charter a Boat?

With so many varied waterways to explore, it's no wonder boat ownership is so popular in the Northwest. But if you have only an occasional taste for salt water, if you live far inland where owning a cruising boat isn't practical, or if you don't want to make the investment such a boat requires, you can charter a boat, enjoy your cruise of a weekend, a week, or a month and not worry about boat maintenance next winter.

Cruising boats with sleeping accommodations, galleys, and heads are available for charter in sizes from about 20 feet to more than 100 feet. You can charter sailboats or power boats (power boats are more popular in Northwest waters). Costs range from about $25 to $600 per day or $150 to $1,600 per week. A fully equipped 30 to 35-foot boat, with sleeping quarters for four, six, or eight, will charter for $300 to $600 per week.

In addition to this fee, you pay for fuel and short-term insurance and provide your own food. Even allowing for this, when two families charter a boat together, the total costs are often no more than for other travel vacations.

Both take-it-yourself and skippered boats are available. To qualify for a skipper-yourself boat, you must convince the charter service that you are capable of handling the vessel and piloting it through the waters of your planned cruise. This means more than steering; you should be familiar with inland water navigation, chart reading, and the operation of electronic navigational aids (most boats have radios and depth finders; large yachts may have radio direction finders and radar).

If you don't feel qualified or would prefer to relax and let someone else do the work, you'll need to arrange for a skipper at an additional cost of $25 or $30 a day. Your skipper will add much to a relaxing cruise—he knows the waters, the points of interest, and boat operation.

Generally, you should contact a charter boat agency and make reservations well in advance. The agency will provide considerable advance information on request: kinds of boats available, costs, suggested marine guides, even proposed cruise destinations within your interests and timetable. For a firm reservation, a deposit of one-third the charter fee is usually required.

Inquire whether a boat is equipped with a crab trap and pot, a double-sided round-pointed oyster knife, fishing tackle, and a shovel and bucket. These may help you keep down the cost of food; market prices run a bit higher here than in most other areas of the West. You don't need a license for salt water fishing. Utensils, pots, and pans come with the boat. You must bring personal articles, sheets, towels, and sleeping bags.

For a list of Northwest charter boat agencies, send a stamped, addressed return envelope to *Sunset* Magazine, 1009 Tower Bldg., Seattle 98101.

STURDY CHARTER BOAT speeds through Strait of Juan de Fuca off Port Angeles toward adventure.

Exploring the San Juan Islands

FAMILY RETURNS to their chartered boat after a day of clamming along shores of tiny San Juan isle.

AERIAL PHOTOGRAPH shows proximity of the San Juan Islands. One of the longest stretches, from Anacortes to Blakely Island, is only 8 miles. Island hopping here is easy to do.

KILLER WHALE sighted off Orcas Island rises to the surface about 50 breathtaking yards ahead.

MOORED charter boat beneath Victoria's Empress Hotel.

WHEN A BOY catches the evening meal and it's a crab—good news.

Sampling the Olympic Peninsula

Not many people live on the Olympic Peninsula. From the top of snow-washed Mt. Olympus to the spongy floor of its moss-festooned rain forests, this peninsula is the province of nature. A visitor here quickly realizes the priceless value of the mountains, forests, and beaches that are preserved within the 1,400-square-mile expanse of the Olympic National Park.

The peninsula is dominated by an isolated mountain mass with an icy chunk of Greenland at its center and the best of the Temperate Zone's rain forests on its flanks. The upthrust fingers of Mt. Olympus reach 7,965 feet, enclosing an ice reservoir kept filled to overflowing. In half a dozen glaciers radiating from the summit ridge and basins, ice flows smoothly into valleys or breaks away to tumble over cliffs.

Olympus itself is not easy to see from afar. Here is no Rainier or Hood looming up from a low horizon, no Whitney spire jutting stark and clean from a serrate scarp. The summit is a puzzling cluster of crags that are barely clear of the ice cap, nearly lost in a jumble of peaks of almost equal height.

Two distinct climates coexist on the small Olympic Peninsula. On the western side of the Olympic Mountains, the measured annual rainfall averages 140 inches, resulting in a luxuriant growth of towering, shallow-rooted trees hung with thick moss—the rain forests. It's a safe guess that in some years Mt. Olympus itself gets the equivalent of 200 inches or more of rain.

But Olympus and its neighbors act as a barrier to the moisture-laden winds from the Pacific, protecting the eastern part of the peninsula from heavy precipitation. In an average year, the town of Sequim, 3 miles from the Strait of Juan de Fuca, gets little snow and less than 17 inches of rain.

OLYMPIC HIGHWAY DISCOVERIES

If oyster beds, Victorian architecture, epic views, lakeside recreation, nature trails, salmon fishing,

MASSIVE DRIFTWOOD boulders scattered across First Beach at La Push make epic frame for sea stacks.

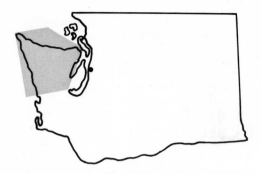

driftwood, lush rain forests, Indian reservations, archeological digs, and Paul Bunyanesque logging camps touch your interests, then motoring around the Olympic Peninsula should be high on your list of things to do in Washington.

U.S. Highway 101, starting in Olympia, circles the peninsula to Aberdeen, and U.S. 12 closes the loop. The driving distance is 334 miles, but you'll want to take several side trips of 20 miles or more to reach peninsula highlights. Sample the best that the Olympic Peninsula has to offer by visiting Port Townsend, the Olympic Game Farm at Sequim, Hurricane Ridge, Lake Crescent Lodge, Sol Duc Hot Springs, Ozette Lake, Cape Alava, the coastal strip from La Push to Ruby Beach, the Bogachiel

or Hoh rain forest, Kalaloch Beach, Lake Quinault Lodge, and the lower coastal resort area between Pacific Beach and Moclips. Three days is not too much time to allot for a leisurely tour of this exceptionally rich vacationland.

From Olympia to Discovery Bay

Leaving Olympia, the state capital, U.S. 101 runs north through land logged so long ago that second-growth fir forests are well on their way to maturity. You'll pass these points of interest as you drive:

Shelton. The city of Shelton is headquarters for one of the larger lumber companies that has pioneered in treating timber as a perpetual crop. It is also the center of a thriving Christmas tree business and home of the annual Forest Festival.

The Hood Canal. You reach Hood Canal at its "fish-hook" bend. "Canal" is actually a misnomer for this 80-mile-long, natural inlet. Its discoverer, Captain George Vancouver, named it "Hood's Channel" in 1792 for Lord Hood of the British Admiralty.

Resorts catering to tourists and fishermen line both sides of the channel, especially in the lower canal area. On sunny days the gravelly beaches are dotted with clam diggers. Washington state parks are scattered along or near the canal—Potlach and Lake Cushman State Parks (Cushman has camping and trailer hookups) near Hoodsport and Dosewal-

A WELCOME SIGHT for weary or weather-harried hikers in Olympic National Park is the inviting Soleduc shelter, ringed by giant Sitka spruce and hemlock trees.

lips State Park near Brinnon on the west shore; Scenic Beach and Kitsap Memorial State Parks on the east shore of the upper canal.

For some 40 miles, U.S. 101 is a marine drive along the serene Hood Canal. Its beaches furnish fresh oysters to wayside cafes—as the expansive monument of oyster shells in Quilcene harbor testifies. At Eldon, north of the Hamma Hamma River, there's an unusual Northwest Carving Shop. Seal Rock, above Brinnon, offers both an extensive rhododendron nursery and a public campground: Seal Rock Forest Camp. Three additional campgrounds are located a bit farther on toward Quilcene at Spencer Creek, Rainbow, and Falls View. At Quilcene you'll become engrossed with what's to be seen at the National Fish Hatchery.

Hood Canal Floating Bridge. A turn off U.S. 101 onto State 104 will take you to the impressive Hood Canal Floating Bridge, an important connecting link between the Olympic and Kitsap peninsulas. Though the toll can be expensive (it rises with each additional auto passenger), the bridge considerably shortens the time needed to drive from Seattle to the northeast corner of the Olympic Peninsula.

Port Townsend...a Victorian museum

Port Townsend is a town so steeped in 19th century culture that even a hoopskirt wouldn't seem out of place here. Around 1887 it was perhaps the most promising seaport in the Northwest—until the railroad and real estate failures of 1891 reduced its population from 20,000 to less than 2,000. To reach the city, turn right off U.S. 101 onto State 113 at Discovery Bay and drive 14 miles.

With some justification, Port Townsend was known in years past as "the wickedest city north of San Francisco." Until 1912, the present town bakery was a Chinese grocery store with a sign above the door reading "Coffee—Tea—Opium." Manresa Castle, formerly a Jesuit school, was later transformed into a pleasure palace, complete with belly dancing in the prayer room. And the scantily clad figures in the "Four Seasons" frescoes by Otto Chapman on the ceiling of Starrett House's tower are said to have caused proper ladies to blush.

But today, sin is less evident than structure, for Port Townsend is most remarkable for its extensive collection of restored Victorian buildings.

A stop as you enter town at the Chamber of Commerce's Visitor Information Building will equip you with a map of the town's major tourist sights. Because fascinating Victorian structures are scattered throughout the bluff area above the business district, the map is especially helpful.

You might begin your Victorian excursion from the County Historical Museum in the City Hall at Monroe and Walter Streets (State 13). Here you can visit Jack London's basement jail cell.

GLISTENING VICTORIAN, Port Townsend's Starrett House, left, built in 1889, is now a restaurant. Above, spectacular highway climbs to crest in Olympic National Park from gateway city of Port Angeles.

OLYMPIC PENINSULA **65**

MEN SCRUTINIZE mountains, left; marmots scrutinize men, above. Party of climbers has reached an especially scenic Hoh Valley ridge.

The Rothschild House, built in 1868 and now owned by the State Parks Commission, is one of the oldest surviving houses in Port Townsend. Its pre-Victorian architecture shows a strong New England influence. Restoration and refurnishing were done with attention to authenticity; even its flower and herb gardens are much the same as in the 19th century.

You can visit three historic churches. The Episcopal Church was built in 1865, then moved in 1883 to its present location. The Methodist congregation, organized in 1851, constructed its church in 1871. The Presbyterian Church was built in 1889.

In addition to its colorful history and architecture, Port Townsend has some good art galleries and specialty shops. Fort Worden State Park—established on the ghost of a full-scale Army base —is worth a look. The town also celebrates with a yearly salmon derby and rhododendron festival. A popular Summer School of the Arts and a summer ballet school add interest to the village.

Here, too, on a cliff overlooking the Strait of Juan de Fuca, is an unusual country inn of exceptional quality, The Farmhouse, run on weekends by a University of Washington drama professor and his wife. Telephone 523-4625 in Seattle or 385-1411 in Port Townsend for reservations.

Along the northern peninsula

Shortly after leaving Discovery Bay on U.S. 101 heading west, you'll pass through land directly on the lee side of the mountains where the countryside is so dry that farms must be irrigated. Some of the highlights along this northern stretch of the Olympic Peninsula are given below:

Gardiner. Most interesting to tourists here is Loboland (just off the highway), a collection of seven subspecies of wolf, ranging from Mexican to Arctic varieties. After having been a top tourist attraction in Pennsylvania for 40 years, Loboland moved to the Olympic Peninsula in 1972.

Sequim. Well-equipped for campers, Sequim Bay State Park is the one closest to the road leading from Port Angeles into the Olympic National Park. For noncampers, resorts, hotels, and motels are scattered throughout this area.

You may want to make use of the stores and restaurants along the highway in Sequim. Here signs direct you to a right turn that will take you to the Olympic Game Farm (see p. 72).

Dungeness. It's a short drive north from Sequim to Dungeness, where crab is king. A seafood restaurant here has a magnetic appeal; accommodations near the 7-mile-long Dungeness Spit (longest natural sandspit in the United States) are available. Near here, the Voice of America beams its broadcasts westward to the Pacific.

Port Angeles. The peninsula's largest town, Port Angeles invites you to penetrate the interior of the peninsula on a 20-mile side trip. Just outside the city, on the road leading to Hurricane Ridge, is the park's main visitor center—the Pioneer Memorial Museum.

Alternative route. West of Port Angeles, U.S. 101 swings inland, cutting through a corner of Olympic National Park at Lake Crescent. If you prefer to stay along the coast, though, take State 112, which passes through Clallam Bay and Sekiu on its way to Neah Bay.

Ozette Lake. North of Sekiu, a 20-mile spur road off State 112 leads to Ozette Lake, one of Washington's largest lakes. Although its east shore is open to logging, its west shore is in the park. A resort at the northern tip of the lake has housekeeping cabins, groceries, a cafe, boat rentals, and a trailer park. A Park Service picnic area is across the Ozette River from the resort. Trails strike out from Ozette toward the beaches: a unique plank trail ends at Capa Alava (3.3 miles), and another trail ends at Sand Point (3 miles).

Neah Bay. This village is the center of the Makah Indian Reservation. You can see few remains of the culture of these Indians, however, except for some Indian dugout canoes on the beach and the Makah baskets for sale locally. The present-day Makah engages in logging, commercial fishing, or running sport fishing facilities (Neah Bay is renowned for its salmon fishing). The tribe has a salmon barbecue and "Makah Days" celebration in August every year; visitors are welcome.

Cape Flattery. You can reach Cape Flattery at the tip of the peninsula after a pleasant hike of less than a mile from the end of a 6-mile road from Neah Bay. Pick up a free map of the area at resorts or stores. At the Cape, the Pacific is at your left, the Strait at your right, and lonely, rockbound Tatoosh Island, with its lighthouse, stands just offshore. A hundred feet below, the noisy surf pounds away, carving great caverns and blow holes in the cliff.

The beach just south of Neah Bay (a few miles by dirt road, muddy and impassable during very bad weather) is attractive for picnicking and exploring. Park on Portage Head, the bluff above the beach, and walk down to the beach. Point of Arches, at the south end of the beach, is a photogenic formation

What Does Dungeness Make You Think Of?

The appetizing task of catching Dungeness crabs in Puget Sound can be easy. Basic equipment and technique are simple.

Crabs live just offshore, most often in eel grass, less often in kelp and seaweed beds. You'll have to wait for very low tides (tides of minus 2 feet or more are best), don a pair of waders, and go out no more than waist-deep.

Walk smoothly and quietly—too much turbulence will send crabs racing into deep water and increase water turbidity. Watch closely for crabs; underwater they lose their bright orange color and appear only as dark outlines. Polarized sunglasses help reduce water glare.

Once you've spotted a crab, you can bring it to the surface quickly with a small-mouthed, shallow-meshed dip net (easiest to use) or a bamboo lawn rake. If you use the rake, first pin the crab to the bottom, entangle the crab in the rake teeth, then flip the rake over and quickly lift the crab to the surface. Canvas gloves will help you avoid pinched fingers. Regulations prohibit using a spear or other sharp tool that might penetrate the shell of the crab.

The crab limit is six; no license is required. Only male crabs, 6 inches across the shell in front of the points, may be kept. Female, soft shell, and smaller crabs must be returned. Males have narrower abdomens (underbellies) with a long triangular section of shell near the tail; females have a wider abdomen with much smaller triangular section.

DELIGHTED crab raker deposits in sack catch scooped up from Puget Sound waters.

PERENNIAL CHALLENGE: reaching the summit of Mt. Olympus. Here three mountaineers are on top; another intrepid party approaches at left.

of wavecut arches, offshore rocks, and sea caves. Together with the impenetrable brush back from the shore, it forms a barrier to further beach passage.

Access roads to the park's upper coastal strip. You can reach the northern part of the Olympic National Park beach strip via the Ozette Lake road from Sekiu.

Your next opportunities to reach the beach by car are at La Push and Rialto Beach, on opposite sides of the Quillayute River. The La Push road leaves U.S. 101 north of Forks and continues on to La Push and the Quillayute Indian Reservation. There is a Park Service campground at Mora. To reach it (and gain access to the north wilderness strip), drive back to the Rialto Beach turnoff, 6 miles toward Forks.

Just before U.S. 101 swings out to the coast at Ruby Beach is a junction with a gravel road to Oil City. This road follows the Hoh River for 12 miles and reaches the coast just north of the Hoh Indian Reservation. There are no public facilities at Oil City, but it is a splendid place to begin a walk on the south wilderness portion of the ocean strip. There is a parking area, and at most times you can reach the beach over a good three-minute trail. At high tide the trail may be submerged under the Hoh River; then you must do a little bushwhacking over the bluff to your right.

The beach trail. The trail that takes you along the splendid wilderness coast is largely the beach itself. It divides naturally into the two sections: Oil City to La Push and Rialto Beach to Cape Alava.

The only predictable aspect of travel along the Olympic wilderness strip is that no two trips are quite the same. Easily walked, hard-packed sand beaches on one trip may be soft and tiring on the next. Headlands easily negotiated on your way to a picnic may be under high, crashing waves on the way back. A beach strewn with Japanese glass fishing floats and other jetsam treasures at 5 a.m. may have been carefully picked over by 7.

As to difficulty, your own sense of what is passable and what is not will be your best guide. A tide table is necessary if you wish to plan your time schedule with any certainty. Headlands may be passed in minutes at low tide, but the necessary trip over the top at high tide may take an hour.

Scenery along the headland bypass trails is as varied and rich as the beach itself. Mostly you pass through virgin Douglas fir forest. The trails, as you'd expect, are muddy, and they often go over or along slippery logs. But they are well marked with red and orange metal tags.

Perhaps the most popular wilderness site available to daytime hikers and weekend backpackers is Toleak Point, 6 miles from Third Beach at La Push. Here bald eagles flourish in one of their last strongholds outside Alaska.

The Lake Crescent area. If you stay on U.S. 101 west from Port Angeles, you'll drive along the southern shore of lovely Lake Crescent, a camping and resort area. Halfway along the lakeshore, you'll come to a left turnoff that leads to the park's Storm King Visitor Center. Shortly after you leave the lake, a spur road to the left leads 12 miles to Sol Duc Hot Springs, where mineral water baths are popular during summer months.

The western leg of the highway

Swinging southward at Sappho, U.S. 101 provides access to two major areas of interest before it reaches the park's coastal strip.

La Push. This Quillayute Indian village is set on a wildly dramatic beach punctuated by massive, offshore sea stacks. The beach can be reached on three marked trails. Food, lodging, boat rentals, and grocery stores are available here. Turn right

off U.S. 101 one mile north of Forks for the 14-mile side trip to La Push.

Hoh rain forest. Leading east from U.S. Highway 101 about 6 miles south of Bogachiel State Park, a paved, 19-mile road swings past the Minnie Peterson Campground and Recreation Area and the little resort called Westward Hoh (store, gasoline, cabins) and enters Olympic National Park. The visitor center and museum here is open most weekends when staffing permits (only one ranger is stationed here year-round). Two nature trails are maintained all year.

The park's lower coastal strip. Shortly after crossing the Hoh River, U.S. 101 veers west to reach the park's lower coastal strip at Ruby Beach. From here to the southern boundary of the park's coastal strip just north of Queets, you drive along 11 miles of ocean beach, with the shoreline only a minute's walk away. The few signs of civilization are six markers pointing to beach trails, a highway viewpoint from which you can see Destruction Island just offshore, the Kalaloch Ranger Station, and Kalaloch Lodge and cabins. Kalaloch's beautiful driftwood-sprinkled beach (good clamming and surf fishing for smelt) and its comfortable lodge

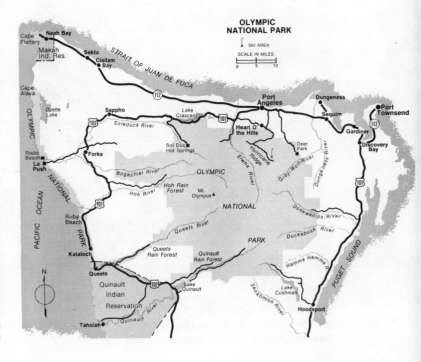

BACKPACKER PAUSES near Ozette Lake to inspect monument to Norwegian crew lost in 1903 shipwreck.

MOUNTAIN GOATS roam the foggy crags in Olympic National Park, sometimes visit campsites.

make this a welcome stopover spot or weekend retreat. Except for this 11-mile stretch, the highway does not go into the ocean strip.

Most visitors to the park explore the ocean strip along short trails. You can walk several miles out and back in a day from any of the departure points reached by car. In no more than a half a mile you are in tideland wilderness, still practically as it was when the now-extinct Olympic wolves roamed this coast. But if you are a self-reliant hiker, you will want to walk some or all of the 30 miles of pristine shoreline.

Queets rain forest. Crossing the Queets River and turning inland, the Olympic Highway soon comes to a graded dirt road about 6 miles east of Queets that takes you 14 miles into a narrow arm of Olympic National Park. Watch for elk in the meadows of abandoned homesteads. There's a small auto campground at road's end. From here you can hike a short, picturesque trail along the Queets River back to the ranger station, or you can follow other short trails along the Sams River through deserted homesteads.

Quinault rain forest. Groceries, gasoline, and accommodations are available at Amanda Park, at the community of Quinault, and along the north shore of Lake Quinault. There are numerous improved campgrounds on the lake and river, both in Olympic National Forest and Olympic National Park. A short nature trail starts near Quinault Ranger Station. Depending on water conditions, steelhead fishing on the river is good to excellent.

(Interesting sidelight: Lake Quinault is under a tri-partite administration. The lake itself is controlled by the Quinault Indians; part of the shore is administered by the U. S. Forest Service and part by the National Park Service.)

Along the southern shore of Lake Quinault is a charming resort—Quinault Lodge—that is steeped in Old World flavor. Set above the lake in the dense Olympic National Forest, this lodge is one of the peninsula's most attractive places to overnight. The forest has self-guided trails, and this is the western jump-off point for trips into Enchanted Valley.

Paul Bunyan-type logging reached its peak 40 years ago in the region from Quinault south. Hoquiam and Aberdeen were Wild West towns where loggers celebrated payday. The cities are still centers of the timber industry, shipping lumber from Grays Harbor.

A side trip to south peninsula beaches. State 109, a winding forest road, leads west from Hoquiam to the 20-mile-long stretch of beach running from Ocean Shores in the south to Moclips at the border of the Quinault Indian Reservation in the north.

Though you may find that some of the commercially-developed resort areas here lack the charm of the lodging and eating concessions within the Olympic National Park grounds to the north, there are exceptions. Perhaps the most pleasant resorts are those found in the vicinity of Moclips—Ocean Crest, Iron Springs, Trade Winds, and Beechwood. To the south, Ocean Shores is an extensive resort development with a wide variety of accommodations set on a flat, treeless beach area.

OLYMPIC NATIONAL PARK

The heart of Olympic National Park is a dedicated wilderness. Without question, it is not for everyone; yet despite the aloofness of haughty Olympus itself, few other wilderness areas are more inviting, more unlocked, or more approachable.

Park accommodations

Olympic National Park has 17 campgrounds and a number of cabins, lodges, and trailer parks.

Campgrounds. Most park campgrounds consist of individual campsites with tables and fireplaces; piped water and toilet facilities are usually near a cluster of campsites. Neither showers, laundries, nor utility connections are provided in these campgrounds. For more detailed information on campgrounds in Olympic National Park, write to the superintendent, 600 East Park Avenue, Port Angeles 98362. Inquire at the Pioneer Memorial Museum in Port Angeles before attempting some of the approach roads with a trailer.

Some campgrounds at lower elevations are open all year, but high-elevation areas are covered by snow from early November to late June or early July. It is not possible to reserve campground space prior to your visit. Fire permits are not required in the automobile campgrounds. Fees are charged for overnight camping in most campgrounds.

Cabins, lodges, and trailer parks. For information about concessioner-operated cabins, lodges, and trailer parks at Sol Duc Hot Springs, Lake Crescent, La Push, or Kalaloch, write to park superintendent.

Outside the park. Information about other accommodations on the Olympic Peninsula may be obtained from the Olympic Peninsula Resort and Hotel Association, Colman Ferry Terminal, Seattle 98104.

What to see and do

Aside from being a feast for the eyes, the park offers many educational and recreational opportunities:

Interpretive programs. As an introduction to understanding and enjoying Olympic National Park, the National Park Service has three visitor centers—the Pioneer Memorial Museum near Port Angeles (open all year), Storm King Visitor Center at Lake Crescent, and the Hoh Rain Forest Visitor Center. At these centers are audiovisual programs, talks, exhibits, and numerous interpretive publications and maps. Self-guiding nature trails, located throughout the park, sample many different life communities. In the summer, rangers lead guided walks and present evening campfire programs. For a printed program of interpretive activities, write to the superintendent.

OLYMPIC PENINSULA beaches, lakefronts abound in driftwood; harvest bleaches at Ozette Lake.

MARINE BIOLOGY students from Port Angeles measure formaldehyde to preserve catch at Dungeness.

Animal Extinction Resisted Here

You could drive straight through Sequim on U.S. 101 and perhaps overlook the small signs that direct you to turn right toward the Olympic Game Farm. But if you did, you'd be missing one of the peninsula's prime tourist attractions: a small but highly specialized zoo.

The game farm actually has two purposes. For the past 25 years, the Walt Disney Studios have boarded here all of the North American animals used in their films.

A more exotic collection of animals is also maintained here—for a much more practical reason. Lloyd Beebe and Bill Hodge, game farm managers, are vitally concerned with breeding wildlife that are in danger of extinction.

Among the rarest of the Olympic Game Farm's endangered animals is the Asian clouded leopard, a cat that reaches 45 pounds. Another is the Siberian tiger from Manchuria, attaining 500 pounds at maturity. Cages also hold spotted and black leopards, golden cats, red wolves, jaguars, cougars, and bighorn sheep.

The importance of the game farm's program is underlined by the fact that in the past 73 years, 84 mammals, as well as many birds and fish, have become extinct.

On this 86-acre site, many routine and not-so-routine activities take place. Using a recipe that originated in 1927 in the Philadelphia zoo, keepers bake hundreds of loaves of nutritious brown bread in large ovens weekly for the diet of the grizzly and polar bears. To house the lazy Canadian geese that migrate in, men have had to construct over 500 nests. Most vital to the fight against extinction, though, is the experimental program of artificial insemination. Recently, a female timberwolf was bred from frozen sperm and produced a robust litter of seven pups.

The Olympic Game Farm is open seven days a week. There is a nominal admission.

Asian Clouded Leopard

Motoring. U.S. 101 provides the main access to the park, with numerous spur roads leading to the rain forest valleys, the higher country, and the Pacific Coast Area. Since the main body of the park is dedicated for preservation in its natural state, no roads pass through its rugged heart.

Rain forests can be seen along Hoh, Queets, and Quinault River roads. Two nature trails begin at the Hoh Rain Forest Visitor Center. On the north side of the park, there is a good road from Heart o' the Hills to Hurricane Ridge. Hurricane Ridge affords visitors an excellent opportunity to look into a superb part of the Olympic wildland. On clear days, the sculptured, ice-clad peaks of Mount Olympus and the Bailey Range delight photographers. The wildflower display in the fragile subalpine meadows is best seen about mid-July.

The Pacific Coast Area is accessible from U.S. 101, directly at Kalaloch and by spur roads to the mouth of the Hoh, to La Push, and to Rialto Beach.

Hiking. Roads provide access to about 600 miles of trails. Some short trails provide easy trips requiring one day or less; longer, more difficult trails may take up to one week or more.

Trails are cleared of obstructions as snow melts and summer progresses. Trail conditions vary from year to year, depending on the severity of the previous winter and the rate of snow melt in late spring. Inquire at any visitor center or ranger station for the current trail conditions.

Horseback riding. Though there are no riding stables or packers available within the park, you can obtain a list of Olympic Peninsula packers outside the park by writing to the superintendent. There are restrictions on and closures to pack stock in certain sections of the park's back country; further details can be obtained by inquiring at a visitor center or ranger station.

Mountain climbing. Some peaks may be climbed safely by novices, but technical climbs should be attempted only by or with experienced climbers who are wise in the ways of Northwest mountaineering.

Ask a park ranger for information. For their own protection, climbing parties are asked to register at the ranger station on their route and to show that they have standard climbing gear. Never engage in off-trail activities alone.

Fishing. No license is required for fishing in the park's many lakes, although a special punchcard issued by the Washington Game Department is required for fishing for steelhead trout. Seasons are generally the same as for adjacent state waters. Regulations are available at visitor centers and ranger stations.

The park's eastern side

Spur roads from U.S. 101 approach or enter this part of the park on the Puget Sound side of the peninsula by going up the narrow valleys of the Skokomish, Hamma Hamma, Duckabush, Dosewallips, and Quilcene rivers, often in the deep shade of second-growth hemlock, fir, and cedar.

North fork Skokomish river road climbs from the somnolent village of Hoodsport through cut-over foothills to Lake Cushman, which extends back to the edge of the park. The road skirts the lake and takes you to a campground near beautiful Staircase Rapids, then goes 3 miles farther to the beginnings of trails into some fine high country.

Approaching from the north

At this most accessible and most popular side of the park, several entrance roads lead in, and there are campgrounds, resorts, lakes and streams, and many trails into the forest.

Lake Crescent. This is by far the largest lake in Olympic National Park. It fills a deep east-west glacial trough on the north side of the mountain. Fairholm campground (the only campground) is nicely developed. There are places to stay around the lake, most of them offering housekeeping cabins. All of them have boats and fishing and housekeeping supplies. Lake Crescent Lodge, the largest resort, has lodge rooms, cottages, restaurant, and cocktail lounge.

Soleduck River. The river road passes through logged-off hills and goes for 12 miles to an improved campground and a cabin resort. Two miles upstream, the road ends at the beginning of an excellent trail that leads to Soleduck Falls and some of the park's finest woodland.

Elwha River. Elwha and Altaire campgrounds have the usual improvements and are in attractive forest settings.

Hurricane Ridge. Here you settle into a grandstand seat at 5,200 feet, overlooking the Olympic National Park alpine wilderness, crossed only by trails. A still more remarkable view is yours from Hurricane Hill, on a dirt road 2½ miles north. It looks down on the Strait of Juan de Fuca and Port Angeles, over to Vancouver Island and the San Juans, and farther on to Mt. Baker in northern Washington.

Plan on a full day, take your time, and go all the way to Obstruction Point (6,450 feet). Starting

MATCHSTICK PATTERN of floating logs awaits shipment along Port Angeles spit (center left).

LAKE CRESCENT LODGE is flanked by many cottages, nestles among trees on inviting lakeshore.

CLAM that got away: on Kalaloch Beach, right, boy stops on early morning hike to regret missing razor clam. Below, Indian summer haze at Point Grenville, where wooded hills meet sea.

early, you can include the hike to Grand and Moose lakes. There are picnic areas on the ridge but no camping. Hurricane Ridge Lodge, perched at the edge of Big Meadow, has a lunch room and souvenirs but no overnight accommodations. Park naturalists give 15-minute talks four times a day. Skiing and sledding here in winter makes Hurricane Ridge the most important winter sports center on the peninsula.

Adjacent to the lodge, a marked nature trail meanders through alpine meadows and forest; a trailside "mountain finder" helps you identify visible peaks. Naturalists conduct hour-long nature walks over the trail four times a day.

Deer Park. Drive to Deer Park for views similar to those offered by Hurricane Ridge. The gravel road is fun for most people, torture for the very timid. It's a rare occasion at Deer Park when you don't see deer—lots of them. You will also see marmots. Among the tight little clumps of alpine fir, you'll find several campsites overlooking the canyon of the Gray Wolf River and the broad strait.

The wet western side

After visiting it, you'll probably feel that the Pacific Ocean-facing side of the Olympic wilderness is the main reason for being of the national park. Its

FISHERMEN PROCESS haul, below left, of winter black-mouth (young, sea-going king salmon) at Sekiu. Below right, the tranquil eastern shore of the Hood Canal.

valleys, longer and less steep than those on the eastern flank, contain preserved examples of the rain forests that once extended from Alaska to Cape Mendocino and have no equal anywhere else in the world.

If you've formed a mental picture of the rain forest without seeing it, you're likely to be surprised. Not a dark, gloomy wood, it is filled with soft green light, reflected and refracted by the mosses and the translucent maple leaves. The trees that grow in the rain forest also grow in other places. The differences are not so much in species as in habit. Water-loving things, be they microbes, mushrooms, or Douglas firs, are in their element.

Trees in the rain forest are shallow-rooted, as they can be only where water and food are plentiful—and where the forest cover is so uniform and continuous that the wind can't get a "bite."

The forest aisles are kept open partly by the browsing of the peninsula's most famous wild creature, the handsome elusive Olympic elk. You'll see fewer elk in the rain forest in summer, when they migrate to the high meadows; but for nine months of the year, this is their home.

Bogachiel River. The trail through the Bogachiel Valley is mostly level, the scenery wonderful, and the fishing excellent, especially in fall when sea-run cutthroat start their annual migration upstream to spawn. The park boundary is 4 miles by car plus 2 miles on foot from U.S. 101. From the boundary, a trail follows the Bogachiel River upstream for 12 miles and then begins to climb, following the Bogachiel's North Fork, into the Olympic Mountains. Few hikers use this route into the high country, for it is much longer than the approaches in the Hoh River Valley to the south. But many hike along the lower river for the 11 miles between the park boundary and Flapjack Shelter; a two-day round trip allows plenty of time for fishing, photography, and quiet contemplation.

This valley is transitional, lusher than a typical Pacific Northwest forest but less overgrown than the climax rain forests (such as those in the Hoh, Queets, and Quinault valleys).

The trail weaves through stands of moss-mantled spruce, fir, hemlock, and maple, and past extraordinary fern gardens. If you walk quietly and talk softly, you may see some of the many wild creatures that live in the Bogachiel Valley. It isn't hard to approach elk, both on the trail and along the river. And the deer seem as interested in hikers as the hikers are in the deer. Grouse and eagles are common in the valley, and if you don't see coyotes, bears, and cougars, you'll probably find their tracks on the trail. Trail shelters are located 5 miles from the park boundary, 11 miles from the boundary, and 15 miles from the boundary on the North Fork. Between the park boundary and Flapjack Shelter, you'll find good camping spots along the river bars. Upstream from Flapjack, though, where the river courses through a rocky gorge, good campsites are hard to find.

In some ways, winter is a better season to visit the rain forests than summer — particularly for serious wildlife watchers. The red alders and maples have dropped their leaves by January, and you can see farther through the forests than at other times of year. Perhaps the most frequently encountered animals are elk, down from the high mountains for the winter. With luck, you may also see deer, coyotes, even cougars or a bear. Along river bars, especially near logjams, look for raccoon and skunk tracks.

Archeological Finds in an Ancient Indian Village

Long-buried artifacts of an ancient Indian culture are attracting explorers to the Olympic National Park's Coastal Strip.

At the Ozette dig near Cape Alava on the Pacific Ocean, archeologists from Washington State University have unearthed the remains of six houses and their contents, buried by massive mud slides 150 to 500 years ago. Among the finds have been awls, carved wooden boxes, bowls, woven blankets, bows and arrows, bone combs, beaver tooth chisels, fishing gear, and decorative screens. More than 7,000 artifacts have been cataloged. Most are now housed at Neah Bay, but there is a representative display at the Ozette site. Free tours of the excavation are conducted by archeology students every few hours daily in the summer.

The 3.3 mile trail begins at the northeast tip of Lake Ozette, 21 miles southwest of Sekiu on the Hoko Road. This hike to the ocean is level and easy—much of it over raised cedar planking—but muddy stretches call for lug-soled boots.

Mud that buried the village sealed the houses and preserved their contents by stopping oxidation, bacterial action, and other weathering. Ozette is thus one of the best preserved archeological sites yet discovered on the north Pacific Coast, as well as one of the largest and oldest south of Alaska.

Indian Bone Comb

Indians who lived here harpooned whales, seals, and sea lions from their ocean-going canoes as early as 2,000 years ago (and possibly much earlier) and as recently as the first part of this century. The village was abandoned in the 1920s when the Indians moved to Neah Bay.

UPSTREAM from Flapjack Shelter, hiker leaves the trail to watch Bogachiel River rush through gorge.

OCTOBER CATCH of cutthroat trout in Bogachiel measures 12-16 inches.

Out of this World: a Rain Forest Hike

YOUNG BUCK surprised only 20 feet from tent at a spring dawn. Soon his velvet becomes hard antlers.

TRAIL RESEMBLES garden path for first 11 miles into Bogachiel River Valley.

SWORDFERNS carpet much of forest floor; soft green light filters from above.

Olympia & the Southwest Corner

Though it's apt to be overlooked by visitors to Washington who beeline straight to the Puget Sound area, the southwestern coastal region between the mouth of the Columbia River and Grays Harbor is popular with many who live in the Pacific Northwest. Rewarding in summer, this area also holds much of winter interest. Its harbors, bays, islands, points, and shoreline are rich in wilderness life, beaches, sport fishing opportunities, historical lore—and drama on the dunes.

Washington's southwest corner nestles between the Columbia River to the south and Puget Sound to the north. Two major highways traverse it: Interstate 5 on the east and U.S. 101 on the west. In this chapter, we'll first move north from the Oregon border on U.S. 101 to tour the North Beach Peninsula and the countryside around Willapa Bay. Then we'll head south from Olympia, the state capital, on Interstate 5, cutting over to the coastal Grays Harbor region.

NORTH FROM THE ASTORIA BRIDGE

Though the completion of the Astoria Bridge simplifies access on U.S. 101 from northern Oregon into southwestern Washington, it isn't likely that the bridge will change the North Beach Peninsula very much. The peninsula is not on a through highway, as are the Oregon coast beaches and some of Washington's northern beaches. People who visit this section of coast come because they want to.

(The name "North Beach Peninsula" is the official designation by the State of Washington; but many North Beach residents prefer to call it "Long Beach Peninsula," and most locally printed maps, brochures, and real estate advertising refer to the area as "Long Beach.")

Just after you've crossed the Astoria Bridge into Washington, you'll come to a historical marker indicating Lewis and Clark's campsite from November 16th to 25th, 1805. Seeing the Pacific Ocean's thunderous breakers from here, they knew that

DEDICATED CLAMMERS give their all: use tubelike devices to simplify digging, draw out shy ones.

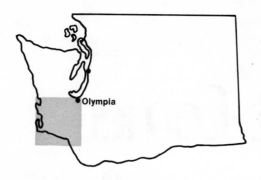

the journey assigned them by President Thomas Jefferson had ended successfully.

North Beach Peninsula

As early as 1876, stagecoaches carried passengers along the 28-mile-long sand beach of the North Beach Peninsula. By 1895, North Beach was a popular vacation area for Portlanders who came downriver on steamboats to Ilwaco, and then boarded the Ilwaco Railroad and Steam Navigation Company's narrow-gauge train to reach Seaview, Long Beach, Ocean Park, and Nahcotta. Roads finally replaced the steamers and the railroad.

North Beach's cottages, hotels, and motels are strung along State 103 from Ilwaco to Ocean Park. A list of them is available from the Peninsula Resort Association, Long Beach 98631.

The oldest hotel on the peninsula is the Shelburne in Seaview, which dates back to 1896. By the week, quiet accommodations, including dinner and breakfast, are quite inexpensive. Reservations are necessary.

At least two small restaurants in Ilwaco and one each in Long Beach, Ocean Park, and Nahcotta serve good local seafood.

Though North Beach's tourist facilities aren't as gleaming and modern as those of more recently developed vacation areas, in charm and recreational attractions the Peninsula can hold its own with practically any other portion of the Pacific from San Diego to Cape Flattery.

Here are some Peninsula high spots:

Columbia River. For an unparalleled view of the Pacific and the mouth of the Columbia, go to Bellevue Park at rugged North Head, near Ilwaco.

Browsing. In Ilwaco, Seaview, Long Beach, Ocean Park, and Nahcotta, you'll find combination antique and junk shops that carry merchandise ranging from Chinese vases to sea-washed pop bottles. There is only one art gallery on the Peninsula—the Sea Chest in Seaview.

If you're interested in gardening, visit Clarke Nursery and Cranguyma Farms on Peninsula Road along Willapa Bay. Clarke's is one of the Northwest's largest wholesale-retail suppliers of rhododendrons and also has an excellent collection of heathers. Cranguyma Farms, which encompasses one of the largest cranberry bogs in the West, has rhododendrons, azaleas, holly, and cranberry products for sale.

Oyster ogling. Oysters put Willapa Bay on the map, but you may not collect them, since all are on

FOR KEEPING WARM on sandy Columbia River beach near Astoria Bridge, nothing is more effective than game of tag. Family crossed from Washington to Oregon's Clatsop Spit.

privately owned tidelands (oyster farms). You can purchase them, however, and Northwest Oyster Farms in Nahcotta offers a tour of its oyster processing plant. While in Nahcotta, drop in on the Washington State Shellfish Laboratory. It's open Monday through Friday. Oysterville is so small you can drive through it in 30 seconds, but it's one of western Washington's oldest communities, and a few of its moldering buildings date back to the 1860s. You may want to explore it on foot.

Leadbetter Point. As you approach the northern end of the Peninsula, the road deteriorates and finally ends at Leadbetter Point, an undeveloped Washington state park. Leadbetter is beautifully desolate—a good place to see birds and small animals (or their tracks in the sand), explore sand dunes, and dig bay clams.

Clamming. More razor clams are annually dug on the long sandy shore of North Beach than anywhere else in the world. You can also dig for littlenecks and other bay clams at Leadbetter Point and on Long Island in Willapa Bay (rent a small boat in Nahcotta to reach the island).

Fishing. Long Beach residents are proud of the fact that they can fish for salmon in the ocean, trout in the lakes, and sturgeon in the bay. There is excellent surf fishing all along the Peninsula and rock fishing from headlands and jetties on the peninsula's south end. You can catch planted rainbow trout in fresh-water Loomis Lake. But the main attraction is salmon, and Ilwaco is the place to go. You can go out with a charter boat with an experienced skipper for under $20 a day. For informa-

tion, write the Ilwaco Chamber of Commerce.

Horseback riding. One of the most pleasant ways to explore the dunes and beaches is on horseback. You can rent saddle horses inexpensively at Seaview Riding Academy and at Sea Horse Stables at Surfside Estates, north of Ocean Park.

Beach driving. The most convenient way to explore the 28-mile-long sandy beach (one of the longest driving beaches in the world) is by car. Speed limit is 35 miles an hour, and it's illegal to drive in the razor clam beds near the water line.

Willapa Bay

As U.S. 101 heads north from the Columbia River to follow the eastern shoreline of Willapa Bay, it provides a 13-mile stretch of breathtaking beauty for the motorist. This short stretch of U.S. 101 between Ilwaco and South Bend would surely be a finalist in a contest to select Washington's loveliest road.

Along it you'll find these attractions:

Willapa National Wildlife Refuge. Located about 12 miles north of Ilwaco, this large refuge consists of 9,600 acres of federally owned land and water and about 10,000 acres of state tidelands and water. Leadbetter Point is a recent addition to the refuge. It was established in 1937 to provide a protecting wintering area for Pacific black brant, who nest on the arctic tundra of Alaska and Canada and winter at the refuge from October through May. Other birds who stopover here include the dusky race of the Canada goose and dabbling and diving ducks.

(continued on page 83)

ASTORIA BRIDGE, left, soars high over Columbia River traffic on Astoria side, continues at water level for most of its 4-mile length. Above, Hoquiam Castle overlooks city of Hoquiam.

LOOP TRIP: Up Long Beach and Past the Columbia's Mouth

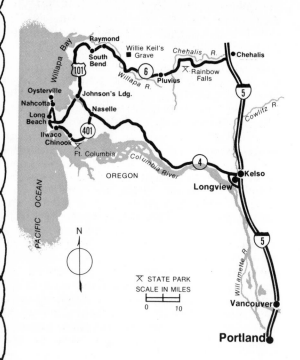

Lonely lighthouses, rocky coastlines, and ancient forests—all are just off the main route. Travelers driving into Washington via Interstate 5 from Oregon will find this 336-mile loop intriguing.

Vancouver (7 miles from Portland). Site of an early outpost of the Hudson's Bay Company and the oldest community in the state, Vancouver preserves some concrete reminders of the fur-trading center which operated from 1824 to 1846. Outlines of the original stockade and buildings are still visible; sturdy Covington House was built in 1846; the Ulysses S. Grant Museum houses a collection of memorabilia concerning the president and displays of Indian arts and crafts.

Kelso (47 miles). Featuring pioneer and Indian artifacts, a doll collection, anthropological and natural history displays, and items from various wars, the Cowlitz County Historical Museum is open all day Tuesday through Saturday and on Sunday afternoons. From Kelso, Interstate 5 follows the Cowlitz River north along the old Vancouver-Puget Sound state line.

Chehalis (83 miles). Here at Lewis County seat, swing west along State 6. Three miles from town stands the Claquato Church, one of the oldest in Washington, whose bronze bell was cast in Boston in 1857 and shipped around Cape Horn. Winding along the Chehalis River, the road leads to Rainbow Falls State Park, then 25 miles farther to Willie Keil's grave (see page 85).

Raymond (135 miles). Lumbering and shipping supply jobs for Raymond's townspeople. Travelers can feast on oysters and blackberries at South Bend, southwest on U.S. 101. At Johnson's Landing, bear right over the Naselle River.

Seaview (179 miles). The long, fingerlike peninsula of North Beach jutting out from Seaview is the prime feature of your loop tour. Here are opportunities for swimming in surf or bay, fishing, clamming, boating, stalking duck and deer, visiting cranberry bogs and oyster beds, taking dozens of photographs . . . or just lazing in sun.

Long Beach (181 miles). Combing beaches for driftwood or Japanese glass fishnet floats and going after clams and crabs are only two of the activities that have made Long Beach a center of attraction. It really does have a long beach— 28 miles of hard sand. You can drive along the beach (above the clam beds!) but beware of the swift incoming tide.

Ocean Park, surrounded by shipwrecks and rotting old ships, sports a house constructed of flotsam and jetsam among its antique homes. Other beach towns farther along the peninsula are Nahcotta (look for a good restaurant here) and Oysterville.

Ilwaco (207 miles). Past Ilwaco, nestled in a sheltered cove on the Columbia estuary, you'll pass the Fishing Rocks on a small peninsula to the south, favorite of sportsmen seeking perch, sea bass, flounder, skate, or halibut. Farther along are the rocky cove of Beard's Hollow, North Head Light, North Jetty (first-rate driftwood collecting and fishing), and old Fort Canby. At the wide mouth of the Columbia River towers Cape Disappointment Light. From Ilwaco, follow U.S. 101 southeast along the shore of Baker Bay.

Chinook (212 miles). Weathered homes of fishermen recall the past here. Two miles away, atop a promontory dominating the river, stand the Spanish-American War buildings and batteries of Fort Columbia State Park. Visitors can walk through a museum telling the history of the fort, then enjoy a picnic-with-a-view. Follow State 401 north toward Naselle.

Junction with State 4 (230 miles). A right turn here takes you south along Columbia River past dairy country, old Wahkiahkum and Cathlamet Indian lands, river islands, and river towns.

Longview (289 miles). The first planned city in the Pacific Northwest offers tours of the world's largest integrated wood products plant. Across the river is Kelso, from which you can follow Interstate 5 back through Vancouver.

Portland (336 miles). Now shake the sand out of your shoes.

(continued from page 81)

A major part of the refuge is Long Island, 6 miles in length and just offshore from refuge headquarters. The island is approximately 70 percent federal property; a private timber company owns the rest. The entire island has wildlife refuge protection and abounds with blacktail or mule deer, black bear, and raccoon. A canoe trip to Long Island could be the highlight of your visit.

Bruceport State Park. Set on a bluff overlooking Willapa Bay about 5 miles south of South Bend, Bruceport makes up in charm for what it lacks in size. Overnight camping is permitted here; each vehicle is charged a nominal fee. This wooded setting is planned as the future home of the Pacific County Museum, presently in South Bend.

South Bend. An oyster processing town, South Bend also brags (with real justification) about its blackberry pie—available during the summer season. Perhaps the most interesting sight for the tourist is the Pacific County Museum, which stocks everything from a 12-foot saw to the notorious Forks Creek still. The Pacific County Courthouse, clinging to a hill above town, looks as if it stepped out of a tale by Nathaniel Hawthorne.

SOUTHWEST FROM OLYMPIA

Traveling to the southwest corner of the state from Puget Sound, the gateway into the area is Olympia, Washington's capital and itself a target for tourists with a thirst for new experiences.

Olympia ... State Capital

The capital city of Washington state resembles the national capital in Washington, D. C. not only because of the architectural style of its capitol building but also because, like the eastern capital, it is very near water. Olympia is situated at the extreme southern end of Budd Inlet, off Puget Sound.

In and around this carefully groomed, parklike community, you'll want to explore these offerings:

State Capitol Buildings. Dominating the city are the state capitol buildings. The Legislative Building, with its Roman-Doric architecture and lavishly detailed interior, is the central structure of the group. Organ concerts are given in the rotunda. As you walk into the rotunda, notice the massive brass chandelier (created by Tiffany Studios of New York) suspended from the 185-foot-high ceiling. The State Library to the south of the Legislative Building has outstanding sculpture, mosaics, paintings by outstanding Northwest artists, and a broad collection of books.

Beautifully landscaped capitol grounds comprise approximately 55 acres of lawns and gardens. The Sunken Garden and the other flower beds on the grounds provide a gorgeous display of color most of the year. In the spring, the Japanese cherry blossoms along the street east of the Temple of Justice present a spectacle of color. The Tivoli Fountain, a replica of Denmark's Tivoli Fountain, offers a dramatic display of changing colors.

One block off Capitol Way, at 211 West 21st Street, the State Capitol Museum is housed in the handsome old Lord mansion. In some ways it is the most interesting of all state buildings to visit. Exhibited are Indian art and artifacts, memorabilia of Washington's pioneer days, an old general store, and a permanent collection of work by Pacific Northwest artists.

Capitol Lake. Varied water recreation is available on this lake formed by a dam at a point where the fresh water of the Deschutes River empties into the salt water of Budd Inlet. From atop the dam during spawning season in mid-August, you can see thousands of fighting salmon making their way upstream. Deschutes Parkway skirts the shore of Capitol Lake, providing a view of the State Capitol.

Tumwater Falls Park. South of Olympia off Interstate 5, this 15-acre city park on the Deschutes River is a good picnicking and playground spot.

Crosby House. Near Tumwater Falls Park is Crosby House, of interest because it was the home of Bing Crosby's grandfather.

STATE CAPITOL at Olympia rises beside the Deschutes River just before it empties into Budd Inlet. Its setting at southernmost tip of Puget Sound makes Olympia an especially handsome capital.

DUNE SLIDING at Leadbetter Point on tip of North Beach Peninsula is good—but gritty—fun.

Olympia Brewery. Probably the most popular—and certainly the most immaculately clean—tourist attraction near the capitol is the Olympia Brewing Company in Tumwater, 2 miles south of Olympia.

Free tours of the brewery (including free samples of the product) are conducted every day except Christmas Day. In addition to watching beer being flavored with hops and bottled under closed-circuit television supervision, tourists see a film of the brewery's history. Highlight of the film is the scene during Prohibition in which federal agents are spraying holes with machine gun bullets into beer-filled kegs.

Visitors enjoy browsing in the plant's gift shop at the end of their tour.

A southeast spur. At Tenino, about 18 miles southeast of Olympia on a spur road off Interstate 5, there's a unique swimming pool in an old quarry. From this quarry, stone was hewn for Olympia's courthouse and for the footings of the state capitol. At Tono, 4 miles farther along the same spur road,

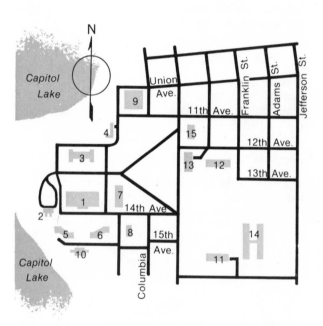

THE CAPITAL

1 LEGISLATIVE BUILDING
2 GOVERNOR'S MANSION
3 TEMPLE OF JUSTICE
4 GREENHOUSE
5 PUBLIC HEALTH BLDG.
6 PUBLIC LANDS BLDG.
7 INSURANCE BLDG.
8 INSTITUTIONS BLDG.
9 GENERAL ADMINISTRATION
10 STATE LIBRARY
11 EMPLOYMENT SECURITY
12 HIGHWAYS-LICENSES
13 ARCHIVES AND RECORDS
14 HIGHWAY BUILDING
15 THURSTON COUNTY COURTHOUSE

FOOTBRIDGE crosses river from highway to Rainbow Falls State Park, 28 miles west of Chehalis.

Where Willie was Laid to Rest

You'd be hard pressed to find a more unusual tourist attraction in Washington than Willie Keil's grave.

Visiting graves is not your idea of a vacation treat, you say? But this is a grave with a difference. For Willie was a 17-year-old lad from Missouri whose parents, Dr. and Mrs. William Keil, leaders of the Bethel Colony, were putting together a wagon train in 1855 to move west. Willie was especially excited about the project, for his father had promised him a position of honor during the trip—as driver of the lead wagon.

Unfortunately, Willie died a few days before the trip was to begin. A Missourian to his core, Dr. Keil was not to be daunted. After an appropriate period of mourning, he placed his son in a lead-lined box, filled it with alcohol to pickle Willie's body, and set the casket in the front wagon, remodeled as a hearse.

As the wagon train moved across the Indian plains, word spread among the braves that a dead man was leading the expedition. Never has a more effective form of trip insurance been devised: not a single arrow flew; not a single scalp departed from its rightful position.

When the family arrived in Washington, they buried Willie in an aromatic, candlelight ceremony atop a hill near Menlo (about 8 miles south-east of South Bend), overlooking the farmland where members of the Bethel Colony settled.

Reason enough for a look?

HISTORIC MARKER at right tells the story of Willie Keil, buried under trees on hill.

is a huge Washington Water and Power Company power plant and a strip mining operation.

Centralia and Chehalis

About 30 miles south of Olympia, Centralia takes its name from the fact that it is located about midway between Portland, Oregon, and Seattle. Centralia's prime tourist sight—Borst Blockhouse and Borst Farmstead in Fort Borst Park—is 1 mile west of the city off Interstate 5. Built to ward off Indian attacks at the confluence of the Skookumchuck and Chehalis rivers, the fort was moved here after its original site was flooded. Hewn log walls support upper fortifications that have loopholes for rifles. The park also contains an early steam locomotive and a small zoo.

Scattered southeast and southwest of Chehalis are a number of sites of historical or recreational appeal. They include the John R. Jackson House (2 miles east of Interstate 5 on U.S. 12) at Mary's Corner, an early day building constructed with peeled logs and split cedar (the first residence

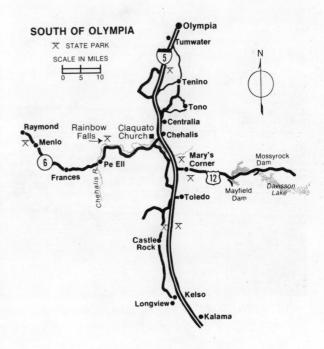

UNIQUE STEEPLE crowns Claquato Church. Tree beside church was planted day of Lincoln's assassination.

established by an American in the Washington Territory and later used for a courthouse); and Mayfield and Mossyrock Dams, both farther along the same highway and both with recreational developments.

Heading west on State 6

As State 6 heads west from Chehalis to Raymond, you pass through farmlands that are reminiscent of European countryside. Several points spark interest along this road:

Claquato Church. A striking church located 3 miles west of Chehalis, Claquato Church was built in 1858 with hand-forged nails and lumber sawed in a water-powered mill. It lived a double life, serving both as a church and schoolhouse—the Claquato Academy. Claquato was an important stopping place for pioneers traveling between the Columbia River and Puget Sound.

Rainbow Falls State Park. About 28 miles west of Interstate 5, you'll come to a footbridge and car bridge over the Chehalis River leading to this 122-acre campground. Filled with tall evergreens, the park is set in a lush forest beside a large, open meadow. The park has a community kitchen.

Pe Ell. This town was first named "Pierre" but became "Pe Ell" because the Indians were unable to pronounce the letter "r."

Frances. One of Washington's most attractive country churches, the Catholic Church of the Holy Family rises on a hill above the highway in Frances.

SPORT FISHING BOATS by the hundred move into Westport harbor as day of offshore salmon fishing draws to close. At this Grays Harbor center, many charter companies operate.

Can You Dig It—a Succulent Clam?

One enthusiast has described digging for razor clams this way: "It satisfies a man's basic urges to hunt, fish, and farm, all in one gloriously difficult operation." The comment might be applied to clamming in general.

Most epicures insist that all clams are edible, but clams do vary in flavor. In Washington about 13 species are popular, but numerous other species can also be dug and eaten. Bay clams live in tidal zone muds, sands, and gravels of most of Puget Sound and also in small, sheltered coves along the Pacific Coast. The prize specimens, though, are geoducks and razor clams.

Geoduck clams. The largest clam in the Northwest is the *geoduck* (gooey-duck), which means "big clam" in Chinook. This bowlful of chowder in the rough is the "big game" of clam digging. Geoducks average 3 to 6 pounds and can grow even bigger. Search for them beneath sandy tide flats, where they frequently burrow to a depth of 3 feet or more.

After you locate the fairly large hole left by the geoduck when it retracts its siphon, you can proceed in one of two ways. You can place a large metal tube—perhaps a piece of stovepipe—about 18 inches in diameter and 3 to 4 feet long over the geoduck hole, called a show, and stomp or pound it into the sand to surround and isolate the clam. Then excavate the sand inside until you can reach the clam.

Or you can use a shovel and lots of heart and simply dig down until you expose the geoduck's neck. Then reach into the hole (it may resemble a crater by now) and carefully wiggle out the whole clam. Don't tug-of-war with the neck or you'll break it off.

Razor clams. The most popular clam in the Northwest, one of the most delicious, and the most difficult to dig—that's the razor clam, a hardy inhabitant of the sands of coastal beaches where the surf pounds endlessly.

Of all clams, razors burrow downward the fastest—as much as 9 inches a minute—and digging for them is something of an art. The time-tested method employs a specially designed shovel (clam gun) with a narrow, slightly curved blade.

The smooth and graceful operation of a clam gun by an expert is highly effective. In the hands of a beginner, though, the shovel usually proves lethal for the clam and frustrating for the digger.

To dig a razor clam, watch for a show: small dimples in drier sand, or tiny pits under low water. Looking underwater, you'll sometimes see the top of a razor's siphon, like a small rosette in the sand. With your shovel, scoop a hole 9 to 12 inches deep, and then quickly insert your hand and feel about for the clam. This seemingly simple operation is hard for beginners, but you can usually find an old-timer to give you advice.

There's also a tubelike device that greatly simplifies the digging task and reduces the chance of wastage. The Department of Fisheries publishes explicit instructions available at sporting goods stores and motels.

The razor clam season is closed from July 1 through September 30.

THE BIG REACH is sometimes important when the prospect of eating clam chowder grabs you.

CAPE DISAPPOINTMENT light-house, right, like Circe, suggests both beauty and danger. Many ships (see General M. C. Meigs below) have sunk along coast.

Menlo. Near Menlo are a horse ranch, a salmon hatchery, and the hill on which Willie Keil is buried.

North to Grays Harbor

Just outside Raymond, State 105 branches west off U.S. 101 to parallel the north shore of Willapa Bay and takes you through the small Shoalwater Indian Reservation on your way to the ocean. With its concentration on driftwood, cranberries, and harvesting the sea, this small stretch of coastline has a character all its own. Try these stops:

Tokeland. A rental equipment sign on Tokeland's pier testifies to the versatility of the arrangements possible here: "Charters; Poles and Bait; Clam Guns; Crab Ring Nets." Fishing is good throughout the year from Tokeland's dock, and crabbing is excellent in February.

Grayland. Turn off the main road on any of Grayland's cross streets, and you'll see cranberry bogs that date back to an early settlement of Finnish cranberry growers. Grayland's cranberry growers belong to a cooperative organization that prepares and packages cranberry products. The main plant is located in Markham. Grayland is the home of an annual driftwood show; a restaurant on the dunes serves crab in appetizing ways. The beach here is famous for its well-stocked razor clam beds.

Twin Harbors State Park. There are 380 campsites in the 87 acres of Twin Harbors State Park, as well as a trailer camp with hookups.

Westport. The busy fishing town of Westport is on a sandy point of land that bounds Grays Harbor on the southwest. Its main street is lined with charter boat offices, custom canneries, and general stores that carry everything a fisherman needs—from a salmon plug to a sou'wester. Along the sea wall are launching docks for small boats. A small aquarium in town is worth the price of admission.

The residential part of Westport is on higher ground about a half-mile back from the main street. Here you'll see crab trap floats, looking like huge colored tops, swinging from the rope fences that enclose small, neat gardens.

LOOP TRIP: Ocean Beaches and the Hood Canal

Learn history and geography the easy way— board a famous battleship, drop a line in the salmon-fishing headquarters of the world, and take a voyage across Puget Sound. It's 291 miles of adventure.

From Seattle head south on Interstate 5 past a spectacular view of the Boeing Aircraft plant to your right.

Tacoma (32 miles). View deep-sea freighters being loaded in Commencement Bay, examine the world's largest collection of octopi, a fine zoo, and a tall totem pole. You can rejoin Interstate 5 at the downtown Pacific Avenue or South 38th Street complex.

Olympia (62 miles). A seaport, lumbering and shellfish center, as well as Washington's capital, Olympia is justly famous for its restaurants' excellent seafood. Guided tours are available at the legislative building.

Centralia (83 miles). In the heart of Washington's timber belt, you can visit the famous Fort Borst Blockhouse (1852), center of a 100-acre park with picnic grounds, kitchens, and fishing areas exclusively for children. Going south and west on State 6 takes you past Rainbow Falls State Park along the scenic Chehalis and Willapa Rivers.

Raymond-South Bend (139 miles). The seagull's cry blends with the whine of sawmills in these colorful seaports. Follow the new "Scenic Marine Drive" (State 105) for 2 miles north through North Cove.

Grayland (170 miles). Good tourist accommodations plus a 16-mile stretch of salt spray ocean front for beachcombing or clam digging attract visitors to this small coastal village. This is driftwood country.

Westport (177 miles). Nationally known for deep-sea salmon fishing, Westport rewards strollers with a little main street lined with marine stores, gift shops and, naturally, seafood restaurants. You can stay at a number of private campgrounds in the area or at the big state park at Twin Harbors. Continue north and east on State 105 for 19 miles.

Aberdeen (200 miles). Here you may wish to drive northward on State 109 to beaches at the small resort areas of Ocean City, Copalis Beach, Pacific Beach, and Moclips or the more extensive resort city of Ocean Shores. This alternative will add 82 miles but is well worthwhile if you have time. From Aberdeen, pick up U.S. 12 heading east.

Montesano (210 miles). Serving as the county seat of Grays Harbor, Montesano also was the birthplace of the tree farms, an important part of the selective logging development of the state's timber crop. After driving east for 10 miles, turn on State 8.

McCleary (226 miles). The International Bear Festival is an annual highlight in this typical Pacific Northwest logging town. Take State 108 north from McCleary.

Shelton (244 miles). Site of thrilling logging sports during the Forest Festival in May, Shelton is proud of modern forest-management practices, ranging from tree-planning to thinning and harvesting. Ten miles north of Shelton on U.S. 101, head northeast on State 106 for the Hood Canal drive beginning at Union.

Twanoh State Park (264 miles). Tree-shaded picnic areas and beach scenery reward you on the shores of Hood Canal. Adjoining the park, State 106 takes you from the Webb Cutoff to Bremerton on State 3.

Bremerton (289 miles). Giant flattops roost in dry dock here where the Navy uses the Puget Sound Naval Shipyard for carrier conversion, as well as for major repair of warships. Tours visit the famous World War II battleship *U.S.S. Missouri.* To return to Seattle, motorists can board a ferry for the 45-minute cross-Sound ride. (Or take State 16 over the Narrows Bridge into Tacoma, stopping en route at Gig Harbor.)

Seattle (291 miles). The end of the line.

The Lure of the Cascades

A good case could be made for the Cascade Range being Washington's single most impressive recreational resource. Its monarch, 14,410-foot-high Mt. Rainier, is the fifth highest mountain in the continental United States. Other peaks range from 8,000 to 9,000 feet; some volcanic cones rise even higher.

To these slopes come sportsmen with their skis, toboggans, and inner tubes. Others travel to the mountain lakes with canoes, rowboats, powerboats, water skis. Some carry fishing poles, kayaks, or rubber rafts to the rivers of the Cascades. Still others climb to Mt. Rainier's ice caves or follow the rugged Pacific Crest National Scenic Trail that winds along the crest for the entire length of the summit.

Two of Washington's three national parks are found in the Cascades: North Cascades National Park and Mt. Rainier National Park. The following pages tell you what to look for there, as well as in other areas along this impressive mountain range.

CASCADES TO THE NORTH

More than 1.5 million acres of spectacular mountain scenery have been set aside for public enjoyment within the boundaries of the new North Cascades National Park and two adjacent wilderness areas in northwestern Washington. Additional tourist pleasures in this area are yours for the discovering in the Mt. Baker and Wenatchee National Forests.

North Cascades National Park:
wilderness waits

Rising silently among swirls of gray fog, a dramatic range of ice-scoured peaks lends its name to America's most breathtaking high mountain park. In 1968, Congress designated over 1,000 square miles of the North Cascades as the site of the two-unit North Cascades National Park and the Ross Lake

PACK STRING crosses gravelly ridge, descends into scrubby pine on trip west toward Mt. Rainier.

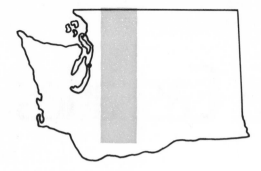

and Lake Chelan National Recreation Areas (see pages 95-97).

The Picket Range, with its silhouette of severe jagged crags, is the major feature of the northern unit of the park that snuggles up to the Canadian border about 100 miles northeast of Seattle. The equally majestic Eldorado Peaks are the outstanding feature of the south unit. Between the north and south sections of the park, along the Skagit River and its series of hydroelectric dams, lies the Ross Lake National Recreation Area. At the southern end of the park is the Lake Chelan National Recreation Area.

Bordering the south edge of the park, as well, is the 468,000 acre Glacier Peak Wilderness, and to the east of the Ross Lake Recreation Area lies the 520,000-acre Pasayten Wilderness. These roadless areas are administered by the United States Forest Service, and no mechanized vehicles of any kind are permitted within their borders.

Through the rugged North Cascades, roads are in scarce supply. A major exception is State Highway 20 (Washingtonians call it the North Cascades Highway); it leaves Interstate 5 at Burlington, 65 miles north of Seattle, and wends through North Cascades National Park to traverse the state, ending at the Idaho border.

The western end of the park may also be reached by State 543 east from Bellingham and on secondary highways that leave State 20 at the towns of Concrete and Marblemount.

Though few roads traverse the North Cascades, the park and adjoining wilderness areas are crisscrossed with many miles of hiking and riding trails, including a segment of the Pacific Crest Trail that extends from Canada to Mexico.

More than 100 years have passed since fur trappers and prospectors first penetrated the area, but the North Cascades still are relatively unexplored and have not been completely mapped. Although there is no exact inventory available yet, park offi-

SHARP PINNACLES of typical North Cascades peak, rock-strewn shores reflect in White Rock Lake.

cials estimate there are at least 150 glaciers in the park and another 90 in nearby Glacier Peak Wilderness. A Forest Service report compiled in 1965 listed 200 miles of trout fishing streams and more than 90 lakes in just one section of the park.

Planners envision future construction of aerial tramways to take visitors to the tops of some of the high peaks; helicopter trips also have been suggested as a way to see the country. At present, charter flights organized by private companies in Bellingham, Anacortes, Seattle, Tacoma, Omak, Chelan, or Yakima offer panoramic park views.

Both the park's North and South units contain many high peaks to challenge the mountain climber. A permit (in advance) is required for backcountry camping. You can request one by mail or phone or in person at ranger stations. Maps are available at park headquarters in Sedro Woolley near Burlington or at the ranger station in Marblemount, 40 miles east.

Write to the North Cascades National Park, Sedro Woolley, Washington 98384, for information on accommodations and services available in the park and in nearby communities.

Plant life thrives in tropical profusion on valley floors only 1000 feet above sea level. Above the low valleys in a subalpine zone grow alder, fir, and ferns; hikers struggling up from the deep valleys can watch the forest thin out and then give way to a climax of color in alpine meadows. On the park's drier east slope, vegetation is scattered but more varied.

Wildlife is not always visible in the park, since animals are partly concealed by vegetation and terrain. Near you (whether you see them or not) are wolverines, otters, martens, mountain goats, blacktail and mule deer, an occasional moose or elk, and perhaps a grizzly bear.

Bird watchers might view white-tailed ptarmigans, bald eagles, ospreys, trumpeter swans, or grouse. Most often you'll see the small animals that abound in the park—squirrels, pikas, and marmots.

North Cascades Highway—a vital connecting link

Cutting between North Cascades National Park's north and south segments as it links western Washington and Idaho, State 20 is the only developed route through the park. Opened in 1972, it is one of the nation's grand scenic routes. Most of the highway leads through national forest, though the road also enters the Ross Lake National Recreation Area. Heavy snows close the highway in winter.

WINTER-TOURING deer, left, in Snoqualmie National Forest ponders directions toward possibly richer feeding ground. Above, Seattle students unanimously enjoy inner tubing down snowy hill.

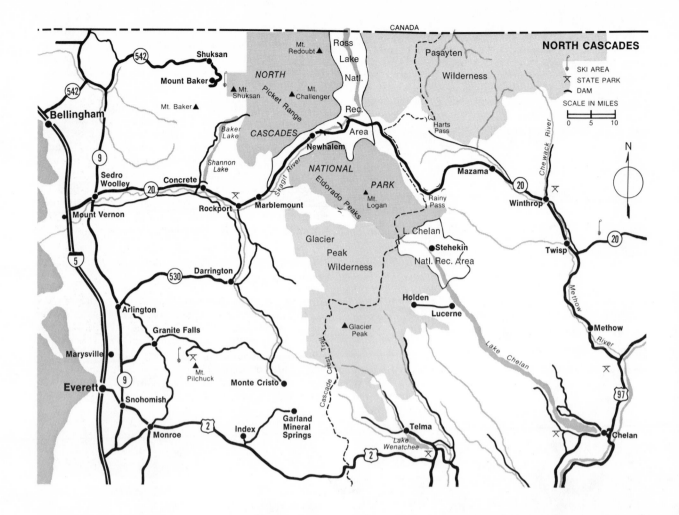

As if providing access to the North Cascades were not enough, State 20 has attractions along the way to make the drive alone worthwhile. Traveling eastward along the route, you'll pass a number of intriguing stops:

Marblemount. A small town at the junction of the Skagit, Marblemount provides an opportunity to stock up with gas and food before entering the mountains, as well as to obtain information at its ranger station.

Newhalem. You can make advance reservations for a Seattle City Light tour of the Skagit Project. Other attractions are the Gorge Powerhouse, Ladder Creek Falls, and an antique steam engine. Some sort of dam has been located at this spot since 1919; the present one dates from 1961.

Diablo. Visitors can see a replica of the first Skagit water wheel powerhouse and ride an incline railway 600 feet up the mountainside. This mountainside vehicle is all that remains of the old Seattle-Skagit River Railway, dismantled in 1954. The trip takes only 6 minutes; then it's a short walk down a gravel road to Diablo Dam.

From Diablo Lake Overlook, the view extends from Thunder Creek to the hanging glaciers on Colonial and Pyramid Peaks. Fine sediment (rock-flour) carried by glacier-fed streams creates the blue-green shade of Diablo Lake.

Ross Lake overlook. Extending 24 miles northward, Ross Lake is the heart of a National Recreation Area. Ten small campgrounds on the lakeshore can be reached by boat.

Rainy Pass. The Pacific Crest National Scenic Trail (see page 96) crosses the highway here. Lake Ann is only 1.4 miles away.

Whistler Basin viewpoint. Here you'll find a close-up view of fragile alpine meadows; bright colors glow in autumn.

Washington Pass overlook. An easy trail to the overlook begins at a parking area ½ mile from the highway. The view encompasses Early Winters Creek, the needlelike peaks of Silver Star Mountain and Snagtooth Ridge, the Cooper Basin framed by Kangaroo Ridge and Early Winters Spires, and Liberty Bell Mountain.

Early Winters Information Center is next along the highway.

Harts Pass. A 23-mile road hewn to serve the 1890s gold rush prospectors branches off State 20 below Mazama. It is passable for automobiles but not for trailers. The pass is the northernmost U.S. access to the Pacific Crest Trail. Unfolding from Slate

Peak is a circular panorama overlooking several hundred square miles of wild, tumbled scenery—from Mt. Baker on the west through the glaciated valleys of the Pasayten Wilderness to the eastern horizon and south to snow-crowned Glacier Peak. Closer at hand are the remains of old mines (private property).

Winthrop. The site of a museum and Forest Service ranger station, Winthrop has been renovated with false-front buildings according to an Old West theme.

A smokejumper base, located 4 miles east of Winthrop on the eastside Methow Road, is open to visitors who want to see the home of the first airborne firefighters in the Pacific Northwest. Sometimes visitors can watch practice jumps.

Two lakes for recreation

Preserved for public enjoyment along with the national park, these two areas are different from each other in one essential way: Ross Lake is manmade, whereas Lake Chelan is an impressive natural fjord.

Ross Lake National Recreation Area. Flowing for 15 miles through a narrow granite gorge, the Skagit River has been harnessed and its power converted into electrical energy by three dams—Gorge, Diablo, and Ross.

• Skagit Project Tour. An excursion through the City of Seattle's Skagit Hydroelectric Project provides a close look at all three dams and their reservoirs, a scenic boat ride on Diablo Lake, and a trip on an incline railway. Tours leave from the powerhouse at Newhalem. Book reservations in advance at the Skagit Tours Office, City Light Building, 1015 Third Avenue, Seattle 98104.

The tour arrives at Diablo Dam by way of an incline railway (page 94) coordinated with the lake boat schedule; elevator trips are about 20 minutes before each boat departure for Ross Dam.

The boat ride provides an unexcelled view of the spectacular narrow gorge leading to the waffle-patterned 540-foot Ross Dam. Guided tour groups inspect the Ross powerhouse. If you're on your own, you may decide instead to undertake the half-hour hike to the top of Ross Dam for a look at the reservoir.

• Colonial Creek. Technically a part of the Ross Lake Recreation Area, Colonial Creek Campground on Diablo Lake (2 miles southwest of Ross Dam) is the largest campground in the park-recreation area complex. It offers boat launching ramps, running water, and indoor toilets. Major hiking trails radiate from the area.

Lake Chelan National Recreation Area. On the National Park's southern border, the glacier-carved trench of Lake Chelan (1,500 feet deep, 55 miles long, and barely more than a mile wide) is a true inland fjord, the only such water entry to wilderness in the United States.

You can launch your own boat or charter a float plane at Chelan, on U.S. 97 about 40 miles north of

PASSING Diablo Lake, travelers share benefits of strategic new North Cascades Highway (State 20).

LAKESIDE CLEARING in North Cascades wilderness provides ideal setting for tenting, campfire.

Wenatchee. Many visitors ride the *Lady of the Lake* or the *Speedway* all the way up to Stehekin at lake's end. (See page 132 for a description of boat service.)

Make the trip a one-day excursion or stop over anywhere en route and board the return vessel on any succeeding day. Instead of boarding at Chelan, you can board the launch farther on at the end of the road at 25-Mile Creek.

• At Lucerne, the boat docks briefly near a small group of resort cottages and a marina. Holden, up a dirt spur road 15 miles away, is the private camp

Hiking the Pacific Crest National Scenic Trail

Strung along mountain ranges for some 2,350 miles from Mexico to Canada, the Pacific Crest National Scenic Trail is one of two such challenges to hikers in the country (the other national trail is in the Appalachians).

The Washington segment of the scenic trail passes through five national forests, four national wilderness areas, and two national parks. Its 450 miles were traced first by Indians, then sections were explored by trappers, miners, stockmen, foresters, and pioneers.

Most adventurers today backpack. Some portions of the trail are impassable for horses, and motor vehicles are forbidden on the trail itself. One necessity is to plan well in advance and prepare supply points, for trail hikers must depend upon their own resources. *Never* travel alone. Few improved camps mark the route, and communication with the outside world is minimal.

You can adapt the trail to suit your time and interests, traveling only one segment at a time or extending your journey with side trips to nearby mountain lakes, the valleys below, or other attractions. Larger lakes provide excellent fishing; nearly all the smaller ones near the trail have been stocked with rainbow, eastern brook, and other trout. Mountain goats roam the highest and most rugged country. Occasionally hikers spot elk; blacktailed deer are common on the ridges and creek bottoms to the west, and mule deer traverse the country east of the summit. During the late summer, you might meet a black or brown bear foraging in a huckleberry patch.

The route's terrain ranges from sharp crags to graded trail. Subalpine open meadows and scattered patches of timber, typical of the high country east of the summit, merge into the sharp alpine peaks, firs, and heavy underbrush of the moister west. Near the Oregon border, the trail skirts a lava bed.

Normally the best period to hike the trail is between July 1 and September 1. Information on packers and outfitters can be obtained by writing to the Forest Supervisors of the five national forests (Gifford Pinchot, Mount Baker, Okano-

WASHINGTON'S SECTION of the Pacific Crest National Scenic Trail traverses lush woods.

gan, Snoqualmie, and Wenatchee—addresses on page 158). You can send for topographic maps of some trail areas from the Geological Survey, Denver Federal Center, Denver, Colorado 80225. An informative folder on the trail, including a trail log and maps, is available from the Pacific Northwest Region, Regional Forester, P.O. Box 3623, Portland, Oregon 97208.

of a religious organization and a starting point for horseback and hiking trips into the Glacier Peak Wilderness (see below). The boat stops for an hour at Stehekin before returning to Chelan.

• From Stehekin, a 25-mile dirt road follows the Stehekin River to dead end at Horseshoe Basin in the southern end of the National Park. Here you'll have access to miles of trout streams and several Forest Service campgrounds. You can rent a car at Stehekin or take a ½-hour bus excursion 4 miles up the Stehekin River road to 312-foot Rainbow Falls. Many combinations of trail riding and pack trips are available.

Several resorts at Stehekin offer modern accommodations (advance reservations are advisable). If you plan to stay at Stehekin, remember to include warm clothes.

For a list of lodgings and also for summer and winter boat schedules, write to Lake Chelan Chamber of Commerce. Hikers can arrange for resort owners to drive them and their gear to a destination along the way, then return for them at a pre-arranged time.

Two wilderness areas . . . paradise regained

Imagine a stretch of land where "the earth and its community of life are untrammeled by man, where man himself is a visitor who does not remain." This quote is from the Wilderness Act of 1964, which created a National Wilderness Preservation System. Two regions in the North Cascades have been designated wilderness areas:

Glacier Peak Wilderness. Surrounding formidable Glacier Peak, an aloof twin to Mt. Baker, are 468,500 wilderness acres. Around the wilderness perimeter, you can camp in roadside Forest Service campgrounds in mountain settings, mostly less than 1,000 feet above sea level and very rarely more than 2,000. A little farther back, but within short drives of the trail country, are modest motels at Concrete and Darrington on the west side and an impressive assortment of resorts and lodges in the town and backcountry environments of Chelan—east of the summer coolness and now-and-then wetness of the Cascade Crest.

On the west side, you can drive up any of the river valleys and camp as you would in mountains elsewhere. But first, for a preview of the kind of mountain grandeur that awaits you beyond, spend a day or the better part of a day driving the 115-mile circuit out of Everett that includes the Mountain Loop Highway—an ambitiously named but actually modest road from Darrington up the main Sauk River—then up its South Fork and over into the watershed of the South Fork of the Stillaguamish past Pilchuck ski resort for the return to Everett.

The highlight of this tour might be a visit to the defunct old mining town of Monte Cristo, at the end of a 4-mile side road. Stop not for the ruins themselves but for their breathtaking backdrop of towering, snow-curtained precipices. Placed at the

CANOERS STROKE along Ross Lake in national recreation area. At rear is Jack Mountain (8,928 feet).

foot of Wilman Peake, Monte Cristo in 1897 was the bustling supply center for six mining companies and had a population of some 800 people. Today, only tumbled wreckage of buildings and twisted cables from ore-processing equipment remain.

On the south side, the roads up the Little Wenatchee, White, Chiwawa, and Entiat rivers, disdained by climbers, should not be overlooked by camping families. They all lead to pleasant camping spots, dead-ending at jumping-off places for streamside trails into wild high country.

On the east are the Methow and Twisp valleys.

Pasayten Wilderness. Just east of North Cascades National Park against the Canadian border, the Pasayten Wilderness has its own distinct character, being somewhat dryer and more open than the western slopes of the Cascades.

Traversing the area are several hundred miles of trails; the Pacific Crest National Scenic Trail crosses 27 miles of Pasayten land from Windy Pass to Monument 78 at the Canadian boundary. Although you might encounter snow on higher elevation trails any time, Pasayten is generally accessible for four or five months a year—from July through October snowfalls.

PICKING THEIR WAY through rock-strewn ridge, right, explorers near the heart of North Cascades National Park. Below, Glacier Peak scrapes clouds in Glacier Peak Wilderness.

If, instead of deer or mountain goats, you meet cows and domesticated sheep, it's because grazing rights, as well as mining claims, existing prior to 1968 are still observed.

The forest supervisor or district ranger near the area you plan to visit can supply you with information about commercial packers and outfitters, maps, and wilderness area rules.

Mt. Baker ... camping par excellence

High mountain meadow country between Mt. Baker and nearby Mt. Shuksan (and along the Nooksack River that springs from their slopes) is an ideal family vacation land. Though the area has few lodges, its campgrounds are excellent and lightly used. When the weather acts up, as it frequently does, you can choose your site anywhere along the Nooksack and hardly see another tent. This mountain has one of the longest skiing seasons in Washington; pleasant pandemonium reigns each spring when the Slush Cup is run.

Northernmost section of the Cascades accessible by road, Mt. Baker is accessible via State 542 east from Bellingham.

At Heather Meadows, rambling Mt. Baker Lodge has steam heated rooms, dormitory accommodations, and a dining room. Beyond the lodge, when

OPPORTUNITIES for cross country ski touring, below left, are abundant in the Washington Cascades. Below right, climber examines entrance to Rainier summit steam cave.

the road is clear of snow, you can drive a little way above Austin Pass to Kulshan Ridge for a magnificent view. The terrain above the lodge is a winter sports area; the double chair lift to Panorama Dome also operates on weekends and holidays during the summer.

If you want to auto-explore, take the spur roads that start here and there along the Mt. Baker Highway (State 542). At the end of the Glacier Creek road (about a mile beyond Glacier) is the crevassed, varicolored snout of Coleman Glacier. Thundering, cliff-walled Nooksack Falls is only ½ mile from the Wells Creek road. From the Shuksan maintenance station, a steep, rough road zigzags to Twin Lakes

campground past narrow, ribbonlike waterfalls. You may pass black bears nuzzling in roadside huckleberry patches.

If you want to hike, trails start at the ends of most of the roads. Map and trail information are available from the Glacier District Ranger Station on State 542, 35 miles east of Bellingham, or from the Forest Service (see Appendix).

South side. To find an isolated lakeside camp or cabin, try the south side of Mt. Baker. Take State 20 east from Burlington. At the ranger station in Concrete, ask for directions to the Baker Lake turnoff, then follow the 20-mile road to Baker Lake.

From this road you can take any of several short

LOOP TRIP: A Swing through Two Cascade Passes

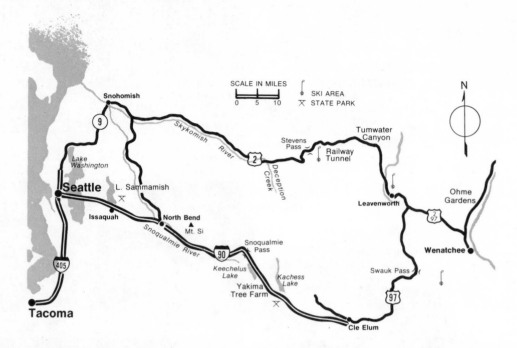

Within the 300 miles of this mountain loop is an amazingly wide variety of sights to see and things to do.

From Seattle drive eastward over the Murrow Bridge on U.S. 10 and Interstate 90 toward Snoqualmie Pass.

North Bend (28 miles). Nestled in the foothills of the Cascades, this charming little rural community is immediately to the south of Snoqualmie Falls and Mt. Si.

Snoqualmie Pass Summit (50 miles). Seattle's next-door ski area and recreation center offers thrilling, year-around sky chair rides. Its Thunderbird Restaurant, overlooking the broad sweep of the Cascades, serves a memorable Sunday breakfast.

Keechelus Lake (53 miles). This man-made reservoir provides storage for the irrigation water that nourishes the fields of central Washington.

Yakima Tree Farm (59 miles). Keep a sharp lookout for deer. Down a connecting roadway is scenic Kachess Lake, a refreshing summer playground.

U.S. 97 (85 miles). Four miles past Cle Elum, turn left for Swauk Pass, a link between Snoqualmie and Stevens Pass in dude ranch country. Mineral Springs Resort is a restful place for a picnic lunch, but watch out for bears. Camping and trailer facilities can be found in the cool forest glade of Swauk Forest Camp.

Junction U.S. 2 (128 miles). The freeway connection takes you 20 miles east toward Wenatchee, the apple center. Worth a stop is Ohme Gardens.

Leavenworth (177 miles). A small Bavarian village that's becoming the ski-jumping capital of the west, Leavenworth is also the site of the world's largest salmon hatchery.

Tumwater Canyon (180 miles). Here is possibly Washington's most fascinating white water scene as the melting snows of the high Cascades turn the Wenatchee River into a boiling, smashing cataract. Especially impressive is the Wenatchee River spillway.

Tumwater Recreation Area (206 miles). Climbing steadily toward the summit of the range, the two-lane highway is bordered by trails and forest roads. Twenty miles along is the Great Northern railway tunnel, longest in the northern hemisphere—17.8 miles.

Stevens Pass Summit (212 miles). Its elevation of 4,061 feet makes Stevens another winter paradise for ski enthusiasts. This area is ringed with peaks, the most exciting of which, Barrier Mountain, protects skiers from the winds.

Snohomish (269 miles). This small logging, dairying, and railroad community is where you turn left on State 9 to merge with State 202. Then take State 522.

Seattle (300 miles). The loop is closed.

access roads east to the lake for camping, fishing, boating, and swimming. Or drive west to a series of stunning views of Baker and Mt. Shuksan. If you simply continue to the end of the 13-mile road to a salmon hatchery, you'll enjoy the view of Mt. Baker en route. In the vicinity are a hot mineral springs, Rainbow Falls, and Upper Baker Dam.

CENTRAL CASCADES: THE ACCESSIBLE MOUNTAINS

Rising through the heart of the Cascade Range, two major roads make this alpine playland easy to reach from either east or west. The middle section of the mountains is perhaps the most developed: it contains the largest, fanciest ski resorts, a popular national park, and facilities to cope with summer crowds.

Along the Stevens Pass Highway

U.S. 2 across Stevens Pass provides a 123-mile link between Everett and Wenatchee. Meandering along gentle curves through sparsely settled country, it crosses the Snoqualmie and Wenatchee national forests, offering eye-widening views along the way. Although it is kept open year around, you may need chains near the summit in winter.

Snohomish. This largest of the eight cities along the route is primarily a residential community. But it is also the center of the Northwest frozen-food processing industry and the site of the Puget Sound power substation, which supplies electricity from Coulee Dam to the northwestern part of the state.

From Snohomish, the highway crosses a broad valley whose alluvial bottom land supports dairy, berry, and produce farms. At Monroe, the rugged tops of the Cascades are clearly visible, dominated by Mt. Baring's twin spires.

Following the Skykomish River, the road enters the Snoqualmie National Forest and begins its gradual climb between hillsides. Wild berries are plentiful. Steelhead swim the rivers, and cutthroat and rainbow trout flourish in the high lakes. Hunters will sight deer, bear, and wild goat.

Skykomish waterfalls. Two miles northwest of Baring, the South Fork of the Skykomish River plunges through deep gorges in a tumult of white water. Right next to U.S. 2, you can see three falls in a 3-mile stretch of the river—Eagle, Canyon, and Sunset. Located at Sunset Falls are a visitor overlook and a fish ladder.

Stevens Pass. Near Scenic is the beginning of the 7.8-mile Cascade Tunnel, through which the Great Northern Railway burrows under the summit of Stevens Pass. Rising above 4,000 feet, the summit joins the Pacific Crest Trail at the boundary between the two national forests. Its location halfway between Everett and Wenatchee and 80 miles from Seattle makes the pass a popular area for winter sports from November to May.

WAVE ON WAVE of mountains rises ahead of pack trip heading west in proposed Cougar Lakes Wilderness.

Lake Wenatchee area. At Cole, State 207 goes north for 4 miles to Lake Wenatchee and nearby Fish Lake. Camping and trailer space are provided at Lake Wenatchee State Park, which has picnicking areas, an airstrip, and boating and swimming facilities. The Forest Service also has camping and picnicking facilities on the lake. Lake Wenatchee is stocked with silvers and rainbow and lake trout. Private resorts border Fish Lake, where perch and bass bite.

Tumwater Canyon. Beyond Cole, U.S. 2 dips south, following the Wenatchee River through Tumwater Canyon. In the fall the canyon blazes with golds and the bright red of vine maple. The Wenatchee River has a run of sockeye (blueback) salmon in August and is also well stocked with rainbows.

In Chinook, "Tumwater" means "rough water"—a fitting description of this stretch—but there are occasional lagoonlike areas where you can paddle a canoe. Sometimes mountain goats are spotted on the crags overlooking the river. Part of the canyon has been made a botanical area because of the rockrose found there.

Near the north end of the canyon, the Tumwater Recreation Area offers camping and picnicking.

After you have driven a few miles beyond the west entrance, look for Drury Falls across the river, one of Washington's highest at 560 feet.

Leavenworth region. Just before leaving the mountains for the flatland of central Washington, the highway passes through the Bavarian-style town of Leavenworth (page 103). Section maps and fishing and trail information are available at the Forest Service ranger station in Leavenworth.

Winter visitors might be able to watch a ski jumping competition; an Autumn Leaf Festival is held in late September. Kayaking on the Wenatchee River is a summertime attraction.

Driving the Snoqualmie Pass superhighway

In 1853, while seeking a route across the Cascade Range for a transcontinental railroad, George B. McClellan met an Indian who told him that the snow at the summit of Snoqualmie Pass was "five squaws deep." Believing this story, McClellan investigated no further and reported the Cascades crossing to be impracticable.

Now, as many as 7,000 cars a day travel over Snoqualmie Pass on Interstate 90, the lowest-elevation major route across the range. The Snoqualmie Pass Highway begins at Seattle's Mercer Island floating bridge and heads southeast as a four-lane freeway for 108 miles to meet U.S. 97 north of Ellensburg. As it crosses the Snoqualmie and Wenatchee national forests, it offers spectacular views.

Close to Seattle. Near Eastgate, the highway skirts Lake Sammamish, a convenient, 9-mile-long lake. At Lake Sammamish State Park you can picnic, fish, boat, and swim.

One of King County's most popular destinations for Sunday drives is the park at Snoqualmie Falls, just west of the town of Snoqualmie. Besides pleasant landscaped grounds, picnic tables, and restaurants, a handsome covered overlook offers fine views of the falls.

North Bend. Continuing along Interstate 90, you cross the South Fork of the Snoqualmie River at North Bend. The ranger station on the east side of town has maps available for hikers (La Bohn Gap is a favorite trail). Past North Bend, the highway follows the river to Snoqualmie Pass, the border between the two national forests.

Snoqualmie Pass. Three miles west of the pass is the Asahel Curtis recreation area. South of the highway, a short nature trail leads you through a majestic grove of trees. Many native plants are labeled.

You can visit several winter sports developments in the Pass area: at the summit is Snoqualmie, and 1 mile north of the summit by gravel road is Alpental, a Swiss chalet-type village.

As the highway descends the east slope of the mountains, it passes Lake Keechelus, headwaters of the Yakima River, and then follows the river. Both Lake Keechelus and nearby Lake Kachess have Forest Service campgrounds with boat launching ramps.

Cle Elum. This is the gateway to a popular recreation area north of Interstate 90. State 903 goes to Lake Cle Elum, where there is a resort and good

WHAT GOES UP, must come down, reasons bemused climber atop sandstone formation near Cashmere.

Leavenworth . . . a Touch of Bavaria

"Willkommen zu Leavenworth" greets you as you drive into this mountain village nestling in the eastern foothills of the Cascades, about 30 miles east of Stevens Pass on U.S. 2. You'll think you've been transported to the Bavarian Alps when you see the gabled roofs, timbered exteriors, painted stucco and overflowing flower boxes around you. If you're lucky, you might hear the crystal notes of carillon bells or vigorous oom-pah-pahs resounding from the bandstand in the park.

Early in 1963 the townspeople of Leavenworth organized a community action program, working with the University of Washington Bureau of Community Development. They decided on an Alpine theme and, under the direction of an architect, began remodeling in authentic Bavarian style. Businesses provided their own financing for refurbishing the original brick buildings. More than 30 structures have been redone with a Bavarian motif. The theme has been further developed by construction of a bandstand in the city park, acquisition of a 25-bell carillon system (recordings are for sale), and establishment of an annual Mai-Fest.

The Bavarian tradition of a May Festival to celebrate the awakening of spring has been adopted wholeheartedly by the citizens of Leavenworth. Visitors and residents wearing Bavarian dresses and lederhosen are treated to two days of entertainment, including a maypole dance.

Families of German descent have moved to Leavenworth and brought their customs with them. Restaurants feature authentic German food; the Edelweiss Dancers perform Bavarian dances in Alpine costumes. Even an annual snowmobile race is dubbed the Bavarian Cup.

It's not surprising that Leavenworth has won a number of awards. In addition to two governor's

IT COULD BE Munich, but it's really quaint Cascade village of Leavenworth, Washington.

awards for beautification programs, the town received first place in a $10,000 Community Improvement contest against national competition. The townspeople plan to develop their alpine theme even further; new construction will be in Bavarian style. Future plans include a multi-acre recreation area and a turreted, covered bridge to Blackbird Island.

---

fishing. In Salmon La Sac, north of the lake, you'll find a campground and resort. From here a loop trail of about 23 miles leads to three alpine lakes that are favorites with fishermen.

Popular Mt. Rainier National Park

The largest and best known landmark in Washington, Mt. Rainier looms above the prairies southeast of Tacoma. Looking from afar like a painted backdrop for a Wagnerian opera, Rainier casts a long shadow over the land in the national park that bears its name.

If you live within sight and easy reach of Rainier, roughly west of the Cascades between Longview and Everett, it is *your* mountain. It becomes a part of your life—a check point, a weather indicator, a subject of conversation, and a playground.

But throughout the state, Rainier speaks to a wide circle of friends. When weather conditions are right, you can see it from north of Vancouver, B.C., south to the Willamette Valley, from the islands of Puget Sound east into Idaho. It's a truly unforgettable sight for passengers flying in.

An individualistic mountain, Rainier stands free of companion peaks. Rising up out of the foothills

CLIMBING PARTY, below, nears 10,000-foot Camp Muir on Mt. Rainier. Right, scaling ice serac on Ingraham Glacier.

If You're Trained and in Shape, Try This

JUMPING CREVASSE, above, challenges Mt. Rainier climber on Ingraham Glacier. Equally daring, right, is swing across perilously yawning crevasse.

on a spreading granite base, it soars over 14,000 feet—a lordly monolith of rock, snow, and ice.

Untouched forests in the park stand as the Indians knew them. Wildflowers carpet the slopes, forming a bright band of ever-changing color between the forests and the glaciers. Four plant belts are crossed by park roads. You can drive from "humid-transition" (the dense fir, cedar, and hemlock forests) through the "Canadian" and "Hudsonian" zones to "Arctic-Alpine" (the open, flower-covered meadows at timberline).

Bumping River. Tucked under the east side of Mt. Rainier just outside Mt. Rainier National Park is a comfortable camping area. An access road leads off the Chinook Pass Highway (U.S. 410) 10 miles to Bumping Lake. Fishermen can find silvers and rainbows in the lake, rainbows in the river, and a few Eastern brook trout in Barton Creek.

Beyond the lake, dirt forest roads extend to an abandoned copper mine hopefully called Copper City, upper Bumping River, and past alpine Granite Lake to a dizzying promontory on Miner's Ridge (6,000 feet). Trails from road ends reach to other crests, lakes, and into Mt. Rainier National Park.

Weather. Rainier's ice-ridden bulk is completely exposed to moist sea winds. The Pacific is only 100 miles away; Puget Sound, 40 miles. When moist winds strike the constant cold of the mountain, they brew up some highly variable weather. July, August, and September are the best visiting months.

Entry roads. Roads enter the park at each of its four corners: Carbon River (northwest), White River (northeast), Ohanapecosh (southeast), and Nisqually River (southwest). The road from the Nisqually Entrance to Paradise and the road along the east side of the park from the northeast boundary through Ohanapecosh are kept open all year, although snow conditions may close them for short periods and you may need chains for part of the drive. The other roads close after the first heavy snow (usually around November 1) and remain closed until spring.

Accommodations and services. Overnight lodging is available inside the park at Longmire (National Park Inn) and Paradise (Paradise Valley Inn). Accommodations are adequate but not luxurious. Look for motels and cabins on the approach roads outside the park boundaries. Park lodgings close in winter, but motels near the Nisqually Entrance are open all year.

Park headquarters at Longmire include a visitor center, service station (open all year), souvenir gift shop, cafeteria, and post office. At Paradise, activities center around Paradise Inn and the Paradise Visitor Center. The Paradise ski shop rents inner tubes and platters, in addition to skis, boots, and poles. Gentle open slopes for sliders are ¼ mile from the ski area.

At Sunrise and Ohanapecosh are visitor centers, and Sunrise also has a cafeteria, gift shop, and service station (open in summer only). At each of the centers, illustrated talks and scheduled nature

INCREDIBLE VIEW of Inter Glacier stops group of hikers on Second Burroughs Mountain near Rainier.

hikes are offered. Ranger-naturalists are on hand to answer questions.

The park's mountain guide service is located in the visitor center at Paradise.

The campgrounds. A number of park campgrounds are open in summer on a first-come, first-served basis. The large ones at Cougar Rock, White River, and Ohanapecosh are equipped with fireplaces, tables, water, and sanitary facilities. Smaller campgrounds at Sunshine Point and Carbon River have similar facilities but are less developed. Mowich Lake has limited camping facilities.

A use fee is charged for camping at any of the campgrounds; a 14-day camping limit is in effect from July 1 through Labor Day. Sunshine Point campground is the only one open in winter.

Trailers may use any of the campgrounds when space is available, but there are no hookups. If you want to rough it, you can camp along the trails at designated spots. Obtain a camping permit in advance from any park headquarters or any park ranger station or visitor center.

Roads within the park. Seven roads take you to points of interest. From them you can explore the different aspects of the mountain:

• The Nisqually-Paradise Road winds uphill close to the Nisqually Glacier—you aren't likely to drive an automobile any nearer to an active river of ice.
• The 15-mile West Side Road traces the Park's western boundary, passing the hanging Puyallup Glacier and the base of Tokaloo Rock.

• Stevens Canyon Road leads to blue Reflection Lake and Lake Louise. Located at Box Canyon is a glacial erosion display.
• The East Side Road is an easy drive along a narrow valley between Mt. Rainier and the summit of the Cascade Range to the east.
• Sunrise Road puts you as high on the mountainside as you can get by car.
• The Carbon River Road penetrates the Carbon River country, passing through some of the finest stands of virgin timber in the west, to a very pleasant campground.
• Mowich Lake Road brings you to the largest lake in the park.

Trails. Most of the trails in the park were designed to give you a close-up look at particular bits of the

---

A Summer Tonic: Mt. Rainier's Ice Caves

LIKE HUGE dollop of whipped cream, sculptured wall of Rainier ice cave dwarfs spelunker.

Hidden beneath snow and ice up to 500 feet thick on the mountain's main summit crater is one of the most intriguing geological spectacles in Mt. Rainier National Park. A series of ice caves, with walls and ceilings like frozen spindrift, form a mile-long passageway three-quarters of the way around the crater's rim.

Although Rainier is a dormant volcano, subterranean fires heat rocks and release steam near the summit, which in turn melts more snow and ice and forms the caves. Some caves were discovered more than a century ago but were not really explored until 1970, when mountaineers learned that they could cross the main crater entirely under ice.

Inside, the caves are totally dark, and you'll need powerful flashlights to see much of anything. In combination with the audible hissing of steam vents, the darkness is eerie. Although some of the caves are so small you must stoop or crawl, most are large enough for upright walking. And sometimes a passageway will open into a magnificent chamber 50 feet across and half as high.

Obviously these caves aren't for everyone. You have to climb Rainier just to get there. But hundreds of people with no previous climbing experience make it to the summit every year under the supervision of the park-approved guide service, Rainier Mountaineering, Inc., 201 St. Helens St., Tacoma 98402. The guide service will take you into the caves as far as you want to go at no extra charge. A one-day mountaineering course and two-day summit climb costs about $70. You must supply your own clothing and climbing gear, some of which can be rented.

Independent climbing parties can also enter the caves but are advised by the Park Service to carry at least two dependable light sources per party and extra batteries and bulbs. No one should enter the caves alone.

Spectacular scenery draws motorists around this 216-mile loop drive. Like the other Cascade trip, it begins in Seattle.

Renton (11 miles). Whirring production lines roll out jet transports for service on the world's air routes. The Maple Valley Highway (otherwise known as State 169) is your route through logging areas.

Black Diamond (28 miles). Coal mining sparked this town in pioneer days. Now rivers have replaced coal as Washington's major source of power.

Enumclaw (36 miles). The many dairy farms in the lush White River valley surrounding Enumclaw show its importance as a major source of Seattle's milk supply. From here, travel east on State 410.

Greenwater (53 miles). Colorful forest scenery rewards the traveler, especially if you follow one of the forest trails leading to timberland laced with swift-running creeks.

Silver Springs (68 miles). Starting point of trails leading to lookout areas, this is where the highway climbs to the Chinook Pass area (open only in summer). As the road ascends, you can see Mt. Rainier — reverently called "The Mountain That Was God" by the Indians. About 3 miles east, Crystal Mountain Ski Area offers soaring chairlift rides year around.

Mt. Rainier National Park (70 miles). The entrance to the park is a popular ski area.

Cayuse Pass Junction (77 miles). Stay to the right on the East Side Road (State 123); Chinook Pass veers off to the east over the highest cross-Cascade route in the state. From Cayuse Pass the highway begins a gradual descent, paralleling Chinook Creek and the Ohanapecosh River.

Stevens Canyon Entrance (88 miles). Leave State 123 and begin a 19-mile stretch on the Stevens Canyon Road, circling the mountains within the boundaries of the National Park. By traveling in a clockwise direction, you keep Mt. Rainier in sight ahead and to the right. When you arrive at the junction to Paradise Valley, turn right and drive 2 miles.

Paradise Valley (109 miles). Visit the tourist center for Mt. Rainier, the huge peak looming 2 miles above the rest of the Cascades.

Longmire (122 miles). Because it's park headquarters, Longmire's visitor center is open all year. Dropping sharply as it reaches Longmire, the asphalt road from Paradise once again enters a region of green forests and swift, glacier-fed rivers. Twenty miles farther on State 706, turn north onto State 7 at Elbe.

Tacoma (184 miles). Metropolitan Tacoma thrives as a lumber-processing center and a principal Puget Sound seaport.

Seattle (216 miles). Time to organize your mountain memories.

mountain's wilderness. They will put you in touch with lakes, streams, wildflowers, forests, and glaciers. You are never far from a good hiking trail that can be covered in one day or less, using your car as a base:

• The Wonderland Trail is an around-the-mountain loop of about 90 miles, with shelter cabins and outdoor fireplaces along the way (remember a fire permit).

• Pinnacle Peak Trail (3 miles round trip) ends with a steep climb but reveals a view of the entire south slope of Mt. Rainier.

• Van Trump Park Trail (5½ miles round trip) leads you past 420-foot Comet Falls.

• Gobblers Knob Lookout (about 5 miles round trip) takes you where you can see the forbidding west face of Rainier and, when the weather is right, the Olympic Mountains to the west.

CHARACTERISTIC lenticular cloud hovers over summit of Mt. Saint Helens, rising above forested slopes of Gifford Pinchot National Forest.

• Indian Henry's Hunting Ground (7 miles round trip) has, among other attractions, a small mirror lake reflecting the mountain.

• Chennis Falls (1 mile round trip) is one of the park's loveliest waterfalls.

• Mt. Fremont Lookout Trail (5 miles round trip) offers a mountain lake, open meadows, a good chance of seeing animals, and the view from the fire lookout.

• Ohanapecosh Loop Trail (3 miles round trip) winds through deep forest to a beautiful waterfall and along a fast-running mountain stream.

• Grove of giant trees (1 mile round trip) contains western red cedars and Douglas firs—some more than 10 feet in diameter.

Summit climb. Guide service at Mt. Rainier brings the summit within reach of anyone who is in good hiking trim. Three times a week in summer, guided parties leave the Paradise Visitor Center for the two-day climb. Most of the climbers have never tried ice-climbing before, yet almost all reach the top. Unless you are already skilled in ice-climbing, you must first attend one of the daily mountaineering classes to learn roped travel on snow and glaciers, belaying, rappelling, crevasse rescue techniques, and use of the ice axe. For a list of equipment (you can rent this at Paradise) and other information, write to Rainier Guide Service, Paradise Inn P.O., Washington 98398.

CASCADES TO THE SOUTH

Variety is the word for the southern Washington Cascades. From vast lava beds to moist, heavily forested terrain, this area offers scenery and activities for everyone. Much of the Gifford Pinchot National Forest is multiple-use land where activities range from thunderous snowmobiling to peaceful cross-country skiing.

Berry picking is a special attraction of these mountains—huckleberries and wild blackberries are gathered by thousands of visitors each year. Huckleberry picking is good in old "burns" (forest fire sites); blackberry vines grow in lumbered-off clearings. In accordance with an old treaty, a portion of the Twin Buttes huckleberry fields are reserved for the exclusive use of Indians, who form teepee encampments each year.

Southern link across the state

If you want to see changing scenery, U.S. 12 is an ideal route across Washington. From it, the trav-eler can sample rolling farmlands in the mountain foothills, high Cascade wilderness, the pine-covered eastern slopes of the mountain range, then go on to parallel and cross the Columbia River and head into eastern Washington's wheatland.

Morton. Just outside Snoqualmie National Forest, this small community sponsors in August a Loggers' Jubilee, an annual two-day competition of lumbering skills. Picnicking, swimming, and camping are popular at Indian Hole Park on the Tilton River. Both the Tilton and Cowlitz rivers have good steelhead fishing.

Packwood Lake. Located in a roadless basin of outstanding alpine beauty in the shadow of Goat Rocks Wilderness, this lake is accessible by trail only. But rental boats and lodging are available at a resort near the lake outlet.

White Pass. Twelve miles to the east of U.S. 12's intersection with State 123 below Mt. Rainier National Park, White Pass ski area presents some of the most captivating scenery of any resort in the Cascades.

Goat Rocks Wilderness. Bleating sharply, little pikas dwelling in slide rock join the whistling

marmots in reacting to intruders into the central, above-timberline portion of Goat Rocks Wilderness. Large animals include Rocky Mountain elk grazing in grassy basins and, of course, shaggy mountain goats.

Several exits off U.S. 12 will take hikers close to wilderness area trails. Skirting the White Pass Ski Area and meandering southward, the Pacific Crest Trail cuts through the wilderness. In all, 95 miles of trail are available. Packing in on horseback is popular, but riders must carry food for their horses to preserve struggling vegetation. Ask for information on guides with pack and saddle equipment from the district ranger at Packwood or Tieton ranger stations.

As in all wilderness areas, motor vehicles are prohibited. The Yakima Indian Reservation bordering the wilderness area on the southeast is closed to the general public.

Dazzling duo—Spirit Lake and Mt. St. Helens

Snow-covered Mt. St. Helens is one of the most symmetrical peaks in the Washington Cascades.

You can drive right up to its base, where Spirit Lake nestles in a green setting of virgin timber and forms the nucleus of a mountain recreation area in the Gifford Pinchot National Forest.

To get to Spirit Lake, leave Interstate 5 at Castle Rock junction—about 130 miles south of Seattle or 60 miles north of Portland—and drive 46 miles east on paved State 504.

The lake. Spirit Lake, at an elevation of over 3,000 feet, lies in an amphitheater of high-timbered cliffs open to Mt. St. Helens on the south. Roughly 2½ miles long, this lake is the result of glacial outwash that dammed the North Fork of the Toutle River long ago. Around its shore, cliffs alternate with driftwood-margined bays that invite exploring.

The main activity at the lake is along the south shore. Here, where the highway ends, is a resort, a ranger station, a Forest Service campground (overnight charge), an information center, and a public dock.

Two smaller campgrounds, Donnybrook and Cedar Creek, and a resort are on the lake's east shore and can be reached only by boat or trail.

Spotted in islands of alpine fir at timberline are several other campsites.

Forest trails north from the lake open up a back country rich in alpine meadows and high lakes.

The mountain. You can drive onto the base of Mt. St. Helens at timberline (there's a surfaced parking lot at 4,200 feet) and look up across slopes of gray-white pumice, broken by dark ridges of basalt out-croppings, to the snowy glaciers that glisten at the top of the 9,677-foot peak. The more ambitious or energetic can safely hike, without benefit of trail, up a thousand feet or more through the shifting pumice. Though it's as tiring as walking in loose, coarse sand, botanists will enjoy looking at the small, silvery mats of lupine and penstemon that grow even in the pure pumice. Several campsites at timberline have tables, benches, and fire rings.

The climb to the summit should be attempted only by experienced climbers. It takes about 7 hours to reach the top and about half that to come down.

Mt. Adams ... choice for recreation and wilderness

On the opposite edge of Gifford Pinchot National Forest and across the Cascade Crest from the Mt. St. Helens area, the Mt. Adams recreation lands offer some of the best family camping country in the state. You can reach Mt. Adams via State 141, which goes north from White Salmon (on the Columbia River Highway) to Troutlake.

Quite open as a result of forest burns of long ago, yet close to ice and snow-cloaked mountain peaks, the Mt. Adams area is essentially primitive in character, with plenty of space to roam. The peak, towering above 12,000 feet, helps to form the axis of the Cascade Range.

Takhlakh plateau. Lakes, alpine meadows, and a group of lava rocks combine with Takhlakh Lake and Olallie Lake to form an intriguing area popular for fishing, boating, and camping. In late summer the waters are barely warm enough for swimming.

North of the two lakes is the Chain of Lakes, 13 of them in a 50-acre area. Canoe exploring is possible along navigable, shallow channels linking the lakes.

Ice caves. Nine distinct glaciers, separated by dark ridge lines, are at work on Mt. Adams' broken cone. Explained by geologists as "bubbles in plastic rock," natural ice caves abound here. One is within a mile of the Troutlake entrance to the area. From a hole 20 feet across, icy drafts issue from the 400-foot cave. You descend a tree ladder to the floor

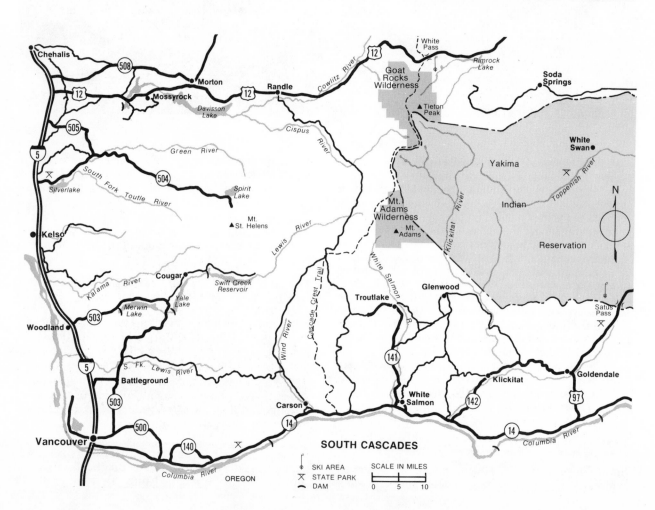

SOUTH CASCADES

SKI AREA
STATE PARK
DAM

SCALE IN MILES
0   5   10

of ice, where you see a wonderland of weird formations resembling stalactites and stalagmites. The entire region south of Mt. Adams is believed to be full of such caves, most of them without openings but known to exist because of the hollow sounds made when horses walk over them.

Reaching the peak. Two roads climb the south side of Mt. Adams to timberline; from the ends of them you can hike to snow level. From Troutlake the two roads start as one, taking a running uphill start for the mountain. Four miles up in a grove of Ponderosa pines, the road branches sharply. Straight ahead is the Cold Springs Road; the road to the right goes to Bird Creek Meadows.

• Cold Springs. This side is the one to yodel from —you can see Mt. St. Helens and Mt. Hood in all their glory. You don't have to hike very far beyond the end of the road to find an intimate look at the crest of Adams. In the deluding clearness, the peak may seem within easy grasp. But it's a long climb of more than 10 hours; to hike it, you need experienced leaders and proper clothing and equipment.

• The Bird Creek Meadows Road. This one leads through Ponderosa pine forests. A few hundred yards beyond the beginning of the road, a sign points to the "Big Tree," one of the largest known Ponderosa pines.

Another reward awaiting you on the Bird Creek Meadows Road is a bevy of lakes. Mirror Lake has a delicate edging of brown-tipped marsh grass; Bird Lake is a remote refuge; down a spur road is Bench Lake, a popular fishing and swimming spot with a spacious campground.

Wilderness Area. Enclosing the mountain peak, this section contains no roads, but the Pacific Crest Trail cuts through it. On the lower slopes of Mt. Adams grows an exceptional variety of trees, shrubs, and flowers, combining species native to both sides of the Cascades, the Sierra Nevada, and the Rocky Mountains.

Mountain Climbing the Easy Way

If you have only limited time or like scaling mountains without the toil of a hard climb, summer-operating chair lifts offer an easy way into the high country. Once on top, you don't have to ride back down immediately; you can take a walk or even hike back down the mountain. With picnickers, photographers, day hikers, and sightseers, chair lifts are especially popular.

The following two chair lifts in Washington's Cascades operate during the summer:

Crystal Mountain. Crystal Mountain's Iceberg Ridge chair lift takes you to the top of 6,872-foot Crystal Mountain from which you can look across to the heights of Mount Rainier. At the Summit House on top you can purchase light snacks.

Trails from the top lead to meadows and alpine lakes. Unusual alpine wildflowers are so abundant here during August that the Seattle Rock Gardening Society makes the area its destination for collecting trips.

The chair lift operates afternoons on weekdays and all day weekends and holidays.

White Pass. White Pass operates a chair lift daily during the summer. It takes you to the top of 6,000-foot Pigtail Peak. Backpackers frequently use the chair lift to get a downhill start into the Goat Rocks Wilderness area which lies directly south of Pigtail. You can ride up and back, or hike down any of several ski trails.

IT'S NO TRICK at all to climb a slope when you've boarded summer-operating chair lift.

North Cascades...
the Newest National Park

HORN/SPITZ/
MATTERHORN PEAK

GLACIATED PEAKS

HORN/SPITZ/
MATTERHORN PEAK

CIRQUE
BERGSCHRUND

SNOWFIELD

CIRQUE

ARÊTE

CIRQUES

SNOWFIELD

SNOWFIELD

ARÊTE

CREVASSES

NUNATAK

CREVASSES

MYRIAD CREVASSES, ever-regenerating, mark awesome face of Boston Glacier in Eldorado Range.

*TRICKLES of melting snow merge into creeks
crashing over boulders in their rush to valleys below.*

BOSTON PEAK'S chunky dome (8,900 feet high) looms above serrated ridge in newly created North Cascades National Park's rugged south unit.

SLENDER LAKE CHELAN, above left, is a fjordlike entry to wilderness on park's southern border. Above right, sharp rock, ice contrast with forested walls of U-shaped valley.

The Columbia: Monarch of Western Rivers

Although the Columbia, like other rivers of the world, varies in color from blue to green to gray to brown, its most appropriate color would certainly be gold. For this formidable river is as important to Washington's economy as the Cascade Range is to its recreation.

From the Pacific Ocean, the Columbia forms three-quarters of the border between Washington and Oregon, then turns north to cut through central Washington on the way to its source in British Columbia. To tame this mammoth river and put it to productive use, Washington has constructed a masterwork of dams—15 of them, including the incredible Grand Coulee. The Columbia contains one-third of the potential water power of America.

In the pages that follow, we've tried another approach to taming the Columbia. To help travelers better focus on the points of historical, geological, recreational, and economic interest along or near the Columbia's banks, the river has been divided into three sections: from its Pacific Ocean mouth to Vancouver; from Vancouver through the Columbia River gorge; and to the meeting of the Columbia, Snake, and Yakima rivers at the Tri-Cities. For places of interest along the banks of the Columbia from the Tri-Cities north to the Canadian border, see the Central Washington chapter, pages 124 to 135.

FROM THE MOUTH TO VANCOUVER

Two great adventurers who met briefly in 1792, an Englishman and an American, contributed to the early exploration of this section of Washington. Captain George Vancouver was an English explorer making a last-ditch attempt to locate the Northwest Passage; although he never actually saw the site, a large trading post on the Columbia was named after him and became the city of Vancouver.

Once a trader in sea otter pelts, Captain Robert Gray (who donated his name to Grays Harbor,

FOG-SHELTERED sunlight illuminates Columbia Gorge, where Cascades intersect Columbia River.

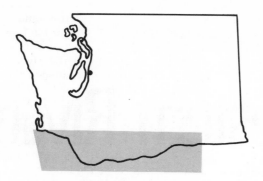

even today, ocean-to-river traffic moves cautiously, for this section of river has claimed hundreds of vessels. From the headlands and from the north jetty, you can watch ocean-going freighters bounce like bathtub toys.

Fort Canby State Park at Cape Disappointment encloses the spot where Lewis and Clark first reached the Pacific Ocean. As a coast artillery fort, Canby (established in 1864) was active through World War II. In the park, visitors can find campsites, picnic areas, trailer hookups, and fresh and salt-water swimming. The Robert Gray drive from Ilwaco to Fort Canby State Park is especially beautiful in winter.

High on a tall headland on the former military reservation, the Fort Canby (or Cape Disappointment) lighthouse is very picturesque. The cape's poignant name was given it by Captain John Meares in 1788 when his search for the suspected river outlet proved to be fruitless.

North Head Lighthouse stands among the rugged, forested bluffs overlooking the ocean and the mouth of the Columbia, warning ships off the North Head above Cape Disappointment. Below the lighthouse is Dead Man's Hollow, named for the lost sailors of the *Vendelia*.

Fort Columbia, an old military outpost near the mouth of the river 1 mile east of Chinook on U.S.

farther up the coast), wrote in his log aboard the *Columbia Rediviva* that "When we were over the bar we found this to be a large river of fresh water, up which we steered." A seaman to the core, Captain Gray named the newly-discovered Columbia River after his ship. His discovery on May 10, 1792, was a decisive step in establishing the United States' claim to the Oregon Territory.

Where the Columbia meets the Pacific

Captain Gray was lucky to have made it over that sandbar and the Pacific's treacherous breakers;

A SENTINEL overlooking the point where the southward-flowing Columbia bends to the west, Two Captains Rock marked Wallula Gap for early wheat barge pilots.

Highway 1, affords an absorbing tour into the past. All of the batteries here were operative until after World War II. Exploring abandoned bunkers can be an eerie experience. One of the barracks has been turned into a museum, open daily.

Driving along the river

Less known and less traveled than the route on the Oregon shore, State 401 and State 4 take in the Columbia terrain at a more leisurely pace. There are side roads to explore, streams and lakes to fish, and historically interesting places to visit. State 4 is especially pleasant to drive as it cuts through marshy land, winds along at river level, and climbs through forested hills.

Almost ghost towns. The stretch of highway between the Astoria-Megler Toll Bridge down to Cathlamet can tell you tales of hope and despair, of prosperity and ruin. Towns that flourished in the booms of the late 19th century include Frankfort (beyond end of logging road east from State 401 between Megler and Naselle), Altoona (south 7 miles on State 403), Pillar Rock (east 4 miles on a gravel road from Altoona), Knappton, and McGowan (1½ miles west of the toll bridge).

Grays River. The last covered bridge in use on a public highway in Washington is located amid idyllic scenery about 3 miles from Grays River.

Skamokawa. In this especially picturesque river town, many people can taxi up to their back doors in their boats.

Cathlamet. Here the road rejoins the river, and you'll pass the Crown Zellerbach Managed Forest. You can cross by ferry to Oregon or by bridge to Puget Island—a locale with a strong Old Country flavor. Prior to World War II, more people here spoke Norwegian than English. For a pleasant side excursion, explore the island's roads, which meander along diked waterways, through green fields and trees, and past small boat docks.

Longview and Kelso. To most intents and purposes, Longview and Kelso are one town. Longview is larger; Kelso, considerably hillier. These twin cities are lumbering centers. Tours are conducted through the gigantic Weyerhaeuser Company mill Monday through Friday at specific times.

Longview—a planned city that began as a lumber company town—contains Lake Sacajawea, where children can boat and fish and see ducks, swans, and geese.

Kelso, a mile away from Longview, was founded in 1847 by a Scottish surveyor who named it for his home town in Scotland. The Cowlitz County Historical Museum, tucked into the courthouse annex at 4th and Church, has an authentic log cabin and replicas of a country store, 1880s kitchen, bar-

BUILT TO WITHSTAND the elements, Fort Vancouver stockade, left, has stood for many years. Bonneville Dam, spillway shown above, masters the turbulence of a great river.

FARM TRAFFIC still moves across the gentle Grays River on this rustic covered wooden bridge.

bershop, and livery stable, in addition to Indian artifacts and other exhibits.

Lewis River. You can leave the freeway at Woodland or Vancouver and suddenly be up in the mountains by taking State 503 along the Lewis River. Snow-topped Mt. St. Helens and Mt. Adams continually appear as you climb. Ten miles from Woodland you'll pass the Cedar Creek gristmill, built in 1876.

The river has been converted by dams into a series of lakes — Merwin Lake, Yale Lake, and Swift Creek Reservoir. Boat rentals are available on the north shore of Merwin Lake; campgrounds are farther into the mountains toward Cougar. Featuring an interpretive display, the Yale Dam Viewpoint is down a turnoff 2 miles south of Yale.

If you continue from Yale to Cougar, you'll enter a region of massive lava flows where tubes formed under the cooling crust as molten lava continued flowing beneath. The Lava Cast Area, with tree trunk images, and Ape Cave, the longest lava tube in the country, are open to the public. By lantern light you can see stalactite formations and, occasionally, hibernating bats.

Historical Vancouver

Metropolis of the north shore of the Columbia, the commercial seaport of Vancouver is strategi-

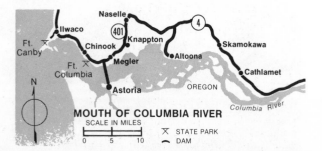

cally situated where Interstate 5 passes from Portland, Oregon, into Washington. Founded in 1824 as Fort Vancouver by the Hudson's Bay Company, Vancouver is the oldest city in the state.

Fort Vancouver National Historic Site. The lone pin-point of civilization in the wilderness of southwestern Washington from the 1820s to 1860s, Fort Vancouver is today a 160-acre national historic site less than five minutes from downtown Vancouver. On Saturday and Sunday afternoons you can take an interpretive hike or hear a lecture.

The north wall of the old stockade, which once surrounded and protected the trading post of the Hudson's Bay Company, has been rebuilt complete with its double gates. Signs within identify the sites of the factor's home, a bakery, smithy, offices, and fur warehouse. The fort is open daily but closed on holidays.

Built in 1961, the Fort Vancouver Historical Site Museum contains a library and Hudson Bay Company exhibits.

U. S. Grant Museum. President Ulysses S. Grant had an office in this log building (now covered with siding) in 1852-1853 when he served as brevet captain. Built in 1849, the structure is the oldest in the Vancouver Barracks. It has been made into a museum housing Indian artifacts, petroglyphs, furniture owned by Grant, and antique glassware and china. You can visit it any afternoon except Thursday; the address is 1106 E. Evergreen Blvd.

Covington House. Built in Leverich Park in 1846, this is the oldest house in the state. It was moved to 41st and Main from a site 5 miles east, near the village of Orchards. This log cabin is open Tuesdays and Thursdays in summer.

Clark County Historical Museum. Located at 16th and Main, Clark County's museum contains such varied collections as a pioneer doctor's office with a complete drug display, an early printing press, an 1890 country store, and Indian artifacts. It is open in the afternoon except on Monday.

THROUGH DAMS TO THE SNAKE

From Vancouver east, the Columbia courses through a desert, potentially fertile dry scrublands, huge geometric blocks of basalt, spring-flowered foothills, and a mountain range. Remarkably, to follow the river through these different worlds takes only hours—a day if you plan a leisurely trip with stops along the way.

Columbia River Gorge

Driving from Camas to White Salmon, you're unmistakably in the Cascades. This is the section of the river containing the Cascade Crest Trail (see page 96) and the famous landmark of Beacon Rock. A cooling ocean breeze presses through the river gorge from the west.

Beacon Rock State Park. Stately trees and jagged rocks rear against the sky atop this towering giant that rises 848 feet above the gorge of the Columbia. Beacon Rock's sheer escarpments look impossible to climb, but a well-maintained, ¾-mile trail ascends to the summit from a parking area off State 14 just west of the rock. Trail improvements include ramps, bridges, steps, handrails, and frequent stopping places for rest in the shade.

The view from the summit is well worth the hike. To the east, the river disappears between folds of forested hills, with Oregon's Mt. Hood balancing the snowy cone of Washington's Mt. Adams. Looking west, you can see the many islands of the Columbia River.

Bonneville Dam. Three miles beyond Beacon Rock and within sight of it is Bonneville Dam, the first public power dam built on the Columbia River. The powerhouse is located between Bradford Island and the Oregon shore; the spillway dam is between the island and the Washington riverbank.

Bridge of the Gods. Just upstream from the dam is the modern steel Bridge of the Gods, named after an ancient natural bridge whose rock remains lie submerged beneath the Columbia. According to Indian legend, an old woman appointed to be guardian of the rock bridge was faithful throughout a fiery war between sons of the Great Spirit in volcano form. After the bridge was destroyed, she was rewarded by being transformed into lovely Mt. St. Helens.

Wind River side trip. A few miles east of Stevenson, past a cove full of anchored tugboats, a paved side road leads northwest through Carson and follows the Wind River for about 15 miles to Forest Service campgrounds at Trout Creek, Soda Springs, Tyee Springs, and Government Mineral Springs. A fork in the road at Whiskey Creek takes you to Goose Lake and the Red Mountain Forest Service Lookout. At one point, you cross the Wind River on a bridge 257 feet above the canyon floor. The most spectacular view from here is to the north, across miles of forest to the perfect cone of Mt. St. Helens.

A short trail 1½ miles from the Red Mountain Lookout road will take you to the biggest Indian artifact ever found in the Northwest—a racetrack 10 feet wide and 1,000 feet long. This racecourse laid out in a high mountain meadow is where Indians assembled once a year from miles around to test their horsemanship.

Spring Creek Fish Hatchery. Near Underwood, this hatchery is situated on one of the frequent river-lagoons along the Columbia. It is part of a fascinating network of national and state-operated hatcheries found throughout Washington. Here adult salmon returning upstream are captured, their eggs fertilized, and fingerlings raised until they're large enough to be released. You can watch all these processes; feeding time at the fingerling pools is full of action.

Goldendale area

Here the land is dryer, with dramatic rock formations and a few poplar trees or fruit orchards. Pine-dotted hills make way for great spring swathes of purple lupine at Goldendale.

The Dalles Dam. Take a short spur road, U.S. 97, to reach this dam upstream from the Bingen toll bridge. On the Washington side is a ship lock often in operation. Approachable from the Oregon shore, the visitor center is on an island between the powerhouse and spillway.

Lake Celilo, the lake formed by the dam, extends for 24 miles upstream to the John Day Dam. Swimming and picnicking are popular or you can launch a boat at Horsethief Lake, 6 miles east of Lyle.

Maryhill Museum. Perched on the bluffs east of The Dalles Dam, Maryhill Museum of Fine Arts and its formal Flemish architecture contrasts sharply with the arid emptiness of the craggy hills around it.

Once known as "Hill's Folly," the massive building was begun in 1914 by Sam Hill, a son-in-law of railroad builder James J. Hill who by coincidence had the same surname. Intended originally to be a family home, it became instead a nonprofit museum. Hill's good friend, Queen Marie of Rumania, took part in the dedication ceremonies in 1926, and her coronation crown and royal throne are part of the display.

Today the isolated mansion houses one of the most diversified collections of art in the Pacific Northwest. In its 22 galleries is a sampling of work from such late 19th century French Impressionists as Renoir, Pissarro, Vuillard, Gaugin, Corot, Manet, Cezanne, and Daumier. Among its other treasures are paintings by Rembrandt and Van Dyke, sculpture by Rodin, a fine collection of Northwest Indian artifacts, a gallery of chessmen, and some early Greek pottery. The museum is open daily in summer; picnic facilities are available.

MONOLITHIC BEACON ROCK was mentioned by Lewis and Clark as an important Columbia landmark.

Klickitat County Historical Museum. If you take U.S. 97 up to Goldendale, 10 miles north of the river, you can stop at a cozy old house on Broadway to see reminders of the town's pioneer heritage. A porch swing and an impressive array of Victorian furnishings create a nostalgic mood; star of the show is a collection of 115 old-time coffee grinders —none of them alike. Parked in front of the building is an ancient Russell steam engine, fired up on occasion to assume a place of honor in town parades. Both the house and a shelter next door for farm equipment and large displays are open daily in the summer.

Stonehenge replica. Another strange sight is visible from State 14, just east of the Maryhill Museum. Sam Hill constructed a concrete replica of Stonehenge as a memorial to World War I casualties from Klickitat County.

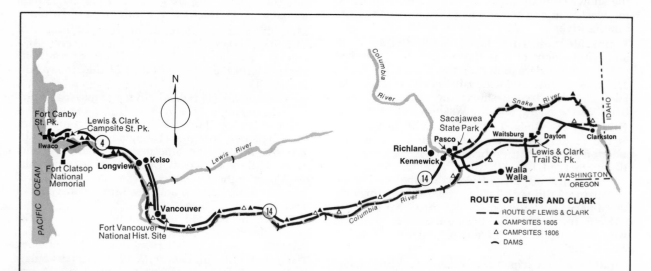

Washington: Lewis and Clark Country

When Meriwether Lewis and William Clark set out on their famous expedition to the west in 1804, the great rivers were the safest and most reliable highways available. The expedition intended to explore, map, and establish a claim to the land for President Thomas Jefferson. And they were finding a way westward for "those who may hereafter attempt the fur trade to the East Indies by way of the Columbia River and Pacific Ocean." The leaders knew that, although perils and discomfort still lay ahead, once they reached the mighty Columbia the worst of their trip would be over. The expedition entered what is now the state of Washington on October 11, 1805, near Clarkston.

A few reminders of the Corps of Discovery still remain along the course of their Columbian voyage. Washington State Route 14 between Ilwaco and Clarkston is known as the Lewis and Clark Highway. At the confluence of the Snake and the Columbia River, 5 miles southeast of Pasco, is Sacajawea State Park—named for the Indian girl who helped to guide the Lewis and Clark expedition. In the Interpretive Center, Indian artifacts are exhibited in her honor. Sacajawea's presence was a sign to Indians they met along the way that the band of men was on a peaceful mission.

Almost to the mouth of the river, the party rested from their trip. Lewis and Clark Campsite State Park, two miles south of Chinook on U.S. Highway 101, commemorates the site where they made camp within sight of the ocean.

Fort Canby State Park, on Cape Disappointment 2 miles west of Ilwaco, marks the spot where Lewis and Clark reached the Pacific Ocean. In his journal entry on December 1, 1805, a disgruntled Clark insisted on referring to the ocean as the Great Western because he hadn't seen one pacific day since his arrival. The expedition wintered on the coast, awaiting a supply ship that never came, then returned eastward. Fort Clatsop National Memorial in Oregon has a replica of their winter quarters.

Almost at the Idaho border lies the Lewis and Clark Trail State Park, on U.S. Highway 12 at the Touchet River between Dayton and Waitsburg. The park contains a grove of pines in which the members of the expedition camped.

The journals of the Lewis and Clark expedition make fascinating reading. A folder describing their route through Washington and some of their experiences along the way is available from the Washington State Parks and Recreation Commission, P.O. Box 1128, Olympia 98501.

John Day Dam. Once the dam was finished, it took only 48 hours to fill Lake Umatilla, the 76-mile-long pool reservoir behind it. North shore visitors to the dam have an excellent view of the spillway and can visit the navigation lock, fish ladder, and fish counting room; a visitor center is on the Oregon side.

TRI-CITIES REGION: THE BEND IN THE RIVER

Yes, there really is a desert in Washington, in spite of the mighty Columbia—but there might not be one much longer. The forces of agribusiness and atomic energy, centered in the three communities of Pasco, Richland, and Kennewick, are busily planting a shiny new oasis. Abundant sunshine and deluxe accommodations make this area increasingly popular as a resort and convention center.

Horse Heaven Hills

Between the Yakima Valley and the Columbia River is a remote country where wild horses used to run in herds over the rolling, grassy hills (some might still exist in the upper reaches) and where you can drive for miles without meeting another car. Horse Heaven rises higher and higher to the west toward the Yakima Indian Reservation and the Cascade wilderness around Mt. Adams.

Agribusiness. Though you might not be able to see the effects from State 14, the Horse Heaven Hills are rapidly being irrigated and developed by huge agricultural corporations. A remarkable variety of crops can be grown on this rich soil, from sugar beets to grapes to alfalfa. Movable overhead sprinkler systems provide the water to convert the hills into vast fertile fields.

McNary Dam. Though not as high as Grand Coulee, McNary Dam is half again as wide. On the Washington shore, the navigation lock and its operation may be seen from the lock wall or from the visitors' area in the lock control building.

The Twin Captains, two basalt columns on the riverbank at Wallula, were once used as landmarks by sternwheeler pilots. Slightly north is Hat Rock, overlooking a sheltered park. You can hike to the top of the rock for an unobstructed view of Wallula Gap and McNary Dam.

Roping school. Western traditions are still alive here—there's even a roping school between the towns of Richland and Prosser. On Tuesday and Friday nights, you can watch roping demonstrations from a cafe next to the open arena.

Recreation at the river confluence

The Columbia, the Snake, and Yakima rivers combine to create a variety of water recreation possibilities in and around the Tri-Cities. One of the last remaining free-flowing sections of the Columbia is above Richland, past the McNary Dam pool.

MOTORING HOME along a river highway in Skamokawa, a fishing village near mouth of Columbia.

PEAK-ROOFED MANSION in Goldendale holds Klickitat County Historical Society pioneer displays.

If you prefer your sport on land instead of water, the six Tri-City golf courses are just one of the many possibilities here. Irrigated lands on three sides of the Tri-Cities abound in Chinese pheasant, quail, and chukar. The McNary Wildlife-Recreation Area peninsula south of Burbank and the Wahluke Wildlife Recreation Area north of Ringold have excellent duck and goose hunting.

Ice Harbor Dam. First completed dam of the Snake River series (see page 150), Ice Harbor was named for a tiny, ice-free wintering cove used by steamboats and river craft in the gold-rush days of the 1860s. The cove is now submerged by Lake Sacajawea. You can take a self-guided tour to nine points of interest beginning at the visitors' over-

NUCLEAR REACTOR PLANT is explained to visitors at the Hanford Science Center in Richland.

look on the south shore, including a rare look at the working hydroelectric units within the powerhouse.

Lake Sacajawea. Though it's fun for Tri-City boaters to just take their craft through the Ice Harbor Dam locks, most stop at one of the parks along the shores of Lake Sacajawea. In fact, one of the parks, Big Flat, is accessible primarily by boat.

One of the most surprising sights in the area is a juniper forest thriving in the sand dunes, almost midway between Ice Harbor and Lower Monumental dams.

Parks. Several miles of shoreline and an island west of Kennewick along Lake Wallula on the Columbia River have been set aside as Columbia Park. In addition to a golf course, campground, game and picnic areas, a natural area with trails has been designated near the park headquarters. Sacajawea State Park, east of Pasco on the site where Lewis and Clark camped in 1805, contains a small interpretive center with exhibits of arrowheads, petroglyph photos, stone mortars and pestles, and other artifacts.

Boating. Climaxing a two week water follies celebration, the Atomic Cup Unlimited Hydroplane Races are run on Lake Wallula each year in July—best viewing spot is Columbia Park. Boat rentals are available at a marina in Kennewick, and launching ramps are numerous.

Fishing. Anglers can try for steelhead and sturgeon on the Columbia, Snake, and Yakima rivers or catch trout and crappie in nearby lakes. Ringold, on the Columbia River above Pasco, is the site of both salmon and trout hatcheries and probably offers the best steelheading. At the 4-foot-tall Horn Rapids Dam on the Yakima River (off State 240 at

the edge of the Hanford lands), Indians still net salmon in season.

The burgeoning Tri-Cities

Pasco, Kennewick, and Richland—three neighboring communities—have a friendly rivalry going in some things, but in most ways they operate as a unit. Residents think nothing of living in Pasco, working in Richland, and shopping in Kennewick —or any combination of the above.

Annual events include pari-mutuel horse racing (quarter horse and Appaloosa) at Tumbleweed Track in the Benton-Franklin County Fair grounds in Kennewick on weekends in February, March, and June; the Benton-Franklin County Fair and Tumbleweed RCA approved rodeo in August; the Three Rivers Gem and Mineral Show at the Richland Community Hall in March; and the Washington State Water Ski Championships in August.

Richland. In 1943 over 1,000 settlers were abruptly moved out of the area surrounding Hanford, Richland, and White Bluffs by the United States government—without explanation. Then thousands of workers were rushed into the evacuated area to build a nuclear reactor to produce plutonium for the first atomic bomb. Plutonium from Hanford was used in the historic nuclear explosion at Alamogordo, New Mexico.

Richland was the community headquarters of scientists and other workers who could only guess about what they were building. Owned by the government from its inception, Richland finally came under private operation in 1958 and acquired the taxes and city government of ordinary towns.

Hanford Science Center. Located in the Federal Building in Richland, this exhibit traces the development and uses of atomic energy. Visitors can work a glove box and a master-slave manipulator similar to the equipment used to handle radio-

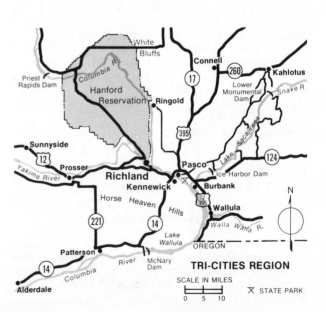

active materials. Displays illustrate the aims of the Arid Lands Ecology Reserve, as well as explain how the breeder reactor concept will enable a nuclear power plant to produce more nuclear fuel than it consumes. The Science Center is open all day during the week, on Sunday afternoons, and closed Mondays. Admission is free.

Around Pasco. Groups can visit an extremely modern, well-kept dairy on Star Route 1 to see areas for milking, feeding, raising, and caring for dairy cattle. Farther away from town, about 2 miles along U.S. 395 going north, you'll pass a railroad tower on the left where there's a computerized switching station open to the public. It's most active about 2 p.m. on Monday and Tuesday.

River road. North of the Tri-Cities, the Columbia River retains its old pre-dam character as it rolls along between the high hills on its east bank and the semi-desert of the Atomic Energy Commission's Hanford Works reservation (where travel is restricted) to the west. A dead-end gravel river road follows the east shore for 10 miles past fishing holes, willow-covered islands, and the ash-white clay bluffs, calcite concretions, and pressure-cemented pebble bed of the Ringold deposits. Rockhounds come here to find agates; kingfishers and great blue herons fish on the river.

To get to the White Bluff Road, drive west in Pasco on Court Street to Franklin County Road 68, then northwest for about 5 miles.

The Great Salmon Mystery

THRASHING SALMON lunges through water.

For a fish that might defy even Jacques Costeau's research wizardry, consider the salmon. This amazing specimen continues to baffle the scientist, disturb the conservationist, and delight both the angler and the gourmet.

Perhaps the most remarkable fact about salmon is that, after two to five years at sea, they will return to the place they were born to spawn —even to the artificial pond of a hatchery.

Scientists disagree as to the mechanism salmon use to locate their birthplaces. Current theories include a fantastic memory for shapes, an instinct for upstream movement, a strong sense of smell, and celestial navigation.

A second mystery almost as intriguing as migration is the rapid aging process and subsequent death that follows spawning. In a matter of days, even hours, the fish pass through changes that take years in other animals.

When they mature and return to fresh water, salmon stop feeding. Nevertheless, they continue striking bait and lures (probably in anger) far upstream.

From March through November, salmon of different species follow each other up the Columbia River to spawn.

According to their anthropomorphic traditions, the Indians of the Columbia believed that the salmon returned to the streams of their birth to bring food to the tribe. They welcomed the first fish swimming upstream as a welcome guest and relative. But they had little compunction about capturing the rest of the migrants with spears and long-handled dip nets.

The five salmon species found on the eastern side of the Pacific are labeled with their common names in Russian as scientific names. *Oncorhynchus tschawytscha* (otherwise known as king, tyee, Chinook, spring, or quinnat) is the biggest salmon in the world and the West's most popular game salmon—its average weight is 20 pounds. The other popular game fish is *O. kisutch*, usually called silver, coho, or silversides.

Many hatcheries are located along Columbia River tributaries. Wells Dam has its own hatchery, where you can see several stages in the complex life cycle of salmon.

Central Washington... the Heartland

From apples to Indian artifacts, from pears to petrified wood, from rodeos to river roads—the range of discoveries in central Washington is as wide as the vistas on its broad plains.

Access to central Washington is comfortable and quite direct on two important highways. Crossing the area from south to north, U.S. Highway 97 leaves Oregon on a toll bridge over the Columbia and enters Washington near Maryhill. From there it winds up through Toppenish and Yakima into Ellensburg, cuts north through the Cascade foothills near Cle Elum and Wenatchee to Chelan, then follows the Okanogan River up to the Canadian border into British Columbia.

Stretching west to east, Interstate 90 runs from Seattle over Snoqualmie Pass and crosses central Washington on its way to Spokane and western Idaho. On the way, it skirts Ellensburg and Vantage and cuts through Moses Lake.

The next several pages expand upon some of the midstate attractions that you will pass along both of these principal highway routes.

SOUTHCENTRAL LORE

If you drive north on U.S. 97 from the Columbia River into central Washington, you won't travel many more than 25 miles before reaching important Indian country. Once through Satus Pass (3,149 feet), you have entered the Yakima Indian Reservation—at one million acres, the second largest reservation in the state after Colville. To the east after leaving Satus Pass, you'll see the Horse Heaven Hills, named for the wild horses that roamed there until the area became more settled.

Another 35 miles leads to the city of Toppenish, doorway to Indian culture.

Toppenish: an Indian name, an Indian region

Bearing an Indian name meaning "people from the foot of the hills," Toppenish is of tourist interest

WILD COW resists milking during Washington's biggest rodeo, held Labor Day weekend in Ellensburg.

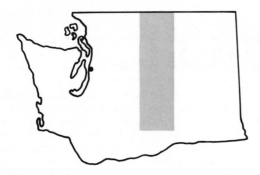

principally because the Yakima Indian Agency is here and because nearby are historical and cultural sights.

Fort Simcoe. At Toppenish, a paved side road (State 220) goes west for 28 miles to Fort Simcoe State Historical Park. The fort was established during Indian hostilities. During its short life as an active post (1856 to 1859), Fort Simcoe was a base of considerable importance, for the site gave troops strategic command of two principal routes (one from Oregon, the other over the Cascades).

Several of the fort's original buildings have been restored and furnished with period pieces. A small museum is devoted chiefly to Indian relics. Included is a collection of native food plants and preparations the Yakimas have made from them.

White Swan Indian Celebrations. At White Swan, 23 miles west of Toppenish on State 220, two summer Indian celebrations are held. The first is an All-Indian Rodeo that lasts for three days in early June; the second is a colorful Indian Encampment on July 4.

Yakima and its valley

Rude canals dug by early Yakima Valley settlers in the late 19th century turned a desert and sagebrush area into a rich agricultural region. Today, Yakima County ranks first in the United States in production of apples, mint, and hops.

In and around Yakima, these are some of the opportunities for exploration or recreation that you might enjoy:

Central Washington Fair. Held during the last week of September on the outskirts of Yakima, the fair includes a full-scale carnival, talent shows, rodeo, band concerts, food and food exhibits of all types, and a broad sample of agricultural and livestock demonstrations.

BROTHER LEADS SISTER along the bank beside the Rocky Reach Dam, spanning the Columbia River near Wenatchee. Here visitors watch salmon from underwater viewing room.

Yakima State Park. Located 3 miles south of the city, the park has campsites and trailer hookups. In the 210 acres are picnic tables, spacious lawns, a children's playground, and even a small zoo. Children also enjoy the five lakes where those 14 and under can fish.

Painted Rocks. Historic Yakima Indian pictographs appear on these rocks 7 miles northwest on U.S. 12.

Skiing. From Yakima, White Pass Village in Snoqualmie National Forest is only 55 miles to the northwest on U.S. 12. Here you'll find novice-to-expert slopes, three double chair lifts, Pomalift, rope tow, and rentals.

Dip net fishing. On three modern irrigation dams on the Yakima River, you can still see Yakima Indians patiently fishing for salmon as their ancestors did centuries ago—with dip nets, from platforms suspended over the water on stilts.

Wapato Dam is just below Union Gap, 5 miles south of Yakima, and is visible from U.S. 12. The second dam, Sunnyside, is farther southeast, about half a mile north of Prosser; best vantage point is across the river on State 22. The third dam is about midway between Benton City and Richland; drive out of Benton City on the west side of the river (along Horn Road).

The Indians are within their treaty rights to fish these dams; the dams are adjacent to the Yakima Reservation. However, the Washington Department of Fisheries has urged the Yakimas to let more fish through, for the number of escaping salmon is decreasing each year.

An event that dates back farther than the oldest Indian can remember is *Cow-a-wit*, the feast of the first salmon. It is prepared each May as part of a two-day festival, always held on a weekend. Traditional games and dances are climaxed by a feast which features salmon roasted over an open fire. Festivities are open to the public without charge.

Fruit orchards. Between Yakima and Prosser, a pleasant drive is a loop trip down one side of the river on U.S. 97 and State 22 and back on U.S. 12 on the other side of the river. It's a total distance of about 90 miles, but you can shorten the drive by crossing the Yakima River on any of the six bridges between Yakima and Prosser. You'll pass fruit orchards, hop fields, and vineyards, and there will be plenty of chances to buy produce in the fall (sometimes you can pick your own).

Some of the larger peach orchards in the valley are near Granger and Zillah. The frilly blossoms are usually at their peak in mid-April.

YAKIMA RIVER, left, flows through canyon between Ellensburg and Yakima. New U.S. 82 runs atop canyon. Above, Kiowa Indian dancer's costume includes buckskin apron, knee bells.

YOUNG BLACKFOOT Indian wears beaded fringe over eyes as part of dance costume during annual Indian Festival held in summer at Soap Lake.

Tracking Indian Art and Culture

Washington's Indian heritage is very much in evidence these days. Along with other ethnic groups in the state, Indian tribes are daily becoming more aware of their own cultures. The result has been a resurgence of their art forms, legends, language, dance, and religion.

The Indian population of Washington state now is 25,000 to 35,000. Approximately half of this number live on reservations. Washington has 23 recognized Indian reservations, ranging in size from the sprawling Yakima, with 1,134,830 acres, to the Puyallup, with only 33 acres remaining.

Concerned with maintaining their unique way of life, Indian tribes throughout the state have begun to question the broken treaties, fishing disputes, and cultural insensitivity which have too often characterized white men's interactions with the Indians. The ensuing legal and political juggling has brought to the state's Indians a new pride in their past culture. Here are some manifestations of that pride:

• At Neah Bay on the Olympic Peninsula's northwest corner, site of the Makah reservation, you will find local artisans busily engaged in carving totem poles, masks, and small figures. The schools on the reservation teach the Makah language, and the University of Washington accepts this course of study as fulfilling the foreign language requirement. Legends, carving, basketry, and dancing are taught in the elementary schools; every attempt is being made to strengthen ties with, and pride in, the past.

• Ariel, Washington, a rural community 40 miles north of Portland, offers a rare opportunity for the visitor to witness firsthand ceremonies and legends of the Indians of the Northwest coast.

Sponsored by the Oregon Museum of Science and Industry (OMSI), Don Smith (his Indian appellation is Lelooska, the woodcarver) welcomes you to a 2-hour performance encompassing dancing, displays of costumes, jewelry, masks, traditional Indian tools, and explanations of Indian legends. Lelooska, considered by many as a top authority on Northwest Indian art, has a workshop and museum on the grounds.

To attend any performance, you must write to the OMSI Education Office, 4015 S.W. Canyon Road, Portland 97221; telephone (503) 224-9500. A nominal admission is charged.

• Interest in the renaissance of Indian folklore is not limited to Americans. European buyers often appear at Seattle's Indian Center to shop for Indian arts and crafts. Exquisite beadwork, jewelry, and carvings are sold here; sometimes you can observe artisans at work on the premises. The Seattle Indian Center is located in the Second Avenue and Cherry Building in Seattle.

• An engrossing experience for a visitor interested in Indian life is a visit to a powwow. Usually lasting for several days, these celebrations occur in various parts of the state, bringing together Indians from the entire Northwest area. It is not unusual to see 50 or 75 teepees at a large powwow. Indian dancing, both competitive and pleasurable, continues through the day and night. Craft booths offer a variety of Indian work, and there is usually some native food available — salmon and Indian fried bread, for example.

Dates for powwows vary from year to year, so check with the Seattle Indian Center (telephone 206-622-3701) for information.

Near Yakima, there are large apple orchards to explore on grids of lazy country roads. Drive toward Naches on whatever country road you come across.

Yakima Canyon. North of Yakima, the Yakima River, the Burlington Northern Railway, and the old Yakima-Ellensburg road all squeeze through a deep, narrow canyon for 36 miles. High above the canyon, U.S. 82, a new, four-lane divided highway, speeds traffic north and south, leaving the canyon floor road free for leisurely exploring.

And there's reason to explore. Kayaking is a popular pastime on the Yakima River. And the canyon is a good hunting area for agatized and opalized wood, formed when trees fell into ancient lake and river beds and were covered by lava flows which sealed them into mud where they gradually hardened and petrified. Today you can find many bits and pieces of these trees.

If you visit the canyon in the spring, you'll find a wider variety of spring-blooming wildflowers than you may have thought possible.

THE HEARTLAND

You'll parallel the ridges and peaks of the Cascade Range lying to the west as you drive along the top

FOSSILIZED WOOD exerts a strong attraction for visitors to Ginkgo Petrified Forest Museum.

of Yakima Canyon on U.S. 82 to Ellensburg, the seat of Kittitas County.

Within this county, you'll see examples of Washington's two faces: to the west, lakes and crags; to the east, irrigated farmlands and sagebrush prairies along the Columbia River.

Ellensburg: the geographic center

Ellensburg has grown in respectability by shedding its former name of "Robber's Roost" and becoming the home of 7,000-student Central Washington State College.

You can locate the exact center of the state of Washington at 4th and Pine streets in Ellensburg. Better not try doing this on Labor Day weekend, though: that's the busiest time of the year here, for the Ellensburg Rodeo is taking place. Horse racing, calf roping, steer wrestling, wild cow milking, Indian dances, and many other events make the Rodeo Field a lively and popular site in September.

The Kittitas County Fair runs in tandem with the rodeo on Labor Day weekend.

Ginkgo Petrified Forest State Park. At Ellensburg, a side trip of about 28 miles east on Interstate 90 will take you to the Ginkgo Petrified Forest State Park near Vantage. Here, petrified logs in drift piles, where they were washed up onto the shores of ancient lakes, lie sealed and opalized between

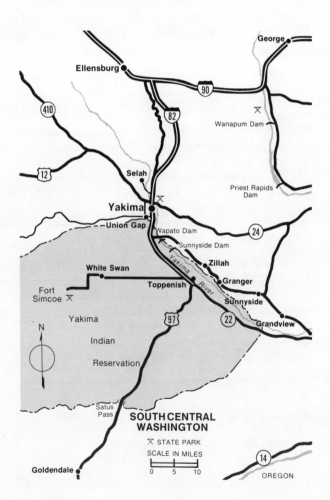

SOUTH CENTRAL WASHINGTON

✕ STATE PARK

SCALE IN MILES

0   5   10

OREGON

lava layers. More than 200 kinds of trees have been identified at this site. Nowhere else can you find a petrified ginkgo tree.

Ginkgo Park displays these trees in two places. Three miles west of Vantage, signs and a large stone building on the north side of the highway mark a canyon trail that leads to numerous open pits in the lava, where you see logs as they have lain for perhaps 15 million years.

If you don't feel up to hiking the trail, an easier exposure to petrified wood can be had at the museum—2½ miles farther east. The museum is open daily except Mondays and Tuesdays from 10 a.m. to 5 p.m. Situated high on a hill, it commands a splendid view of the Columbia River and of the Saddle Mountains.

Wanapum Dam. Roads on either side of the Columbia can take you 6 miles downstream from the Vantage Bridge (on Interstate 90) to Wanapum Dam. Most of the visitor facilities are on the east river bank, although there is a state park with boat ramps and a picnic area on the west side between Vantage and the dam.

Any time of year you can take a self-guided tour of the generator hall or visit the glass-paneled fish viewing room. From April to November you can tour a museum containing artwork, a dugout canoe, and dioramas, including one of early steamboating. The dam's twelve 50 by 65 foot Taintor gates in the spillway are probably the world's largest.

From Ellensburg to Wenatchee

Though the highway from Ellensburg is an up-to-date one, some of the sights along the way are definitely out of the 19th century.

U.S. 97 branches off Interstate 90 just before Cle Elum, about 20 miles west of Ellensburg. In another 2 miles it reaches Teanaway, where many a prospector has wet his whistle. Along the 42-mile northbound stretch of U.S. 97 between Teanaway and Peshastin, you will find many evidences of past and present mining—caved-in shafts, rotting flumes, forgotten towns, mine tailings, and the inevitable never-say-die prospector. Gravel mounds along Swauk Creek north of Teanaway are the result of some of the early dredging operations.

Farther north on U.S. 97, you wind up to the summit of Swauk Pass. The popular Swauk recreation area, consisting of a large picnic and camping

---

A Timetable for Blossom Watchers

APPLE ORCHARDS blossom in valley near Monitor (between Wenatchee and Cashmere).

From March through early May, blossom watchers can always find fruit trees in bloom somewhere in Washington. Here is a timetable of the typical blooming periods for various kinds:

Apricots. The white blossoms appear during the last week of March and first week of April. Approximately 4,500 acres of apricot trees grow in southcentral Washington.

Peaches. Blossoms open the first and second week of April. You'll see some 5,000 acres of peach orchards in southcentral Washington, 3,000 acres in northcentral Washington.

Pears. Both Bartlett and Winter pears bloom in the second and third weeks of April. There are plantings of 14,000 acres in Yakima County and 8,000 acres in northcentral Washington.

Apples. The abundant pink and white blossoms open during the last week of April and the first week of May. Look for them in northcentral Washington (40,000 acres) and southcentral Washington (35,000 acres).

Prunes. Blossoms open in the first and second weeks of April. About 3,500 acres of prune trees bloom in Benton and Yakima counties.

ground in a grove of ponderosa pines, is 2 miles south of the summit.

Beyond Tronsen Creek, the highway descends along mine-scarred Peshastin Creek. Look for remnants of the old town of Blewett—scattered water wheels, a ramshackle mill, a few rickety buildings, and a stone arrastra.

Leaving Blewett, the highway follows Peshastin Creek and enters the Wenatchee Valley. Here you meet U.S. 2, which goes northwest to the resort area around Lake Wenatchee and on across Stevens Pass to Everett or southeast to Wenatchee.

Wenatchee—where the apple is king

Little wonder that Wenatchee is called the "Apple Capital of the World"; this city ships more apples than any other city in the world. The annual Washington State Apple Blossom Festival is held here in the spring. In the fall, the region is bustling with harvest-time activity and various fairs and festivals. Then you can visit the packing houses and see apples being sorted, packed, and readied for shipment.

Around Cashmere, at the bottom of the east Cascade slopes, U.S. 97 passes through an orchard-filled valley surrounded by pine and fir forests. Cashmere's Willis Carey Historical Museum, featuring Columbia River history, is open daily May through September.

From Wenatchee, a classic loop tour of the apple-growing country takes you up either side of the Columbia River to Chelan, where you cross the river by bridge and then return on the other side (U.S. 97 on the west side, U.S. 2 and State 151 on the east side). Or you can cross by toll ferry just south of Entiat if you prefer a shorter drive. On the Chelan County side (U.S. 97), you pass several points of interest, including Ohme Gardens and Rocky Reach Dam. The best close-up views of apple orchards are on the 26-mile stretch of State 151 below Chelan Falls.

Ohme Gardens. Three miles north of Wenatchee, these 7-acre, mountain-top gardens are rustically landscaped with native trees and low-growing alpine plants. On all sides you'll have sweeping views —of nearby mountains, the Columbia and Wenatchee Rivers, Wenatchee, and the Wenatchee valley. A lookout tower is located at the highest point.

Rocky Reach Dam. Seven miles upstream from Wenatchee, the Rocky Reach Dam spans the Columbia River. It has an underwater viewing gallery where you can watch the salmon as they swim upstream by means of a 1,350-foot-long fish ladder.

Crescent Bar recreation area. One of the most developed sites along the Columbia, this park is located on a man-made island at the base of soaring basalt cliffs. Its camping area and service building are open year around. You can reach the park via a spur road off State 28, seven miles west of Quincy.

Douglas County Historical Museum. On your right as you enter Waterville on U.S. 2 from Wenatchee,

MIDCENTRAL WASHINGTON

this free museum is open daily from May 1 to October 1. It features the usual pioneer and Indian articles, but you'll also find some of the unexpected things that reward attentive museum browsers. There's an extensive mineral exhibit, a collection of 650 mechanical pencils, and a homemade 20-car circus train. Best of all—and occupying an entire room of its own in the basement—is a large animal horn collection, including a narwhal's long spike, along with horns from gazelles, antelopes, gnus, elands, and deer. The massive rack of an Indian sacred bull dominates even the horns from a Texas longhorn and an African buffalo.

Mission Ridge. Thirteen miles southwest of Wenatchee is the Mission Ridge ski area, with three chair lifts, three rope tows, a day lodge with cafeteria and dining room, and ski shop.

NORTHCENTRAL HIGHLIGHTS

The hand of man is boldly evident in much of central Washington. You see it in the tamed Columbia River, the irrigated prairie, the sweep of super-highway, the disciplined rows of apple trees.

But as you drive north of Wenatchee on U.S. 97, the handiwork of nature dominates.

Spectacular Lake Chelan

You can skirt the southeastern end of Lake Chelan, give its popular resort area a passing glance, and never realize you have missed anything. From U.S. 97 you see an unspectacular stretch of calm water surrounded by apple orchards, summer-dry brown hills, and lakeside homes, not unlike the scene at dozens of similar lakes in the West.

But Lake Chelan is a remarkable body of water. What you don't see from the highway reaches 55

REGATTA held on lower end of Lake Chelan inspires much activity among sailing buffs during summer.

miles into the heart of the Cascades and is accessible only by boat or float-plane. Beyond the realm of automobiles, towering ramparts squeeze the fjordlike lake into straits less than ¼ mile from shore to shore and give it a maximum depth of 1,489 feet (in this country, only Crater Lake and Lake Tahoe are deeper). At the lower end of the lake are warm, sunny beaches, water sports, and busy resort facilities; at the upper, pristine wilderness.

Boating on the lake. If you intend to cruise the lake in your own boat, you'll find launching ramps at Manson, Chelan, Lake Chelan State Park, and 25-Mile Creek. Frequently, afternoon high winds on the lake above 25-Mile Creek make the journey hazardous for small boats; authorities advise you not to attempt the trip in an open power boat of less than 16 feet. (Marinas at the lower end of the lake rent only small fishing or water-ski boats, unsuitable for the trip.)

Passenger boat service. Lake Chelan Boat Company runs regular passenger boat service on the lake daily from May 15 to September 30 and on Monday, Wednesday, and Friday from October 1 to May 14. The run to uplake resorts and to Stehekin, at the upper tip of Lake Chelan, takes 4½ hours one way on the "Lady of the Lake," moving you from the desert of the Columbia Basin to the foot of the rugged North Cascades mountains.

Pack trips into the Cascades originate from Stehekin (close to the summit) and Holden. To reach Holden, debark at Lucerne and hire a taxi to take you the rest of the way (a 15-mile trip).

Charter plane service. Chelan Airways, based at Chelan, operates a float-plane charter service to points uplake and will fly you into Domke Lake, Trapper Lake, or other remote alpine lakes for fishing or camping.

The resort of Chelan

In addition to a cluster of waterfront motels in Chelan, you'll find resort facilities scattered along the road to 25-Mile Creek, up the west side of the lake. Weekend accommodations are scarce during the summer; it's advisable to write for reservations. Lake Chelan Chamber of Commerce (see Appendix) will supply information.

Trailer and tent camping facilities are located at Chelan State Park and 25-Mile Creek. Two lakeside city parks have picnic tables.

The Lake Chelan Golf Club has a par 72 championship course, and within the Chelan city limits are two well-groomed parks.

Branching west through the Methow Valley

As you drive north from Chelan, State 153 leaves U.S. 97 at Pateros to follow the Methow River northwest through pastoral Methow Valley. Two miles from Pateros, a side road goes to Alta Lake, where a state park on the west shore has campsites, a picnic area, playground equipment, boat launching ramp, and swimming float.

The newest cross-Cascades road: State 20. At Twisp, State 153 intersects with State 20, the new North Cascades Highway that branches off Interstate 5 just north of Mount Vernon and terminates in Idaho. Completed in 1972, State 20 is a major addition to Washington's tourist offerings. It provides an easy-to-drive route to some top-of-the-world vantage points in North Cascades National

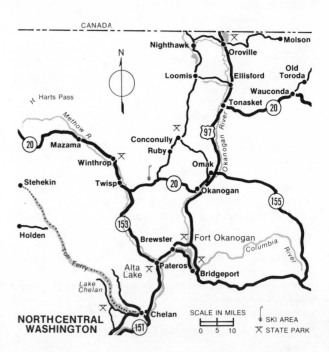

NORTH CENTRAL WASHINGTON

Park— the nation's newest federally recognized recreation area.

Because of the heavy snowfalls in this region, though, State 20 (which swings across the head of the Stehekin watershed to Rainy Pass and then descends along Granite Creek to Diablo Dam) is closed to traffic during the winter months, sometimes as early as October.

In and around the Okanogan Valley

The charm of the Okanogan Valley lies in its tranquility. It is a wild yet friendly country that pleasures you in much the way a Swiss valley might—sticking in your memory and coloring your descriptions with enthusiasm.

In its quiet way, this valley is a highly satisfying summer resort area. Resorts vary from dude ranches and hunters' cabins in Washington to lakeshore boating and fishing places in Canada and mountain lodges in the back country.

The Okanogan River runs along the eastern flank of the North Cascades; from U.S. 97 you look out across sagebrush foothills toward the high mountains. This region is full of small lakes, offering legendary trout fishing and gravel side roads for exploring. Along the river all the way to Armstrong, British Columbia, you encounter fruit orchards and roadside produce stands.

Wells Dam is 12 miles north of Chelan, near Azwell off U.S. 97 between Wenatchee and Pateros. Two unusual features mark this dam: an advanced design known as "hydro-combine" and a spawning channel, one of only three in the state, where Chinook salmon spawn naturally. In addition, there's a conventional fish hatchery. On a vista point above the west end of the dam is a display of painted Indian pictographs, more rare than carved petroglyphs, and a display with a recorded message. The self-guided tour of the dam includes a slide and tape show on the geological history of the Columbia Basin.

Brewster Earth Station. On the flats above Okanogan River near Brewster, Washington, a huge antenna directs its radio signals to and receives signals from a satellite orbiting 22,300 miles above the Pacific Ocean. This 58-inch cylinder is a microwave repeater that picks up radio signals from the earth and amplifies and retransmits them to other antennae at earth stations throughout the Pacific Ocean area.

A recently constructed visitor center contains exhibits showing how the station functions and explaining space technology only dreamed of a few years ago. It is open seven days a week, 10 a.m. to 6 p.m.

Fort Okanogan. The confluence of the Okanogan and Columbia rivers in northcentral Washington has been a natural crossroads for centuries. The teepee-shaped building of the Fort Okanogan Historical Museum, sitting on a hill near the junction of State 17 and U.S. 97 about 5 miles east of Brewster, is at an appropriate location.

ANGLING FOR FISH in the briskly running waters of the scenic Cle Elum River near Salmon La Sac.

THORP MILL, just west of Ellensburg, once ground flour by water power, now is graceful ghost.

On Okanogan's Ghost Town Trail

QUAINT GOLD town of Molson has been reconstituted from old buildings and artifacts found in local area.

WITHIN A MILE of the U.S.-Canadian border at Nighthawk stands this abandoned log cabin.

SIGN OF THE TIMES makes a prophecy the passing decades have given the lie to.

RUBY MILL stands beneath towering hill at Nighthawk; 1896 San Francisco newspaper was found nearby.

INSIDE Ruby Mill, ghost town explorer looks over rusted drum and early machinery.

Okanogan and Omak—towns on the move

Located 5 miles apart, Okanogan and Omak are presently small towns that seem slated for inevitable growth because of the completion of U.S. 20 across the North Cascades, addition of a third powerhouse at Grand Coulee Dam to the east, and industrial and recreational expansion in the Okanogan Valley.

The Okanogan-Omak area has at present one hotel and eight motels with a total of 162 rooms. A dude ranch in the county is the Sunny M—part of the Sun Mountain operation in Winthrop.

One of Okanogan's two city parks is distinguished by the fact that General Goethals, during his Pacific Northwest explorations in 1883, camped here. Later, Goethals engineered the building of the Panama Canal. Omak is home of the famed Omak Stampede and Suicide Race (held on three days in mid-August), in which riders race off a cliff and across the Okanogan River.

Ghost towns galore

Down gravel roads, in overgrown fields, and among pineclad hills moulder the remains of once-prosperous homesteads and businesses. Some are true ghost towns; others still retain a few loyal residents. This northcentral Washington region of gold strikes and railroad booms is now partially incorporated into the Okanogan National Forest. If you'd like to explore it in detail, you can purchase a map from the National Forest Service (see Appendix, page 158). The map on page 132 can be used to roughly locate most of the towns.

Okanogan's story tells of small, scattered mineral strikes at a time when gold fever had infected Western adventurers. Settlements sprouted and withered as fast as rumors could travel. Some towns were mining camps; others sprang up as supply and communications centers; still others served farmers and ranchers.

Here are a few of the ghost or semi-ghost towns of the Okanogan with directions on how to find them:

Molson is perhaps the most traditional ghost town, developed more than most. Besides artifacts and false front buildings, you can see the remains of an automobile-age resettlement that didn't work out.

Where it's found. To reach Molson, take Tonasket Creek Road east from Oroville 7 miles, then travel north on Mud Lake Valley Road for 6 miles.

Nighthawk began when James M. Haggerty, an attorney from Portland, Oregon, stayed on after helping settle the estate of Hiram F. "Okanogan" Smith. Haggerty established three prosperous mines in an area with many nighthawks. Later, a supply center developed. Access to Nighthawk is via footbridge, although formerly a ferry ran across the Similkameen River.

Where it's found. Again using Oroville as a hub, drive 12 miles west on a gravel road to visit Nighthawk.

AT CHELAN DOCK, *passengers wait patiently while freight is loaded for transportation uplake.*

J. H. Loomis, a cattle rancher, started a trading post and then operated a large general store which grew into the town bearing his name. Mining for a variety of metals gradually overtook ranching as the town's principal activity.

Where it's found. Branching west from U.S. 97 at Ellisford (south of Oroville), an 11-mile gravel road leads to Loomis.

Conconully was once the county seat (after a fierce competition with other towns) but fell victim to fires, floods, avalanches, Indians, and the 1893 silver panic. The area is now a state park and Okanogan serves as county seat. Ruins of concrete and rock vaults that once held courthouse records are still visible. Conconully's notorious jail—one that just couldn't seem to hold prisoners—was a frame structure and has vanished.

Where it's found. South of Loomis along a stretch of gravel road, Conconully is also accessible from Omak.

Curlew, founded in the 1880s by trappers, retains rows of boarded-up false-front stores.

Where it's found. Curlew is farther east, just off State 21 near the Canadian border.

Orient, another former gold mining town, was laid out in 1900. Its mines had such fanciful names as Easter Sunday, Little Gem, First Thought, and Gold Stake. Orient boomed during railroad construction, but neither the railroad nor the gold was enough to keep it from declining.

Where it's found. Orient is along U.S. 395 just south of the Canadian border.

Indisputably Grand...
the Coulee Country

To French fur trappers of the 1800s, the words "grand coulee" meant "great canyon"—the name they gave this dramatically stark region of Washington.

To geologists, "coulee" means a sheet of solidified lava or a deep gulch cut by rainstorms or melting snow.

To travelers, Grand Coulee means still other things: a mammoth dam, a huge, manmade lake, slices of nature in the raw, and some fine recreational country.

The two large coulees of eastern Washington—the Moses Coulee and Grand Coulee—are parallel depressions eroded into lava plateaus by the fading glaciers of the Ice Age. Immense Grand Coulee is 52 miles long and, at certain points, 5 miles wide. In the heart of this region rises the Grand Coulee Dam, key link in the great chain of dams, siphons, canals, and reservoirs that makes up the Columbia Basin Project.

South of the dam and spreading east and west from the Grand Coulee is a region of wonders: dry river channels, fossil caves, and exposed ancient lava flows. North of the dam, Franklin Delano Roosevelt Lake—the largest in the state—is surrounded by a recreation area so worthwhile it has been preserved under national authority. In addition, both the refreshing Sanpoil Valley and the huge Colville Indian Reservation add to the attractions north of Grand Coulee Dam.

THE COULEES BELOW THE DAM

If you simply parallel the length of the Grand Coulee by driving along State Highway 155, you'll pass ten different flows of lava that built up the coulee walls.

About 100,000 years ago, the great Cordilleran ice sheet shouldered its way south to cover much of this land. When the ice began to melt, it formed the greatest river known to man—a river bigger than

DEEP IN GRAND COULEE is Steamboat Rock, the 2-mile-long rock formation at top right.

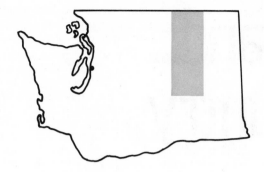

the present Columbia, Mississippi, Fraser, Yukon, and McKenzie combined.

In its torrential wanderings, this river giant scarred the old lava plateau with a maze of rock-walled valleys—scabland channels and medium-sized coulees—that spread from Moses Coulee in the west to Spokane in the east. At the present site of Coulee Dam, the river was diverted from its regular course by a huge ice dam, the Okanogan Ice Lobe. Moving down what is now known as Grand Coulee, the river's main torrent plunged for more than 400 feet over what is now Dry Falls.

When the great mass of ice finally melted away, the river resumed its former course, leaving the Grand Coulee high and dry.

Upper Grand Coulee—a lakeland

The wide, deep upper portion of the Grand Coulee is now mostly inundated by Banks Lake, an irrigation reservoir kept filled by the pumps of Grand Coulee Dam. From several boat ramps you can launch out for spiny-ray or trout fishing; here there's no closed season. Campgrounds are available at Coulee City and at Steamboat Rock State Park.

Steamboat Rock. An impressive peninsula on the east side of Banks Lake called Steamboat Rock marks a glaciation line and once divided the flood channel that cut back the upper coulee. In ancient times, the rock was an island between twin falls that had a combined width of 2 miles and a drop of nearly 800 feet. Now it's a state park, with picnic tables as well as boat-launching ramps.

Barker Canyon. In all, 25-mile-long Banks Lake has 10 access areas on its south and east shores. On the undeveloped western side, the Barker Canyon access might be less crowded.

A WONDER OF THE WORLD when first constructed (some skeptics said it couldn't be built), Grand Coulee Dam is vitally important to the Coulee region's economy.

At the Barker Canyon mouth are boat launching beaches, a small grove of poplars and locusts for shade, and a meandering dirt road that follows the shore to several bays and headlands along a mile or so of the broad alluvial fan.

The Barker Canyon road turns south from State 174 (the Bridgeport highway) just 10 miles west of the town of Grand Coulee. Except as a crossroad, the turnoff is unmarked. From the turnoff it's 6 miles to Banks Lake in an easy descent across old glacial terraces and down a final stretch of walled canyon.

You'll pass grazing cattle here and there and a few abandoned farms—some marked only by the humps of long-unused root cellars.

Since there is no fresh water along the road or at Banks Lake and since it can be quite warm at lakeshore, remember to bring along your own drinking water.

A drive through prehistory: lower Grand Coulee

South of Banks Lake, just past Dry Falls Dam, is the Dry Falls State Park Visitor Center and overlook. A museum contains excellent displays and dioramas showing the ancient river's history, the origin of the Columbia Basin lava fields, glacial events, and the formation of coulees and dry falls.

Dry Falls. Once an immense fall of water, perhaps the biggest in geologic history, Dry Falls is well over 3 miles in width. By comparison, today's Niagara is minuscule. From the museum building, you can see two of the five huge alcoves that formed the falls.

For 20 miles along State 17, basalt walls rise 400 feet above a continuous chain of spring-fed lakes. Beginning with Falls Lake and Deep Lake, these depressions are the plunge pools of a giant waterfall that cut through lava cliffs in prehistoric times, backing up all the way from Soap Lake to Dry Falls. This erosion process formed lower Grand Coulee.

Sun Lakes State Park. For those who imagine Washington to be a totally cloudy, rainy state, Sun Lakes State Park in the Grand Coulee region will come as a pleasant surprise. Desert sunshine and warmth last into September; skies are clear.

South of Coulee City on State 17, 3,546-acre Sun Lakes State Park fills the coulee bottom. This is a vacation spot with distinctive geological trimmings, offering many recreational possibilities. Campsites, tables and stoves, simple cabins, seven

MIND-BOGGLING immensity of Dry Falls, left, dwarfs people on viewing platform. Scale is more comprehensible at Deep Lake, above, where you can launch a boat or raft.

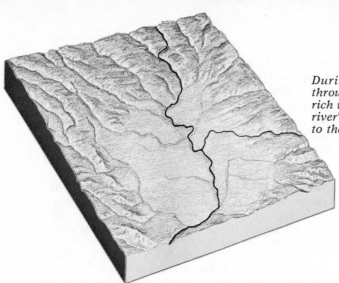

20 million years ago, a verdant river basin.
During the Miocene Epoch, the Columbia swept through a central Washington warm in climate and rich in varied plant and animal life. No one knows the river's old course; possibly it followed a route similar to the one shown in this diagram.

15 million years ago, the lava flows.
In late Miocene and also in early Pliocene times, repeated lava floods covered central Washington's hills and valleys. For some 10 million years, flood after flood of basalt built up to thicknesses of 6,000 feet, forcing the river around the lava fields.

A Crash Course in Geology

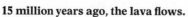

A million years ago, the ice flows.
With the beginning of the Pleistocene, the climate cooled. Conditions favorable to the formation of glaciers developed, and vast sheets of ice moved south, blocking the Columbia and forcing its waters to cut new channels across the lava fields.

Today, the water-eroded coulee country.
Some 12,000 years ago, the last glaciers melted, and the river returned to its old course between lava fields and the mountains, leaving vast scars across the lava fields in the form of immense coulees, dry falls, and water-eroded scablands.

BACKDROP OF VOLCANIC cliffs rises behind golfers playing in clear, dependable sunshine.

fishing lakes, boat rentals, excellent swimming, a cafe and grocery store, a nine-hole golf course, horseback riding, and plenty of remote country-side to explore make this one of Washington's most popular state parks. Winter visitors can even go ice skating.

One of the park's most unusual features is a herd of fallow deer, the only ones roaming free in this country. These natives of India are frequently seen, especially by hikers and trail riders.

Lake Lenore Caves. On the east wall of the coulee, 14 miles south of Coulee City just off State 17, you can visit the Lake Lenore Caves Heritage Site. Melting glacial waters carved these caves out of volcanic basalt. Prehistoric men inhabiting the coulee region found caves like these useful as shelters. Because few artifacts have been found, archeologists theorize the ancient population consisted of nomadic hunters and gatherers. A wood marker in the parking area directs you to a foot trail leading to the caves.

Soap Lake. At the southern end of the Grand Coulee, the town of Soap Lake bounds the region with a large collection of cabins, hotels, and motels. The lake is noted for its highly mineralized water, believed to be of some therapeutic value. Suds 'n Sun Indian Encampment is usually held here in July.

Summer Falls. During summer, Billy Clapp Lake (on a spur road off State 28 east of Soap Lake, near Stratford) is filled with water flowing over Summer Falls. The falls form the outlet of the main irrigating canal of the Columbia Basin system, which follows the course of an ancient streambed. A public access area near Pinto Dam supplements the facilities of Summer Falls State Park.

Ephrata. Just southwest of Soap Lake, the regional center of Ephrata contains the Grant County Historical Museum with exhibits including replicas of a typical homestead summer porch, a country store stocked with pioneer trade goods, and a period kitchen.

The rock-strewn upper Moses Coulee

Like Grand Coulee, Moses Coulee to the west has an upper and lower section.

Jameson Lake. In the upper Moses Coulee, Jameson Lake offers rainbow trout, sometimes abundantly; you can reach the lake from Mansfield or, from the south, via a spur road off U.S. 2. At each end of the lake is a small resort, with supplies, rental boats, public picnic areas, and boat launching ramps. But no through road leads past Jameson along the coulee, so you must backtrack on either approach to the lake, from north or south.

Waterville Plateau. A side road trip in this region takes you onto the Waterville Plateau. Three miles south of Bridgeport, on State 17, a fork in the road turns slightly westward. This paved country road connects with State 172 about 12 miles farther south, after passing through a belt of "haystack rocks." Broken from the basalt lip of the plateau by the last glacier, these chunks of lava were strewn over the whole northern region of the Waterville

Plateau as the ice melted south to the head of upper Moses Coulee.

Fertile lower Moses Coulee

From Moses Lake, the main population center in the lower Moses Coulee region, you can adventure in several directions. Driving south 12 miles on State 17 takes you to Lind Coulee; a west turn from there leads toward O'Sullivan Dam and Potholes Reservoir. People are not new to this area; carbon from Indian hearths dates back 9,000 years.

Moses Lake. Sunny Moses Lake is hub of a relaxing fishing, swimming, and hunting region. Mid-August visitors can enjoy the Grant County Fair.

A visit to the Adam East Museum at Fifth and Balsam Streets will inform you about the history and geology of the area. The museum also contains one of the largest single collections of Indian artifacts in Washington. Many of the exhibits were donated by the University of Washington, whose archeologists advise the museum.

O'Sullivan Dam. Filling a whole valley, a vast inland sea was created by this 3½-mile-long earth dam, which you can drive across. Below the dam, among ancient glacial-age river channels, trout fishermen can follow winding gravel roads to over 50 lakes formed by seepage and runoff from Potholes Reservoir. Some of the lakes have launching ramps. Brooks Lake on the Stratford Game Reserve is a regular stopover for migrating geese.

Coulee excursion. For a trip into the Coulee itself, turn east off State 28, 18 miles below Wenatchee, on the Appledale turnoff.

The Palisades store and a thin community of small ranches are 11 miles up the coulee. On your way, watch for the natural statuary of Chief Moses and his wife, 2 miles into the coulee on the right (he was the Indian chief for whom the coulee was named).

The road, now gravel, climbs out of the ancient river bottom 7 miles above Palisades and crosses plateau wheat fields toward the community of Ephrata and State 17.

MONOLITH IN THE DESERT . . . GRAND COULEE DAM

Europe's greatest monuments are often enhanced by sound and light displays that transform their subjects against the background of night. So it's suitable that the largest concrete dam in the world, massive Grand Coulee, is also the scene of such a display.

Purposes of the dam. WPA-project Grand Coulee Dam was designed to divert the Columbia's waters back into the channel gouged thousands of years ago by the present river's predecessor. Water pumped 280 feet out of a reservoir floods the ancient riverbed. Having taken eight years to build, the dam provides irrigation, flood control, and electric power. Its spillway is twice as high as Niagara Falls; normally visitors can watch it operate from late May to early September.

If you visit the Grand Coulee Dam, you'll see a structure that's almost overwhelming—it's higher than a 46-story building and wider than 12 city blocks. With a capacity of nearly 2 million kilowatts, the dam will eventually provide irrigation for over one million acres of land in the Columbia Basin. The recently-added third power plant will bring the total electrical output to 5.67 million kilowatts when the first phase of construction is completed in 1974. Future additions will increase the capacity to 9.2 million kilowatts.

Local history. The coulee country was one of the last parts of Washington to be settled. Wheat farmers did not move in until around the turn of the century; the cattlemen had come only a few years before them. Population was sparse. Ranchers had two, three, and four-thousand-acre holdings, half of which lay fallow each year; economic survival depended on rainfall and grain prices.

The Columbia Basin Project. Conceived as a means of reclaiming a million acres of arid land in south-central Washington, this project depends upon six giant pumps at Grand Coulee Dam that lift water from Lake Roosevelt into Banks Lake. From here, water flows by gravity through 2,200 miles of canals

FREE FERRY, operating daily, shuttles cars and passengers back and forth across Roosevelt Lake at Gifford.

and siphons to the project area. To date, over five thousand 40 to 160-acre farms have sprung up on a half million acres of irrigated land extending from Coulee City, 30 miles below the dam, to Pasco, 147 miles to the south.

Constructing the dam led to the growth of such towns as Coulee Dam, Electric City, Elmer City, and Grand Coulee. Coulee Dam is the site of a tour center supplying general information.

Tours of the dam. At the Grand Coulee Dam's Information Center (west end), Bureau of Reclamation personnel present orientation lectures and answer visitors' questions. Photographs and a large relief map of the Columbia Basin help explain things. Tours of the powerhouse and the pumping plant that propels irrigation waters are available, and visitors can walk on the top of the dam.

For views of the forebay, the twelve giant pipes carrying water to the canal from the pumping plant, and the canal's entrance to Banks Lake, drive off State 155 on a spur road to the headworks of the main canal. It's directly above the pumping plant on top of a bluff. Crown Point provides an overall look at the dam and vicinity. To get there, turn off State 174 about a mile north of the town of Grand Coulee.

THE REGION ABOVE THE DAM

Contrasting with the rugged coulee lands just to the south, the territory north of Grand Coulee Dam has been somewhat subdued by man. Vast Roosevelt Lake is the water source for irrigation projects. And the tamed Columbia extends in lake-like calm almost to the Canadian border, where it recovers its identity as a more primitive river.

Boaters find Roosevelt Lake nearly ideal. Small communities along the shore of the lake welcome motorists exploring State 25. As you follow the Columbia north to its headwaters, the terrain becomes hilly and trees rise on the horizon.

Even here there's evidence of glacial activity. To see glacial tracks and erratics, try a side trip northwest to the Okanogan Plateau (pages 133 to 135).

Roosevelt Lake: recreation unlimited

The largest water impoundment on the Columbia River (a beneficial side effect of the Grand Coulee Dam) is Franklin Delano Roosevelt Lake. During low water levels in winter, its waters supplement power production. Along the shores of this reservoir, stretching 150 miles from the dam to the Canadian border, cluster some 20 recreation centers.

Facilities. In the Coulee Dam National Recreation Area, 660 miles of lakeshore have been preserved. Facilities along the lake include boat docks, launching ramps, campsites, picnic areas, and swimming beaches. The 27 campgrounds range from large, highly developed areas (piped water, modern restrooms and bathhouses, tables, fire pits, and trailer sites) to small, primitive boat camps (pit toilets

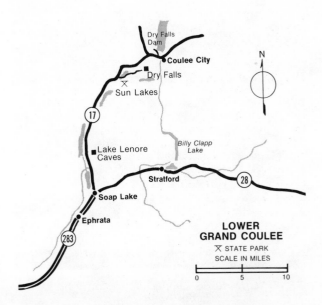

LOWER
GRAND COULEE
X STATE PARK
SCALE IN MILES
0 5 10

and a water well) not accessible by road. At some campgrounds, visitors can attend illustrated programs. Most of the freshwater fish found elsewhere in the state can be caught in Roosevelt Lake.

Natural attractions. On the southern flows and terraces around the lake bloom a profusion of wildflowers. At times the lake teems with waterfowl—Canada geese, mallards, and great blue herons are most numerous. Beaver and muskrat dive in and out of the water; deer roam the lakeshore.

West shore. Don't overlook the possibilities of exploring Roosevelt Lake's west shore. During the busy summer season (late June through Labor Day), its recreation facilities are frequently less crowded than those on the east shore. Motorists along State 25 can cross over to the west shore at Gifford (by ferry), Kettle Falls, and Northport.

Wilbur. From Coulee Dam, you can take State 174 southeast for about 19 miles, joining U.S. 2 at Wilbur. Wilbur has an attractive wooded city park a block off U.S. 2 at the center of town. Tranquil Goose Creek runs through the park, and there are tree-shaded picnic tables.

Map available. All recreation areas (and their respective degrees of development) are indicated on the Coulee Dam National Recreation Area Guide Map, available without charge from the Superintendent, Coulee Dam National Recreation Area, Box 37, Coulee Dam 99116.

Old Fort Spokane

Fort Spokane's military life was brief and unspectacular. Established in 1880, it replaced Fort Colville during a time of tension between Indians, recently moved to reservations, and whites, who illegally settled and mined tribal lands. During the fort's 18 active years, its 45 buildings quartered several hundred troops, none of whom ever fought Indians.

GRAZING HORSES *saunter along slowly beside one of the many lakes in the Grand Coulee basin.*

Now the old fort is an interesting historical site and well equipped recreation facility, with a large campground, supervised beach for swimming, boat launching ramps, and direct access to Roosevelt Lake. To reach the fort, drive west on U.S. 2 from Wilbur, then north at Davenport onto State 25.

Of the fort's original buildings, four still stand and are part of a guide-yourself tour: a restored guardhouse, quartermaster stable, powder magazine and reservoir building, and storehouse. A museum in the old brick guardhouse has a variety of displays, as well as a slide and tape show about the fort's history.

Although the fort's 57-unit campground is usually full on weekends, the many smaller campgrounds along the lake are seldom as busy. After mid-June, water behind the dam is high enough to permit use of launching ramps near the fort as a starting point

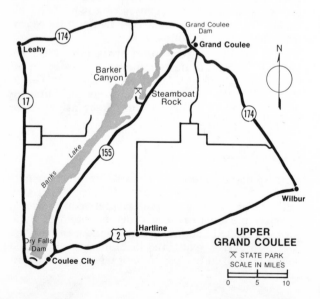

UPPER
GRAND COULEE

X STATE PARK
SCALE IN MILES

0   5   10

for exploration of the lake and the Spokane River.

North from Fort Spokane, you can follow State 25 along the east shore of the lake all the way to Northport, where State 25 crosses the lake and heads northwest for 8 miles to British Columbia.

Colville Indian Reservation

Within the crook of the Columbia River as it flows away from Coulee Dam and bounded on the east by Roosevelt Lake are lands belonging to the Lake, Sanpoil, Nespelem, Nez Perce, Columbia, and other Indian tribes. The Colville Reservation is the largest in Washington.

Across the highway from the Grand Coulee Dam pumping plant is the Indian Agency headquarters. Mystery trees, carved with what appear to be petroglyphs, can be seen on the grounds.

Nespelem. At Nespelem, 16 miles north of the dam on State 155, is the grave of Chief Joseph, a famous leader of the Nez Perce. Known as a strategically minded military leader, Chief Joseph spent his peacetime years fighting for his people's right to return to their lands in the northwest. Though this was, in effect, accomplished, Chief Joseph was not permitted to return to his tribal home and died in exile.

Inchelium, eastern headquarters for the reservation, is on the shore of Roosevelt Lake.

Circle trip through Sanpoil Country

A green contrast after you've seen the stark Grand Coulee and Roosevelt Lake region, the peaceful Sanpoil Valley lies along the western base of the Kettle River Range and can be reached from the upper end of Roosevelt Lake by the Sherman Creek Road west from Kettle Falls.

St. Paul's Mission. Just east of Kettle Falls Bridge, on the north side of U.S. 395, is St. Paul's Mission State Park. The original mission was built in 1845-46 on a site previously occupied by a Hudson's Bay Company trading post, Fort Colville. St. Paul's Mission chapel has been partially restored out of the original timbers. Picnic facilities are available.

The Sherman Creek Road (State 20) crosses the highest highway pass in Washington (5,575 feet). It offers panoramic views of Roosevelt Lake to the east and south and the Okanogan Highlands and Cascades to the west.

The valley. State 21, which follows the narrow river valley south from the town of Republic, makes an excellent return route for motorists who have explored the shores of Roosevelt Lake. It winds through forests of lodgepole pine, grazing land, and small farms. The hillsides are marked with abandoned mines, and you can see unmistakable evidence of earlier placer mining along the streambed.

You meet Roosevelt Lake again just south of Keller. The Keller free ferry takes States 21 motorists across the lake's south shore and to Wilbur on U.S. 2.

LOOP TRIP: Across Grand Coulee and Mining Land

Follow this 373-mile circuit through the impressive Grand Coulee area and the mining country to the north as a guide to what to see and do in a less well-known part of Washington.

In this open, comparatively unpopulated region, accommodations cluster around the centers of Grand Coulee Dam and the city of Spokane. For additional information on attractions along this loop [and possible side trips], refer to the chapters on Central Washington and Spokane & the Inland Empire.

Head north out of Spokane on Highway 395 from Division Street and Second Avenue. Worth a visit is Spokane House, site of an old frontier trading post, in scenic Riverside State Park on State 291. Then loop back to U.S. 395 via an unnumbered road along the Little Spokane River from Nine Mile Falls.

Chewelah (57 miles). From here the road slants westward, passing trading posts, stagecoach stations, and worn-out mines. You'll be heading up the Colville River Valley, flanked by the Huckleberry Mountains on the west and the Pend Oreille Range to the east.

Colville (79 miles). Though Colville is peaceful today, the respectable seat of Stevens County was a brawling frontier town 100 years ago. About 6 miles farther north is the former Indian school

of St. Francis Regis Mission, now a convent. State 20 takes you on into the northwest.

Kettle Falls (89 miles). Rising waters caused by construction of Grand Coulee Dam submerged the original townsite. The present community of Kettle Falls was built near the confluence of the Columbia and Kettle Rivers. Continue west on State 20 across the Columbia River.

Junction with Route 20 (92 miles). Turn left and head south and west on State 20 along Sherman Creek into the wooded mountains of the Kettle River Range and through the Colville National Forest. You'll be crossing 5,575-foot-high Sherman Pass, loftiest in Washington.

Republic (133 miles). Gold ore is still being mined here. An interesting side trip and convenient stopping place is at Curlew Lake State Park, 5 miles up State 21. From Republic, drive south on State 21 down the narrow Sanpoil Valley into the Colville Indian Reservation. Turn due west on a winding country road about 36 miles south of Republic.

Nespelem (182 miles). Memories of the last Northwest Indian uprising led by Chief Joseph linger here where the Nez Perce warrior is buried. Your route now leads south on State 155 along the Columbia River.

Grand Coulee (200 miles). State 155 first passes through the community of Coulee Dam and then past the Grand Coulee Dam itself before arriving at the town of Grand Coulee. Behind the dam, 151-mile-long Franklin D. Roosevelt Lake extends to the Canadian border. State 155 continues southward past Steamboat Rock State Park and along the eastern edge of Banks Lake between Grand Coulee and Dry Falls Dams.

Coulee City (229 miles). This is another community serving the vast Columbia Basin power-irrigation-flood control project. Six miles southwest on U.S. 2 and State 17, you'll pass Sun Lakes State Park and the golden orange-red chasm known as Dry Falls. Farther south on State 17 is Lenore Lake; at the end of a short side road are old Indian caves. When you reach Soap Lake, drive east on State 28 about 9 miles, turn north on a paved country road to Summer Falls, and continue east on State 2.

Davenport (339 miles). An important cattle center, Davenport marks the turnoff north via State 25 to Fort Spokane, where some pioneer structures remain intact.

Spokane (373 miles). Your circle is completed.

Spokane & the Inland Empire

Spokane, Washington's second largest city, is located in a strategic position in eastern Washington. This section of the state is part of a vast mining, lumbering, and agricultural region that calls itself "the Inland Empire." In area, the Empire totals almost 80,000 square miles, including northeastern Oregon, the Idaho panhandle, western Montana, and southern British Columbia. At its hub is Spokane, a natural distribution center for the inland cities.

With its selection as the site for the 1974 World Exposition, though, Spokane has also become known to a great many tourists as the hub of a *recreational* wheel. After visiting Expo '74, they find that a day's drive to the east takes them to Idaho's lakes or Yellowstone National Park; to the south, to Oregon's attractions; to the west, to coastal Washington's richness; and to the north, to Canada's Banff and Lake Louise.

For a look at Washington's role in the Inland Empire, let's start with Walla Walla in the southeastern corner of the state, then move north through the Palouse wheat country and the city of Pullman into Spokane itself and the area to the north.

THE WALLA WALLA REGION

Walla Walla is an area steeped in history. As a stop along the Oregon Trail, as the terminus of the Mullan Road from Ft. Benton in Montana, and as a destination in itself, the Walla Walla valley welcomed early pioneers. Fort Walla Walla was strategically important in conflicts with the Cayuse Indians. And between Waitsburg and Dayton, a state park with camping facilities is a reminder of the Lewis and Clark expedition.

Civilized Walla Walla

Rich farmland nourishes Walla Walla, set emerald-like between the Columbia River and a hazy out-

DINOSAURLIKE combines march across vast acres of ripe wheat in the productive Palouse region.

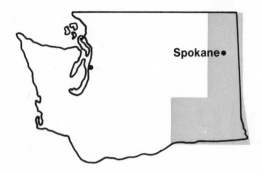

Spokane•

Commerce (address in Appendix). Among the "firsts" claimed by Walla Walla are the earliest railroad in the Washington territory, the first newspaper published between Missouri and the Cascades, the oldest bank in the state (Baker-Boyer National), and the first institution of higher learning in the entire intermountain country—Whitman College.

The cultural level in Walla Walla is pleasantly high. Two little theaters, musical programs, the oldest continuous symphonic orchestra west of the Mississippi, and an art center enrich the city. A former Carnegie Library, the community-sponsored Carnegie Center of the Arts at 109 South Palouse has not only an exhibition gallery but also tastefully furnished rooms.

Walla Walla doesn't have a zoo, but it does have a state game farm on 13th Avenue across from the penitentiary. Visitors to the game farm can observe the breeding and raising of ringneck pheasants.

If you're in Walla Walla over Labor Day weekend, you can attend the Southeastern Washington Fair, where you'll find pari-mutuel horse racing, a night rodeo, free pavilion shows, band concerts, and scientific and educational exhibits.

cropping of Oregon's Blue Mountains to the east. Though its curious Indian name means "many waters," Al Jolson thought it was really "the city they liked so well they named it twice." Shading Walla Walla's wide, peaceful streets are locust, elm, maple, sycamore, and weeping birch trees.

Walla Walla is not only a lovely town (you'd never guess it once had more than 40 saloons) but also a historically important one. You can obtain information on historic spots in downtown Walla Walla and the surrounding area from the Chamber of

EXPO '74 site on Spokane River is in the very heart of Spokane: downtown high-rises are south of Expo (right of picture); shopping centers and suburbia, north.

Fort Walla Walla Park

At the southwestern edge of town on the site of a military reservation established in 1858, Fort Walla Walla Park encompasses Garrison Creek with campsites tucked into cool glens among cottonwoods, water birches, and patches of fennel.

Two attractions of the park stand opposite each other: Fort Walla Walla Cemetery and the Fort Walla Walla Museum's pioneer village. The cemetery is crowded with graves from the Indian wars, especially from the battle of June 17, 1877, near Whitebird Cañon in Idaho, and from the Battle of Boise with Chief Joseph. Nez Perce warriors and U. S. cavalrymen share the cemetery.

Fenced-in log cabins, a one-room schoolhouse, a railroad depot, log blockhouse, and blacksmith shop supply the authentic atmosphere of the pioneer village. Visitors can enter the compound to see settlers' relics and the Russell steam engine at close range during weekends in the summer.

Plans for expansion of the Fort Walla Walla Museum complex include a museum with five display areas, featuring 33 life-sized mules drawing an early farm machine.

Whitman Mission

Seven miles west of Walla Walla, the Whitman Mission is a 96-acre national historical monument. The Protestant mission, founded to educate the Indians, was one of the earliest settlements along the Oregon Trail. Here, on November 29, 1847, Cayuse Indians massacred 13 pioneers, including Marcus and Narcissa Whitman, founders of the mission.

Footpaths lead you to the sites of the first house and apple orchard, the mission house, the emigrant house that served as a hotel, and the grave in which the massacre victims were buried. You can pick up a map of the trails at the visitor center.

THE SOUTHEAST: VARIED LANDSCAPE

Eroded plateaus might remind you of New Mexico, rugged mountain backcountry suggests Wyoming, rolling wheat fields recall the waving grain of Nebraska — but these varied sights are all contained within the southeastern corner of the state of Washington.

DO YOU SEE "Bowl and Pitcher" in shape of boulders, above, at Spokane's Riverside State Park? Left, old scale gets tested on porch at Three Forks Pioneer Village near Pullman.

The lonely Snake River region

From Ice Harbor Dam (page 121) to the city of Clarkston, the rugged Snake River of Idaho is being subdued to provide water, power, and recreation for Washington. You'll find that the Snake is excellent for small boating. Though the twin cities of Clarkston, Washington, and Lewiston, Idaho, are the starting point of expeditions to run the rapids of the Snake through Hells Canyon, they will be slack-water ports when Lower Granite Dam is completed in 1975. After Lower Granite is built, freighters and pleasure boats will be able to sail through locks all the way from the mouth of the Columbia along the Snake into Idaho. The Lower Granite construction site isn't easy to reach—check with the Corps of Engineers for the route past Pomeroy—but it's worth seeing as probably the last project of its kind.

Lower Monumental Dam. Though it's really in the lake formed by Ice Harbor Dam, Windust Park is closer to Lower Monumental Dam. Although there are no formal campsites, camping is allowed for a small fee.

The fresh green grass of Lyons Ferry appears around a bend in the road like a mirage as you

ROARING Palouse Falls spills over lava flow layers, rebounding cool spray high into the air.

drive down State 261. For boaters, it's a spot to buy gas at the marina; campers can swim and picnic. The wooden ferry that used to carry travelers across the Snake is docked just north of the main recreation area—a prime fishing spot.

Stretching across the river high above the highway, Joso railroad bridge, constructed in 1912-1914 by Oriental laborers, was the longest and highest curved trestle bridge of its time.

Just north of Lyons Ferry is the site of the Marmes archeological discoveries, cut short when the construction of Lower Monumental Dam flooded the dig. Although there isn't much to see now (artifacts are on permanent loan to the Pacific Northwest Indian Center in Spokane), you can see the top third of the cave from the water. Because the length of the Snake River was inhabited by ancient Indians, archeologists are working the riverbanks between Clarkston and Lower Granite Dam with an eye to 1975, when that stretch will also be submerged.

Palouse Falls. Check your map carefully when you try to reach this state park; the roads are deceptive. But it's well worth a few minutes to find. It's almost unbelievable to see a 198-foot cataract tumbling in a desert landscape. Along the road to the falls, a rapid transition occurs from grazing land to terraced, southwestern-type rock outcroppings.

The falls aren't the only attraction. The canyon of the Palouse is an impressive sight as brown water foams through the deep gorges. If you aren't deterred by the thought of hiking back up, you can reach the river below in an hour. At the base of the canyon, look in the basaltic bluffs for caves used for shelter and storage by the Palouse Indians. Weaving their own legends about the river's tricks, the Indians believed that the mythological Big Beaver gouged out the canyon and the falls as he fought against four giant brothers. Smaller contemporary beavers still keep busy along the river.

Experienced hikers can trek along the Palouse River from the falls down to Lyons Ferry if they're prepared to deal with the summertime rattlesnake population.

Little Goose Dam. Behind this dam is Lake Bryan, as yet rather undeveloped for tourists except for Central Ferry and Boyer parks. The dam itself (with a fish-viewing window) can be reached from Hooper or Pampa on State 26 via roads to the south through Riparia or, from the south, on paved roads from Starbuck on State 261.

Remote Blue Mountains

It's easy to see how these pine-covered hills got their name—they rise misty and blue in the distance as you drive toward them. The best approaches to the fastness of the Wenaha Backcountry or the campgrounds at Fields Spring State Park originate at Clarkston, on the Idaho border.

Clarkston. Between them, the Clearwater River and the Snake have carved a deep, rugged chasm with two unexpected towns at the bottom—Clarkston and Lewiston, Idaho. Weaving along rolling hills down to the present river level, the highway continually reveals glimpses of the cities below. Clarkston has a Valley Art Center with exhibits in many media, open Sunday and afternoons Tuesday through Friday. However, Lewiston is larger and has a number of attractions for visitors (refer to Sunset's *Travel Guide to Idaho*). Calling itself a "Banana Belt" town because of its mild climate, Clarkston is in the middle of upland game bird hunting territory.

Grande Ronde River. A tributary of the famous Snake, the Grande Ronde River has carved out an impressive canyon of its own near the Oregon border. In the early fall it has steelhead runs.

To see this remote region, drive State 129 south from Clarkston. Past Anatone, red, eroded hills with pine tree epaulets surround the traveler. The Grande Ronde Canyon viewpoint isn't marked, but turnoffs are provided in several spots. Fields Spring State Park, set in thick trees and dappled with light, has many campsites, trails, and a maze of dirt roads heading back into the woods.

Side roads turn into the Umatilla National Forest off State 129, but some aren't passable until July.

Wenaha Backcountry. Two sections in the heart of the Washington portion of the Umatilla National Forest have been barred to motorized vehicles in favor of hunting, fishing, camping, and hiking. Rocky Mountain elk and mule deer roam near streams inhabited by rainbow and Dolly Varden trout. Set between rugged basaltic ridges, rapid streams provide the spawning grounds for salmon and steelhead trout. Scattered stands of Douglas fir and white fir shelter over 150 miles of horse and foot trails. Surprising to naturalists is a stand of virgin western white pine that grows here, far removed from its natural range. District rangers in Walla Walla and Pomeroy can supply you with detailed information.

The rolling Palouse

Roller-coaster hills patterned with the texture of plowed furrows in the spring, green seedlings in the early summer, and golden wheat in the fall are sharply accented here and there by farm buildings surrounding black windmills stuck in the ground like a giant's pinwheels. At the edges of the Palouse wheatlands with their rich volcanic soil are basalt post piles in hexagonal columns, the inspiration for the hexagonal modules used in Spokane's Expo '74.

Pullman . . . a college town. Only 8 miles from the Idaho border, Pullman is the hilly home of Washington State University. Red brick and modern concrete buildings form the lively campus area. You can obtain a map of the campus and a free parking sticker at the Office of University Relations in French Administration Building or at the police office in the Safety Building. The art gallery, two campus museums, the Summer Palace Theater, and

CRISPLY TRIMMED trees and shrubs, geometric flower beds are in Spokane's formal Duncan Gardens.

a new performing arts center-coliseum provide indoor entertainment. The school mascot, a tawny cougar named Butch, is an attraction for children in his cage near the stadium.

Of added interest are the Nuclear Radiation Center located a mile east of the campus (open during working hours; its reactor operates 1-2 p.m. Mondays, Wednesdays, and Fridays), and the Albrook Hydraulic Laboratory (open during working hours), where hydraulic engineering problems are worked out with miniature models of existing or proposed dams and similar construction projects.

Kamiak and Steptoe. Two buttes rise north of Pullman, one named for a Yakima war chief, the other honoring a U. S. cavalry officer.

Between Pullman and the town of Palouse, Kamiak Butte rears its knobby-crested shape above a patchwork of wheat fields. The park at its summit has short trails and picnic and campsites.

Reminders of Lt. Col. E. J. Steptoe appear in three places along U.S. 195 between Pullman and Spokane: Steptoe Butte, the little community of Steptoe, and the memorial at Steptoe Battlefield. Rising 3,613 feet above the fertile plateau, the massive, sliced-off cone of the butte, an eroded remnant of the Selkirk Range, dominates the landscape. A turnoff 2 miles south of the town of Steptoe takes you to the summit, where you can picnic.

At the Steptoe Battlefield Memorial near Rosalia, a 26-foot granite shaft reminds visitors of a battle between Lt. Col. Steptoe and an alliance of Spokane, Palouse, and Coeur d'Alene Indians. The Colonel lost this round and retreated under cover of night to Fort Walla Walla.

Spokane: a city transformed

To a city planner, what has happened to Spokane as a result of the building of Expo '74 would be con-

TOWERS DOMINATE both these Spokane buildings, but that's where the similarity ends. Review-Chronicle Building, top, is 19th-century style; Parkade Plaza, bottom, strictly modern.

sidered a classic case of urban redevelopment. Not only has the Expo site transformed Spokane's skid road into the most attractive part of the city but also the downtown business district itself has been stimulated to create pedestrian malls, planted areas, elevated covered bridges between stores— many visionary improvements that are becoming a reality here in a sudden burst of energy and will.

A river city

Rather than dividing Spokane into two parts, the vigorous Spokane River actually unites it, partly because of the multitude of bridges angling across the river wherever you look.

Spokane is also endowed with other types of bridges—the kind that span time. You can drive from the turn-of-the-century residential architecture in Brown's Addition into the high-rise modern heart of the city in minutes. Festivities range from the action-packed Diamond Spur Rodeo in April to the traditional celebration of spring, the Lilac Festival in May.

Loop drive. In two or three hours you can explore many of Spokane's attractions on a 28-mile marked loop drive, beginning at Howard Street and Riverside Avenue in the business district. A brochure available from the Chamber of Commerce (address in Appendix) outlines what you'll see and also supplies a city map.

Spokane Falls. The climax of a tour of Spokane should be a close-up look at the white water falls of the Spokane River, coursing through the center of the city. The falls powered Spokane's first sawmill and flour mill. Modern spillways supplement the original rapids in providing the city's electricity. The foot of Lincoln Street is a good spot to view the Upper Falls rapids around Cannon Island, especially at night when both sets of falls are illuminated. Gondola rides installed for Expo '74 take you dramatically close to the rushing waters.

Manito Park. Like Seattle, Spokane is a city of parks. One of its most attractive is Manito Park, which contains Rose Hill, in bloom in June; formal Duncan Gardens with lilacs flowering in May, well-groomed topiary and an ever-changing fountain; a Japanese Garden; and a greenhouse-conservatory.

Historical society museums. In the heart of Brown's Addition, gracious, half-timbered Grace Campbell Memorial Museum stands next to the modern Cheney Cowles Memorial Museum. The former home of Amasa Basaliel Campbell, who made his fortune in mining, the house has been restored and refurnished in grand style, down to the tinkling fountain and lush plants in the solarium. Appropriately, there's an extensive mineral collection upstairs with some samples from the Coeur d'Alene mining country.

Connected to the Campbell House by a covered walkway, the Cheney Cowles Museum houses a fine collection of Indian art and pioneer relics, as well as a research library. A fine arts gallery rotates exhibits of contemporary northwest paintings.

LOOP TRIP: Historical Country South of Spokane

Take a weekend to discover scenes of Indian massacres and frontier battles, eye-catching geological formations, awesome canyons, and sylvan forests. Along this 337-mile route you can visit an atomic energy exhibit or stop to look at several historic colleges.

Start from Second Avenue and Maple Street in Spokane along Interstate 90, bypassing Four Lakes, then turn off on State 395 near Ritzville.

Pasco (135 miles). Near the confluence of the Snake and Columbia Rivers, Pasco has an extensive nearby recreation area in narrow Lake Sacajawea, formed by Ice Harbor Dam. Fishing, swimming, water skiing, shoreside picnicking, and camping are a few of the possibilities. Waters above McNary Dam supply Columbia Park with 4½ acres of waterfront for camping facilities, a driving range, and a golf course. By driving westward on U.S. 12 for 15 minutes, you can visit the Hanford Science Center in Richland's downtown Federal Building to view animated exhibits,

models, and graphic displays on the use and development of atomic energy.

Southeast of Pasco along U.S. 12, only about 3 miles away, a spur road right leads to Sacajawea State Park. Lewis and Clark's camping spot is now the site of an Indian Museum. Next, the highway parallels the Caribou Trail sharply eastward, up the Walla Walla River just past Wallula.

Whitman Mission (174 miles). In 1836 Dr. Marcus Whitman and his wife, Narcissa, established Waiilatpu Mission and schooled the Indians until the Whitmans were massacred in 1847. Part of the area has been restored.

Walla Walla (181 miles). Though it began as a fort, this community in the shadow of the Blue Mountains is now a college town, home of Whitman College (oldest in the state) and Walla Walla College. Marcus Whitman is commemorated in the college's Whitman Memorial Museum.

Waitsburg (202 miles). This pleasant, tree-shaded town is about five miles west of Lewis and Clark Trail State Park on the Touchet River. A restful picnic spot, the park marks another camping ground of the 1805-06 Lewis and Clark expedition.

Dayton (212 miles). Set in a V-shaped valley where Indians and pioneers trod, Dayton is an important agricultural trade center. To the east rises Umatilla National Forest. Northward, there is a choice of routes. One takes you via State 126 and U.S. 12 to Clarkston and Lewiston, around the Snake River Canyon, and north on U.S. 195 through the college town of Pullman. The tour route follows U.S. 12 north to Delaney, where a side trip northwestward goes to jagged Palouse River Canyon and Palouse Falls State Park. Here a broad, 300-foot-high cascade gushes from rock.

Dodge (235 miles). Take State 127 north over the Snake River.

Colfax (280 miles). Hemmed in by hills on the Palouse River, Colfax is a prime trade locale in the renowned Palouse wheat-growing region. Fourteen miles north, you can climb pyramid-shaped Steptoe Butte. Kamiak Butte State Park, eastward near Palouse, is similar. The tour route next becomes U.S. 195, heading north.

Rosalia (306 miles). Just south of town, the highway crosses Pine Creek near Steptoe Battlefield Memorial, commemorating a fight between Palouse Indians and troops led by Lt. Col. Edward Steptoe. Wheat fields give way to more broken terrain as you travel north.

Spokane (337 miles). History lesson is finished.

Crosby Museum. A famous alumnus of Gonzaga University, Bing Crosby, donated the funds for a modern library, a gesture honored by Gonzaga in its unique room full of Crosbyana ranging from golden albums to autographed photos.

Riverside State Park. Only 3 miles from the city—close enough to be regularly used—Riverside Park encloses a section of the Spokane River. The rocky river channel, piled with driftwood where it bends and shaded by pines, bisects the park's community kitchens, campsites, picnic tables, and fireplaces. By crossing a suspension footbridge spanning the river, you can explore several forest trails on the west bank. From the bridge or a highway vantage point, you can examine the massive lava formations (called the "Bowl and Pitcher") tumbled in the river canyon.

At the north end of the park, you can turn across a bridge to reach the other side of the river (placid here) and find Spokane House Interpretive Center. Inside an interpretive building is a model of the 1810 North West Company trading post, later administered by the Hudson's Bay Company. Estab-lished under the direction of explorer-geographer David Thompson, this fur trading center was the first permanent white settlement in Washington.

South of Spokane

Making a beeline between Spokane and the Cascades, Interstate 90 passes through the midst of the treeless wheat lands just outside the city limits. Along the way are two worthwhile stops—Turnbull National Wildlife Refuge and the college town of Cheney (on a short loop off the highway), and the wheat center of Ritzville.

Around Cheney. The sidetrip off U.S. 395, along State 904 just after you leave Spokane, takes you to a well-developed National Wildlife Refuge and to one of Washington's four state colleges.

In the town of Cheney, modern brick buildings and pine trees make Eastern Washington State College a pleasant campus. During the school year you can visit the Hargreaves Hall Gallery.

You can reach Turnbull National Wildlife Refuge by traveling 4 miles south from Cheney on the

A Phoenix Rises: Spokane's Pacific Northwest Indian Center

Long before the city of Spokane was founded, Indians trapped fish at Spokane Falls. Now, certain to become a major center for the study of Indian cultures is the new Pacific Northwest Indian Center that has risen between the Expo '74 site and the edge of the Gonzaga University campus in Spokane.

The $1.25 million center is architecturally striking: it includes a five-level, tower museum shaped like a truncated cone and an adjoining two-level research and administration wing. The center has 29,000 feet of floor space. The Chairman of the Board is Father Wilfred Schoenberg of the university faculty.

The purpose of the center is to serve as a repository of information on Indian cultures. Included are a museum, library facility, and art center.

First opened in the fall of 1973, the center preserves collections of original paintings, artifacts, art work, photographs, negatives, and books. A plan is being considered to erect a replica of an Indian village near the center site, complete with demonstrations and performances.

A small admission fee is charged for center visitors (except Indians). Further information may be obtained by writing the Pacific Northwest Indian Center, Terminal Annex, P.O. Box 3044, Spokane, Washington 99220.

MONUMENTAL Indian Center on banks of Spokane River houses art and craft objects.

paved Cheney-Plaza County Road (Badger Lake Road), then 2 miles east on the entrance road. Within 27 square miles of rugged scabrock, pine, aspen, and grassland are interspersed some 20 small lakes and over a hundred ponds and marshes.

Spring or fall migrations present the most spectacular show of birds, but you're almost always sure to see once-rare trumpeter swans at the display pond near the refuge headquarters. Facilities include a 5-mile interpretive automobile route, hiking trails, and a small picnic area.

Burroughs Museum. Ritzville, Washington, has chosen to remember its beginnings with a tribute to a horse-and-buggy doctor: Frank R. Burroughs. The doctor lived in Ritzville until 1929 in the fine Victorian house that he built in 1890. Now open to visitors, the house is unimpressive from the outside, but most of the original furnishings are intact. The Burroughs Museum is at 404 W. Main Street.

North to the Canadian border

Encircled by a necklace of 76 lakes within a 50-mile radius, Spokane is an outdoorsman's dream. Most lakes have gently sloping beaches where you can rent a cabin for a week's stay or a boat for day use.

Big game hunting is popular in the Selkirk Range, which abounds in whitetail and mule deer, elk, and sometimes bear, as well as game birds—pheasant, ducks, and grouse. Fishermen can catch cutthroat, rainbow, and brook trout, along with silver salmon.

The larger lakes, like Loon and Newman, are well developed. Distinctive Department of National Resources wooden signs direct you to small lakes or points of interest.

Mt. Spokane. All the summertime hiking, hunting, fishing, and picnicking possibilities of a state park are complemented by a winter complex of condominiums, ice skating rink, swimming pool, snowmobile trails (snowmobiles can be rented in Spokane), and slopes for all abilities at Snowblaze ski area. From the top of the mountain on a clear day you can see eight blue lakes, three states, and, in the distance, British Columbia. Designated lookout points explain what geographical feature you're looking at.

Newport Geophysical Observatory. Impressively classified under the U. S. Department of Commerce, National Oceanic and Atmospheric Administration, Environmental Research Laboratories, Earth Science Laboratories, this observatory works in the disciplines of geomagnetism and seismology. Visitors can see some of the latest techniques for detecting earthquakes and measuring the earth's magnetic field. Located about 10 miles north of Newport, it can be reached by crossing the Pend Oreille River Bridge off U.S. 2 just east of Newport, turning north on the Le Clerc Creek Road, turning right after 7 miles onto Indian Creek road for about 1 mile, then following the observatory road leading off to the left for about ¾ mile. Visitors are welcome between 9 a.m. and 3 p.m., Monday through Thursday.

WATER-POWERED MILL still stands next to Chapman Lake, just south of town of Cheney.

Manresa Cave. The view from Manresa Cave, the main grotto of the Indian Rock Caves on a cliffside 55 miles north of Spokane on the Kalispel Indian Reservation, looks out to the Pend Orielle River and a broad plain where a century ago the Kalispel and Colville Indians met, traded, and raced horses.

Gardner Cave. Main attraction of Crawford State Park, this is the largest limestone cavern in Washington. It's a pleasant side trip off State 31 into Canada.

Boundary Dam. This unusual dam is set precisely in the solid rock of a canyon. By taking the Vista House road 14 miles north of Metaline Falls, you can view the entire project area. The other turnoff, between Metaline and Metaline Falls on the west side of the Pend Oreille River, takes you right to the dam. Two areas are open to visitors: the antiseptic, gleaming, rock-walled machine hall; and, accessible through a different tunnel, the transformer bays and draft tube gate galleries.

Chewelah. Winner of an All-American City award in 1973, this town has a gem of a museum packed with assorted antiques and almost-antiques. Local history springs vividly to life, illustrated by such items as an assortment of barbed wire, a horse-drawn sleigh, and an authentic trough from the old main street with separate basins for people, horses, and dogs. Most of the displays, including an exhibit of mining equipment, were donated by the area's citizens. Open in summer, the museum is next to Chewelah Industries, Inc., on Third Street.

49° North. This sparkling new ski area is just a few miles from Chewelah, across a creek where miners once sluiced for gold. It is slated for major development. You can rent downhill or cross-country skiing equipment.

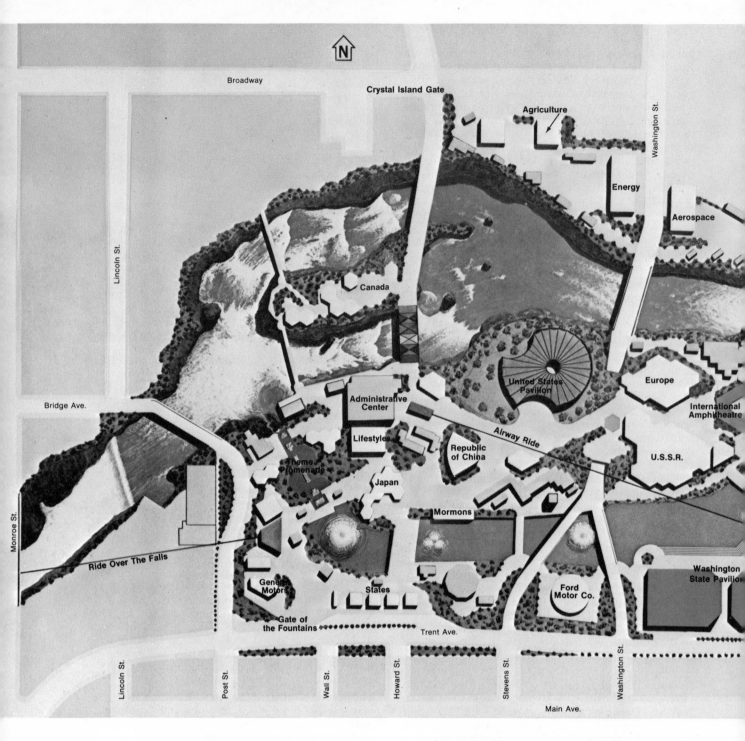

N

Broadway

Crystal Island Gate

Agriculture

Energy

Aerospace

Washington St.

Canada

United States Pavilion

Europe

International Amphitheatre

Administrative Center

Airway Ride

Lifestyles

U.S.S.R.

Theme Promenade

Republic of China

Japan

Mormons

Bridge Ave.

Ride Over The Falls

Monroe St.

Ford Motor Co.

Washington State Pavilion

General Motors

States

Gate of the Fountains

Trent Ave.

Lincoln St.

Post St.

Wall St.

Howard St.

Stevens St.

Washington St.

Lincoln St.

Main Ave.

*RIVER-SPANNING Expo site, above, includes
large U.S.S.R. exhibit, Japanese lagoon,
ride over Spokane Falls. Near right, softshell
tent soars over U.S. pavilion. Far right,
$11.9 million Washington structure houses
Opera House, exhibit hall.*

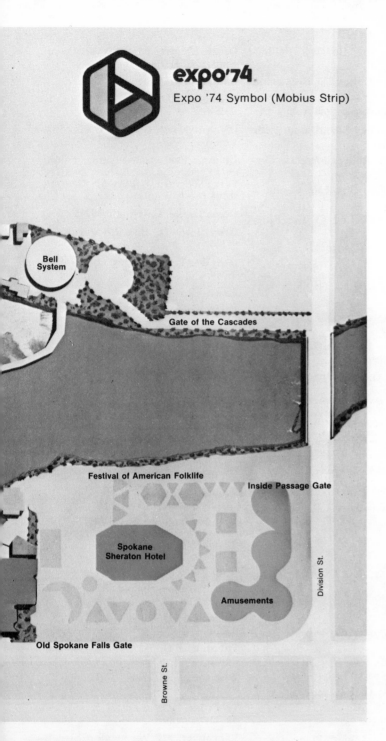

expo'74

Expo '74 Symbol (Mobius Strip)

Bell System

Gate of the Cascades

Festival of American Folklife

Inside Passage Gate

Spokane Sheraton Hotel

Amusements

Division St.

Old Spokane Falls Gate

Browne St.

Expo '74: Spokane's Renaissance

America's first world exposition with a theme of environment and outdoor recreation will open in May, 1974. Expo '74, on a cascading river in the heart of Spokane, will be evidence that progress and natural environment can combine to improve the lifestyle of a community. More than 75 regional, national, and international exhibits will relate to man's ability "To Live, Work and Play in Harmony with His Environment." Among the foreign participants will be the U.S.S.R., and Japan.

The 100-acre site of the exposition is adjacent to the center of Spokane, threading around the Spokane River. It is anticipated that 4,600,000 visitors will be attracted to Expo '74 in the six-month period ending October, 1974. Many of the visitors will be vacationing in the Pacific Northwest, with the fair a major part of their vacation.

Expo '74 grounds along the rushing Spokane River will house more than 75 individual exhibits. Included are a waterfront theater, theme structure, amusement center, riverfront park and recreation area, aerial chair lift ride across the brink of the falls, restaurant and food concessions, state, federal, and international pavilions, and foreign and domestic industrial exhibits. Spokane's tallest building—a 28-story Sheraton Hotel—is also rising at the expo site.

The Expo '74 symbol, called a Mobius Strip after the German mathematician who invented it, has no definable end or beginning but is continuous. Thus it expresses the continuity of life and the harmonic relationship of man and his environment.

The site of the exposition is especially appropriate to the theme. Until recently, the area was obscured by dilapidated buildings and river channels had been filled in; industrial development had all but destroyed the magnificent setting. The area has been reclaimed and transformed into an example of restoration of the natural environment—demonstrating to the world that progress is possible without pollution.

For help in finding lodging in Spokane, write to Hospitality Services, W. 1020 Riverside Avenue, Spokane 99210.

Appendix

HEADQUARTERS ADDRESSES

Coulee Dam National Recreation Area, Coulee Dam 99116

Fort Vancouver National Historic Site, Vancouver 98661

Gifford Pinchot National Forest, 500 W. 12th Street, P.O. Box 449, Vancouver 98660

Lake Chelan National Recreation Area—See North Cascades National Park

Mt. Baker National Forest, Federal Office Building, Bellingham 98225

Mt. Rainier National Park, Longmire 98397

North Cascades National Park, Sedro Woolley 98284

Okanogan National Forest, 219 2nd Avenue South, P.O. Box 950, Okanogan 98840

Olympic National Forest, Federal Building, Olympia 98501

Olympic National Park, 600 East Park Avenue, Port Angeles 98362

Ross Lake National Recreation Area—See North Cascades National Park

San Juan Island National Historical Park, P.O. Box 549, Friday Harbor 98250

Snoqualmie National Forest, 1601 Second Avenue Building, Seattle 98101

Washington State Parks & Recreation Commission, P.O. Box 1128, Olympia 98501

Wenatchee National Forest, 3 South Wenatchee Avenue, P.O. Box 811, Wenatchee 98801

Whitman Mission National Historic Site, Route 2, Walla Walla 99362

CHAMBERS OF COMMERCE

Aberdeen—See Grays Harbor

Anacortes, 14th & Commercial, Anacortes 98221

Bainbridge Island, 264 Winslow Way E., Bainbridge Island 98110

Ballard, 2208 N.W. Market Street, Seattle 98107

Bellevue, 550-106th N.E., Bellevue 98004

Bellingham, P.O. Box 958, Bellingham 98225

Bremerton, P.O. Box 229, Bremerton 98310

Cashmere, Cashmere 98815

Central Whidbey Island, Coupeville 98239

Centralia, 222 Railroad Avenue, Centralia 98531

Chehalis, P.O. Box 666, Chehalis 98532

Cle Elum, P.O. Box 43, Cle Elum 98922

Colville, Colville 99114

Coulee Dam, Coulee Dam 99116

Edmonds, P.O. Box 146, Edmonds 98020

Ellensburg, 436 Sprague, Ellensburg 98926

Enumclaw, 2744 Griffen Street, Enumclaw 98022

Everett, P.O. Box 1086, Everett 98201

Forks, P.O. Box 1249, Forks 98331

Grand Coulee, Grand Coulee 99133

Grays Harbor, P.O. Box 450, Aberdeen 98520

Hoquiam—See Grays Harbor

Ilwaco, Ilwaco 98624

Issaquah, P.O. Box 430, Issaquah 98027

Kelso, P.O. Box 58, Kelso 98626

Kennewick—See Tri-Cities

Kirkland, 113 Lake Street South, Kirkland 98033

Lake Chelan, P.O. Box 216, Chelan 98816

Lake Stevens, P.O. Box 26, Lake Stevens 98258

Leavenworth, P.O. Box 281, Leavenworth 98826

Marysville, P.O. Box 96, Marysville 98270

Monroe, Monroe 98272

Moses Lake, 324 South Pioneer Way, Moses Lake 98837

Mt. Vernon, 310 Pine Street, Mt. Vernon 98273

Newport, P.O. Box 631, Newport 99156

North Bend, P.O. Box 372, North Bend 98045

North Whidbey Island, 5506 Highway 525, Oak Harbor 98277

Ocean Park, P.O. Box 403, Ocean Park 98640

Ocean Shores, P.O. Box 82, Ocean Shores 98551

Okanogan, Okanogan 98840

Olympia, P.O. Box 1427, Olympia 98501

Olympic North Beach, P.O. Box 555, Copalis 98535

Olympic Peninsula, Olympic Peninsula Travel Association, Seattle Ferry Terminal, Pier 52, Seattle 98104

Orcas Island, Eastsound 98245

Oroville, P.O. Box 204, Oroville 98844

Othello, P.O. Drawer O, Othello 99344

Pasco—See Tri-Cities

Port Angeles, 1217 E. First, Port Angeles 98362

Port Townsend, Sims and Kearney Street, Port Townsend 98368

Poulsbo, Poulsbo 98370

Pullman, Pullman 99163

Puyallup Valley, Puyallup 98371

Richland—See Tri-Cities

San Juan Island, P.O. Box 302, Friday Harbor 98250

Seattle, 215 Columbia, Seattle 98104

Sequim-Dungeness, P.O. Box 907, Sequim 98382

Shelton, Shelton 98584

Snohomish, P.O. Box 135, Snohomish 98290

Soap Lake, Soap Lake 98851

South Whidbey Island, P.O. Box 63, Langley 98260

Spokane, P.O. Box 2147, Spokane 99210

Tacoma, P.O. Box 1933, Tacoma 98401

Toppenish, P.O. Box 28, Toppenish 98948

Tri-Cities, P.O. Box 2322, Tri-Cities, 99302

Vancouver, 817 Washington Street, Vancouver 98660

Vashon Island, P.O. Box 281, Vashon 98070

Walla Walla, P.O. Box 644, Walla Walla 99362

Wenatchee, P.O. Box 850, Wenatchee 98801

Westport-Twin Harbors, P.O. Box 306, Westport 98595

Yakima, P.O. Box 1498, Yakima 98901

Index

Photographers

Anacortes Chamber of Commerce: 55 top. **Barry Anderson:** 52 right; 55 bottom. **Ray Atkeson:** 50 top; 53; 58; 64; 65 right; 74 bottom; 86 bottom; 88 right; 98 bottom; 114; 117 right; 118; 121 top; 144; 150; 151. **Robert Bander:** 10; 17 right; 24 bottom; 31; 39; 52 left; 71 bottom; 72; 73; 74 top; 81 right; 84 bottom; 85; 86 top; 152. **Dave Barnes:** 95 top. **Norm Barringman:** 113 top. **Batelle-Northwest Photography:** 122. **Carroll C. Calkins:** 45 right. **William Carter:** 134 bottom left, top right. **Charlotte Casey:** 50 bottom. **Glenn M. Christiansen:** 12 left; 40; 41 top left, center; 51; 57 bottom; 59; 60 top; 61. **John W. Dudley:** 4 bottom. **Dudley, Hardin & Yang, Inc.:** 27; 41 bottom. **Expo '74:** 148; 156; 157. **Keith Gunnar:** 2; 5 bottom left; 11; 14; 20; 25 top; 70 bottom; 75 right; 97; 99; 102; 104; 106; 133 top. **Ruth Kirk:** 9; 76. **Ruth and Louis Kirk:** 69. **Harold Laney:** 130. **Trina LaVine:** 28. **Martin Litton:** 113 bottom left. **Tarcisio Miglia:** 45 left. **Fred Milkie:** 30 bottom; 34; 138; 141. **Joe Munroe:** 135. **Don Normark:** 5 top left; 22 left; 25 bottom; 29 left; 30 top; 32; 33; 35; 38; 41 top right; 47 top right; 66 right; 80; 81 left; 90; 93; 100; 103; 111; 112; 113 bottom right; 117 left; 128; 132; 139. **Northwest Air Photos:** 60 bottom. **Pacific Northwest Indian Center:** 154. **Dick Palmer:** 54. **Hugh Paradise:** 133 bottom; 134 center right, bottom right; 142; 155. **Barbara Parsini:** 127 right. **Port of Seattle:** 15 bottom; 36 bottom. **Jim Poth:** 44; 95 bottom; 98 top; 105. **Mary Randlett:** 146. **James S. Rayner:** 127 left. **Bob Reed:** 70 top; 71 top. **Merg Ross:** 24 top. **Archie Satterfield:** 149 left. **Bob and Ira Spring:** 12 right; 16 right; 57 top; 66 left; 88 left; 92; 116; 134 top left; 136; 149 right. **Paul V. Thomas:** 78; 84 top; 124. **State of Washington, Department of Commerce and Economic Development:** 42; 83; 109; 119. **Elton Welke:** 29 right; 77; 96. **Doug Wilson:** 4 top; 5 top right, 5 center right; 16 left; 18; 22 right; 23; 36 top; 37; 46; 47 center right, 47 bottom left; 67; 75 left; 87; 123; 126; 129. **Darrel Wood:** 48. **Will Youst:** 15 top. **Maureen W. Zimmerman:** 121 bottom.

Sketch of ferry boat on title page by **Joe Seney.**